The theory of social situations

The theory of social situations

An alternative game-theoretic approach

JOSEPH GREENBERG

The right of the University of Cambridge to print and sell all manner of books was granted by Henry VIII in 1534. The University has printed and published continuously since 1584.

CAMBRIDGE UNIVERSITY PRESS

Cambridge
New York Port Chester Melbourne Sydney

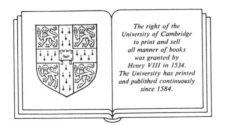

Published by the Press Syndicate of the University of Cambridge
The Pitt Building, Trumpington Street, Cambridge CB2 1RP
40 West 20th Street, New York, NY 10011, USA
10 Stamford Road, Oakleigh, Melbourne 3166, Australia

First published 1990

Printed in the United States of America

Library of Congress Cataloging-in-Publication Data

Greenberg, Joseph, 1948–

The theory of social situations : an alternative game-theoretic approach / Joseph Greenberg.

p. cm.
Includes bibliographical references.

ISBN 0-521-37425-1. – ISBN 0-521-37689-0 (pbk.)

1. Social interaction. 2. Game theory. I. Title.
HM291.G664 1989
302–dc20 89-17467
CIP

British Library Cataloguing in Publication Data
Greenberg, Joseph

The theory of social situations : an alternative game-theoretic approach.

1. Social psychology. Applications of game theory
I. Title
302'.01'5193

ISBN 0-521-37425-1 hard covers
ISBN 0-521-37689-0 paperback

To my parents

איזהו חכם? הרואה את הנולד.

תלמוד תמיד, לב.

Who is wise? He that foresees coming events.

Talmud Tamid, 32.

Contents

Preface

This work was originated during my two-year stay at the economics department of Stanford University in the academic years 1984–6 and my visit to CORE, Belgium, in September 1985. Since then I have had the opportunity (and often the pleasure) of discussing the contents of this research monograph with a number of individuals. I benefited not only from insightful comments made by some scholars, but also from the dogmatic thinking of others, which forced me to be more precise and explicit in my writing. I thank members of both groups.

Special thanks are due to Geir Asheim, Giacomo Bonanno, Edi Karni, Amnon Rapoport, Howard Rosenthal, and Zvi Winer for their very useful and thoughtful comments.

One person, to whom I owe the most for (almost) always being willing to listen, read, discuss, and criticize my ideas, is my friend and colleague Benyamin Shitovitz. His many suggestions concerning both contents and exposition have been extremely helpful.

I have also profited from teaching parts of this book at the following institutions: Haifa University, Israel; California Institute of Technology; G.R.E.Q.E., Marseilles; GSIA, Carnegie Mellon University; University of California at Davis; and the University of Notre Dame de la Paix, Namur, Belgium, where I held the Chaire Francqui Internationale, 1987.

CHAPTER 1

Overview

The purpose of this book is to offer a new and integrative approach, in the spirit of game theory, to the study of formal models in the social and behavioral sciences.

Following Proclus' aphorism that "it is necessary to know beforehand what is sought," the objective of this first chapter is to convey the general ideas behind the proposed theory, and present some of its advantages; the rigorous definitions, complete explanations, the precise underlying motivation, and, of course, the formal results are provided in the next chapters. The reader should not, therefore, expect to master the theory and comprehend its ramifications by glancing at this chapter; its purpose is limited to give the heuristic gist of the theory.

1.1 The scope of the theory

The proposed theory applies to all those models in the social and behavioral sciences in which it is **impossible to impose** a course of action, or an alternative, on the individuals. Rather, I consider only those social environments in which a course of action can be **recommended,** or **proposed,** to the individuals, who are then **free to accept or reject** the proposal. (The source of the recommendation is inconsequential. It might be one, some, or all of the individuals, or, alternatively, the recommendation can be made by an "outside expert," say the social scientist. The crucial point to recall is that the proposer is **not a dictator;** he has **no power to enforce** his recommendation.)

The theory proposed in this book, called the ***theory of social situations,*** applies to all social environments in which each individual is **"a rational free being"** in the sense that he:

i. Understands any recommendation proposed to him.
ii. Chooses the action that yields for him the most preferred result. In particular, he is not bound by the recommendations; he is completely free to ignore them.
iii. Takes into account the consequences of his decisions.

1.2 Social situations

By properties (i)–(iii), the central question that must be addressed is: ***What recommendations will be accepted, or followed, by free rational individuals?***

To answer this question individuals must know the alternatives that are available to them should they decide to reject the recommended course of action. Indeed, one of the building blocks in economics is the notion of alternative or opportunity costs. "Homo-Economicus" makes a "right" or "rational" decision if and only if the action he chooses is such that no other action available to him gives him a higher payoff. It is only on the basis of the options that the economic agent has that we evaluate his choice. An explicit description must therefore be given of the precise alternatives that are available to the individual agent (e.g., the consumer, the firm, or the political party) or group of agents (e.g., the household, the cartel, or political "blocks"); in its absence it is hard to see the criterion for predicting or evaluating the chosen actions.

A useful description of the social environment must, therefore, specify in an explicit and detailed manner the opportunities that are available to the individuals. (As is always the case in science, it is the guiding question that dictates the type of data to be collected and the way in which these data should be organized.) I shall argue that the notion of a **"situation"** (see Definition 2.1.3.) provides an appropriate **representation of the social environment.**

Roughly, the concept of "situation" requires the precise specification of the alternatives that are available to the individuals. A situation comprises the two notions: **"position"** and **"inducement correspondence."** A **"position"** describes "the current state." It specifies the set of **players,** the set of feasible **"outcomes,"** and the **preferences** of the individuals over this set. But the alternatives individuals have are not confined only to choices among the outcomes for the position they are currently in; they may be able "to induce" an altogether different position. This additional information is provided by the **"inducement correspondence."**

The theory of social situations insists that social environments be represented by means of a (social) "situation," which is a pair (γ,Γ), where Γ is a collection of positions and γ is the inducement correspondence which specifies for each group of players the positions it can induce from any given position in Γ, when a particular outcome in that position is recommended. Moreover, all of the induced positions must also belong to Γ.

1.3 Acceptable recommended outcomes

A particular theory in the social sciences is delineated by its recommendations. Properties (i)–(iii) have implications not only for the way social environments ought to be represented, but they also restrict the outcomes that may be adopted by free rational players. In particular, if a given outcome, x, is recommended, then there should be no group of individuals, S, who will find it beneficial to reject x and induce a position in which the **recommended** outcomes render all members of S better off. This property, namely, that the recommendations (or the particular theory) are not self-defeating, is called **"internal stability."**

Internal stability requires that **the recommended outcomes** be consistent. But a restriction on the set of outcomes that are not recommended is also called for. The **exclusion of outcomes should not be arbitrary;** there ought to be a reason why a particular outcome is not recommended. I suggest that the only reason for not recommending a feasible course of action is that were it recommended, internal stability would be violated. That is, if it were proposed, then it would be rejected by at least one group of players who could then induce a position in which the **recommended outcomes** would be preferred by all members to the proposed course of action. This property is called **external stability:** Outcomes that are not recommended are those outcomes that must be excluded for the consistency of the recommendations to hold.

The only requirement imposed by the theory of social situations is that the recommendations be both internally and externally stable.

1.4 Merits of the theory of social situations

In view of the sociology of science, a novel theory, in order to be adopted, or even accepted, has to first prove itself within the existing paradigm (in addition to amending and extending it). It is for this reason that the material in this book is partially biased toward ("classical") game theory. Therefore, although many of the results obtained are of intrinsic value, their prime purpose here is to demonstrate the usefulness of the proposed approach. As Example 3.6 suggests, the fruitfulness of the theory of social situations will be manifested also when it is applied to specific social environments that are of interest to economists, political scientists, or psychologists.

Since a careful reading of the proposed theory might be both time consuming and intellectually demanding, it seems appropriate to provide the reader with the incentive to do so. Therefore, I shall now briefly outline some of the advantages of the proposed approach, thereby hoping to convince the reader that it is worth his while to induce the position in which he is acquainted with the theory of social situations.

Perhaps the most important advantage of the proposed theory is that **the representation of a social environment as a situation forces the specification**

of all the relevant information, information that, thus far, has been overlooked, and, only after being pointed out, is perceived as essential. The inducement correspondence forces the specification of, for example: (i) The beliefs of the players, in particular, the anticipation of a player concerning the possible reactions of the other players to the action he chooses; (ii) the availability of legal institutions, such as the possibility to sign binding agreements; and (iii) the precise negotiation process. (For example, what type of threats are used: "Tender threats" that can be countered and modified, or are the threats in fact commitments that must actually be carried out?)

In Chapters 6–9 I shall argue that the representation of social environments suggested by classical game theory often omits the foregoing vital information. This is true for all three types of "games": characteristic function, normal, and extensive form games.

II

The theory of social situations **recognizes and accommodates the possibility that a group of individuals may choose to coordinate their actions.** (In fact, the theory does not at all distinguish between coalitions and single players; the inducement correspondence has to be specified for both.) In contrast, as Shubik (1984) rightly points out, game theory today is incapable of an adequate treatment of coalitions.

> In much of actual bargaining and negotiation, communication about contingent behavior is in words or gestures, sometimes with and sometimes without contracts or binding agreements. A major difficulty in applying game theory to the study of bargaining or negotiation is that the theory is not designed to deal with words and gestures – especially when they are deliberately ambiguous – as moves. Verbal sallies pose two unresolved problems in game-theoretic modeling: (1) how to code words, (2) how to describe the degree of commitment (p. 293).

A similar observation was made by McKinsey (1952):

> . . . even if the theory of noncooperative games were in a completely satisfactory state, there appear to be difficulties in connection with the reduction of cooperative games to noncooperative games. It is extremely difficult in practice to introduce into the cooperative games the moves corresponding to negotiations in a way which will reflect all the infinite variety permissible in the cooperative game, and to do this without giving one player an artificial advantage (because of his having the first chance to make an offer, let us say) (p. 359).

But, the empirical fact is that our social life is almost entirely conducted within the structure of coalitions. (Individual consumers are households or families, firms are large coalitions of owners of different factors of production, workers are organized into unions, and we organize and govern ourselves in political parties and social clubs.) The theory of social situations overcomes the difficulties mentioned in the above quotes, because the inducement correspondence specifies the opportunities that are available to coalitions, but does not require that an explicit and rigid "process" be given concerning the exact way in which coalitions can form. Thus, for example, we can incorporate tax advantages for married couples without elaborating on the exact way the decision to get married was reached. Similarly, majorities can be endowed with (say, veto) power, although the manner in which majorities form remains unspecified.

III

The proposed approach **unifies the description** of social environments by insisting that social environments, cooperative and noncooperative, be represented as situations. The theory of social situations, therefore, brings together diverse formulations of social interactions. In particular, the three different types of games, those in extensive form, normal (or strategic) form, and characteristic function (or coalitional) form, are all described in the same manner, namely, as a pair (γ,Γ).

IV

In addition to unifying the description of social environments, the theory of social situations, by insisting on the single stability criterion, also offers **a unified solution concept**. A unified theory is useful in clarifying relationships among competing solution concepts thereby indicating which are most useful in particular applications. In their pioneering work, von Neumann and Morgenstern (1947) expressed the desire to integrate social sciences. They realized, however, that this goal cannot be easily reached:

> First let us be aware that there exists at present no universal system of economic theory and that, if one should ever be developed, it will very probably not be during our lifetime. The reason for this is that economics is far too difficult a science to permit its construction rapidly (p. 2).

Indeed, as noted above, game theory offers three distinct representations of a social environment. Moreover, to each type of game, game theory offers an abundance of solution concepts whose underlying motivations differ considerably. In contrast, the theory of social situations insists on a unique representation – "situation" – and a unique solution concept – "stable standard of behavior." Interestingly, important aspects of the proposed approach are (at least formally) closely related to ideas promoted by the founders of game theory, von Neumann and Morgenstern. (See Chapter 4.)

V

The unified description of the social environment as a situation is completely detached from the unified stability criterion for the recommended outcomes. This, again, contrasts with many game-theoretic solution concepts. For example, the well-known Nash equilibrium for normal form games (Chapter 7) involves the description of the beliefs of the set of players. Similarly, the concept of subgame perfect equilibrium for games in extensive form (Chapter 8) incorporates (implicitly) the institutional assumption that no commitments of future actions can be made. Such assumptions ought to be part of the description, not of the solution concept. This is the case with the proposed theory.

VI

The application of the theory of social situations to each of the three types of games, that is, representing a "game" as a situation, **yields several of the better known game-theoretic solution concepts,** such as: the core, the von Neumann and Morgenstern solution for cooperative games (Chapter 6), Nash, strong Nash, and coalition-proof Nash equilibria for games in normal form (Chapter 7), subgame perfect equilibria for extensive form games (with perfect information and without chance moves (Chapter 8), and monotonic social choice rules (Chapter 10).

The characterization of these notions as stable recommendations (for the associated situations), **sheds new light on and relates these currently disparate notions** by pointing out the underlying negotiation processes that lead to them. These conceptual results yield, in turn, **new properties of the existing solution concepts.**

In addition, the theory of social situations enables us not only to redefine, but also to **generalize known solution concepts.** Thus, for example, the concept of coalition-proof Nash equilibrium can be extended to games with an infinite number of players, or to dynamic games with an infinite time horizon. (See Chapters 7 and 8.)

VII

The application of the proposed approach to game theory suggests also **new and interesting solution concepts** by examining different beliefs and legal systems. Moreover, because of its unifying nature, the theory of social situations enables us to "import" game-theoretic solutions from one type of game to another, thereby creating new (analogous) solutions. And, of course, since coalitions are naturally incorporated into the theory, it is also possible to extend "noncooperative" solutions and allow for groups of individuals to coordinate their actions. Among the new solution concepts that we shall examine are: the stable bargaining set (Chapter 6), open negotiations in normal form games – the individual and coalitional contingent threats and the individual and coalitional commitments (Chapter 7), a refinement of subgame perfect equilibrium (Chapter 8), and the notion of coalitional perfect equilibrium paths in game trees and in repeated games (Chapters 8 and 9). It is encouraging that some of these new solution concepts, which naturally emerge from the proposed approach, have been independently suggested, in particular examples and for ad hoc reasons, by other scholars (see Chapters 6–8).

VIII

The theory of social situations **takes most of the "rationality requirements" away from the players and puts them on the recommendations.** Thus, in contrast to current trends in game theory where players are assumed to be engaged in extremely sophisticated inferences, under the proposed approach players have to simply judge the consistency of the prescribed course of action (see Section 11.1).

IX

The theory of social situations allows for **"human rationality" limiting both the perception and the computation abilities of the players.** Indeed, since the notion of situation is sufficiently general, the proposed theory enables the players to simplify the description of the social environment in ways that "classical" game theory cannot (see Section 11.3).

X

The theory of social situations is **simple and intuitively appealing.** Indeed, it seems that when confronted with a specific offer, an individual asks himself, "If I reject the proposed offer, what could be the consequences of my refusal?" Provided with the answer to this question, an individual, or a group of individuals, will then reject an offer if and only if he can, thereby, be made better off.

1.5 The organization of the book

The book is, essentially, self-contained. Most of the material is formal (hence, mathematical maturity is helpful) but does not require advanced technical tools. The prime purpose of the book is to point out the great potential of the theory of social situations. Therefore, I have often sacrificed generality for the sake of simplicity. To further facilitate the reading, the proofs of the theorems are presented at the end of the corresponding chapters.

The theory of social situations is presented in the next chapter (Sections 2.1–2.4) in which the motivation and precise definitions of the notions of "position," "inducement correspondence," and "stability" are given. Chapter 3 provides some examples whose main purpose is to familiarize the reader with the concepts defined in Chapter 2.

The close relationship between (optimistic) stable standards of behavior and von Neumann and Morgenstern abstract stable sets is established in Chapter 4.

General existence and uniqueness results are formulated in Chapter 5. This chapter, which is somewhat technical, can be skipped, at least on the first reading, especially by readers whose main interest lies in the application of the theory to particular social environments rather than in general mathematical properties.

Applications of the theory of social situations to particular classical models in the social sciences are presented in Example 3.6 and Chapters 6–10. The corresponding chapter headings suggest the specific examples that are examined. Each of these five chapters is, essentially, self-contained and can be read independently of the others.

Chapter 11 concludes the book by offering some directions for possible extensions of the proposed theory.

CHAPTER 2

The theory of social situations

The theory of social situations has two main ingredients. First, it offers a unified way to represent social environments, namely, by means of "situations." Second, it offers a unified criterion for the recommendations, namely, that the "standard of behavior" (for the given situation) be "stable."

2.1 Situations

The notion of a "situation" defined below provides a complete description of the social environment. It specifies in an explicit and detailed manner the opportunities that are available to the agents.

To motivate and facilitate the definition of a situation, consider the game of chess. The set of players consists of two individuals: Black and White. There is a collection, say, C, of **"admissible" configurations of the pieces on the board.** For example, every configuration in C must be such that both kings are present on the board and occupy nonadjacent squares. For each pair (c,i), where c is a particular configuration in C and i is one of the two players, there is a set of configurations in C that player i can "induce" from c, if it is i's turn to make a move once c was reached. When this set is empty player i is checkmated. Clearly, all induced configurations must themselves be admissible, that is, belong to C, since the rules of the game apply to such and only such configurations. Chess, then, can be fully described by:

a. the set of pairs (c,i), where c is an admissible configuration of the pieces on the board and i is the player who is to move at c, and
b. the relation, γ, that assigns to each pair (c,i) a collection of pairs (d,j), where d is an admissible configuration that i, by making the first move, can induce from c (and it is player j, $j \neq i$, that makes the first move from the configuration d).

This is, of course, different from the usual way of describing chess. Indeed, the above description does not specify directly how a particular piece can move. It states what configurations (of the pieces on the entire board) can result if it is player i's turn to make a move and i faces the configuration c. As this is a complete description, it is possible (but by no means easy) to derive the rules for "legitimate moves in chess." (Since chess serves here merely to give the flavor of the notion of situation, I ignore the fact that the history that leads to a particular configuration can be important. Castling, for example, is allowed only if the king has not moved previously.)

Since chess is a relatively simple game to describe (but certainly not to play), there may be little advantage in representing it as in (a) and (b). But we shall see that modeling social environments in this manner, that is, as a "situation," proves to be most useful and fruitful.

The two building blocks for the concept of a situation are "position" and "inducement correspondence." A position describes "the current state of affairs." A position specifies, for the given stage, the set of individuals, the set of all possible outcomes, and the preferences of the individuals over this set of outcomes. Formally, a "position" is defined in the following way:

Definition 2.1.1: *A* ***position,*** *G, is a triple* $\mathbf{G \equiv (N(G), X(G), \{u^i(G)\}_{i \in N(G)})}$, *where N(G) is the set of* **players,** *X(G) is the set of all feasible* **outcomes,** *and* $u^i(G)$ *is the* ***utility function*** *of player i in position G over the outcomes, that is,* $u^i(G): X(G) \to \mathbb{R}$. *[That is, for all* $x, y \in X(G)$, *and for all* $i \in N(G)$, $u^i(G)(x) > u^i(G)(y)$ *if and only if i prefers, in position G, the outcome x over the outcome y.]*

The nature of an outcome is completely arbitrary. An outcome is a feasible alternative; it need not be a "predicted," "reasonable," or "rational" alternative. The set of outcomes describes the feasibility constraints at the particular stage, and not the choices that are likely or should be made. The only requirement is that the domain of the utility functions of the players be the set of outcomes, that is, that players in position G be able to evaluate every outcome in $X(G)$.

In chess, for example, we can associate with the pair (c,i), (where c is the current configuration and it is i's turn to make the next move), the position $\mathbf{G = G(c,i)}$, where the set of players consists of Black and White, that is, $N(G) = \{B, W\}$. The set of outcomes, $X(G)$, is the set of all possible "plays" from c when i is the first to move. [That is, $X(G)$ consists of all sequences of alternating "legitimate moves" starting with player i making the first move and ending with either a win or a draw. Recall that the players' preferences must be defined over the set of outcomes.] To complete the description of the position $G = G(c,i)$, we need to specify the utility functions, $u^i(G)$, $i \in N(G)$. Let $x \in X(G)$. If following the sequence of moves x results in player h winning the game, define $u^h(G)(x)$ to be, say, 1, and $u^j(G)(x)$ to be, say, -1, and if following x results in a draw, let $u^h(G)(x) = u^j(G)(x) = 0$.

Another, and more formal, illustration of the notion of position is provided by the following:

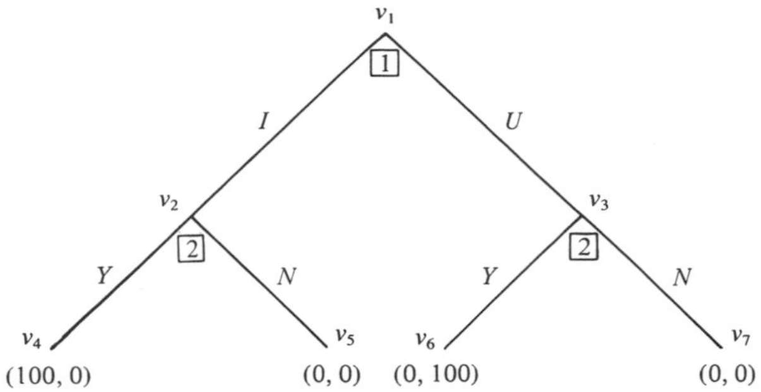

Figure 2.1.2

Example 2.1.2: Two individuals, 1 and 2, are getting divorced and have to decide who will raise their only child. The utility level each parent derives from having (or not having, respectively) custody over the child is 100 (respectively, 0) utils. (Side-payments are not allowed.) If the parents agree on who gets custody, the agreement will be implemented. Otherwise, neither gets custody (and the child will go to a boarding school). Suppose that the negotiation process between the parents is such that 1 proposes who gets custody, and 2 can then agree or disagree to the proposal. Let I and U denote the actions of player 1, where I means "*I* get custody" and U means "You get custody." Similarly, Let Y and N denote the actions of player 2, where Y means "I agree to your proposal" and N means "I don't agree to your proposal." Figure 2.1.2, known as the "game tree" (see Chapter 8), is a graphic representation of this "story." (For a less dramatic interpretation of this game tree replace the child by an "indivisible object.")

The position, G^0, which we shall associate with the beginning of the negotiation between the two parents, is given by

$$G^0 \equiv (\{1,2\},\{(I,Y),(I,N),(U,Y),\ (U,N)\},\{u^1(G^0),u^2(G^0)\}),$$

where

$$u^1(G^0)(I,Y)=100;\ u^1(G^0)(I,N)=u^1(G^0)(U,Y)=u^1(G^0)(U,N)=0;$$
$$u^2(G^0)(U,Y)=100;\ u^2(G^0)(I,Y)=u^2(G^0)(I,N)=u^2(G^0)(U,N)=0.$$

That is, the set of players, $N(G^0)$, consists of the two individuals, the set of outcomes, $X(G^0)$, is the set of the four possible sequences of actions the two players can take, and the utility functions, $u^i(G^0)$, $i=1,2$, specify the payoffs that result from these four courses of action.

Let us now turn to the second building block of the concept of situation – the inducement correspondence. Consider a position G and suppose that outcome $x^* \in X(G)$ is proposed. (Recall that I confine myself to those formal models in which a course of action cannot be imposed, but rather is recommended to the players.) Should player $i \in N(G)$ accept or reject this proposed outcome? In order to answer this question player i must know what are the alternatives that are available to him if he chooses to reject x^*. That is, i must know the set of positions that he can induce from the position G when the outcome x^* is offered. Let $\boldsymbol{\gamma(\{i\}|G,x^*)}$ denote this set.[1] Moreover, in order to decide whether or not he wishes to induce a position $H \in \gamma(\{i\}|G,x^*)$, player i must be able to anticipate what might happen once H is induced. In particular, he has to know what positions can, in turn, be induced from (the induced) position H.

The next step is to apply the same reasoning to a group of individuals. It is quite possible that a coalition consisting of several members of a society can induce positions that cannot be induced by any single individual. (Passing a bill, for example, requires the consent of a majority of the individuals. Similarly, it takes two to get married.) Given a position G and a proposed outcome $x^* \in X(G)$, let $\boldsymbol{\gamma(S|G,x^*)}$ denote the set of positions that a coalition, S, $S \subset N(G)$,[2,3] can induce from G when x^* is proposed. Then, following the same arguments advanced for a single individual, members of S must know not only the set $\gamma(S|G,x^*)$, but also the possible "chain reaction" that might occur should S decide to induce a position $H \in \gamma(S|G,x^*)$.

An appropriate description of the social environment or the social interaction is, therefore, given by the following concept of a situation.

Definition 2.1.3: A ***situation*** *is a pair* (γ,Γ), *where* Γ *is a set of positions, and the mapping* γ, *called* **the inducement correspondence,** *satisfies the condition that for all* $G \in \Gamma$, $S \subset N(G)$, *and* $x \in X(G)$, $\gamma(S|G,x) \subset \Gamma$. (*That is,* Γ *is closed under* γ.)

The requirement that Γ is closed under γ guarantees that "the rules of the game" specify what can happen from any admissible (possibly itself an induced) position $G \in \Gamma$, when a feasible outcome $x \in X(G)$ is proposed.

The only requirement imposed on the inducement correspondence, γ, is that the set of players of each position that a coalition S can induce, includes, but need not coincide with, the players in S. Formally, we have the following assumption:

Assumption 2.1.4: *Let* (γ,Γ) *be a situation. For all* $G \in \Gamma$, $S \subset N(G)$, *and* $x \in X(G)$, *if* $H \in \gamma(S|G,x)$, *then* $S \subset N(H)$.

[1] We shall see that in many social environments the proposed outcome might, indeed, affect the set of positions a player can induce. It is for this reason that γ is allowed to depend on x^*.

[2] A coalition is a *nonempty* subset of the set of players.

[3] All inclusions in this book are weak.

Note that this mild and natural assumption does not rule out the possibility that γ assigns the empty set to some (or even all) coalitions, that is, some coalitions may be unable to induce any position at all. (Indeed, in chess, for example, the end of the game is characterized by such positions.)

Example 2.1.2 will now be used, again, to illustrate the notion of situation. Recall that if player 1 demands custody over the child, then player 2 can either agree (Y) or not agree (N) to this proposal. Therefore, by choosing the action I, player 1 can induce the position G^I, where

$$G^I \equiv (\{1,2\},\{Y,N\},\{u^1(G^I),u^2(G^I)\}),$$
$$u^1(G^I)(Y)=100,\ u^1(G^I)(N)=0,\ u^2(G^I)(Y)=u^2(G^I)(N)=0.$$

Similarly, by choosing the action U, player 1 can induce the position G^U, where

$$G^U \equiv (\{1,2\},\{Y,N\},\{u^1(G^U),u^2(G^U)\}),$$
$$u^1(G^U)(Y)=u^1(G^U)(N)=0,\ u^2(G^U)(Y)=100,\ u^2(G^U)(N)=0.$$

Once G^I is induced, player 2 can choose between Y and N, thereby inducing the positions G^{IY} and G^{IN}, given by:

$$G^{IY} \equiv (\{1,2\},\{(100,0)\},\{u^1(G^{IY}),u^2(G^{IY})\}),$$
$$u^1(G^{IY})(100,0)=100,\ u^2(G^{IY})(100,0)=0;$$

and

$$G^{IN} \equiv (\{1,2\},\ \{(0,0)\},\ \{u^1(G^{IN}),\ u^2(G^{IN})\}),$$
$$u^1(G^{IN})(0,0)=u^2(G^{IN})(0,0)=0.$$

Similarly, once G^U is induced, player 2 can choose between Y and N, thereby inducing the positions G^{UY} and G^{UN}, given by:

$$G^{UY} \equiv (\{1,2\},\{(0,100)\},\{u^1(G^{UY}),u^2(G^{UY})\}),$$
$$u^1(G^{UY})(0,100)=0,\ u^2(G^{UY})(0,100)=100;$$

and

$$G^{UN} \equiv (\{1,2\},\ \{(0,0)\},\ \{u^1(G^{UN}),u^2(G^{UN})\}),$$
$$u^1(G^{UN})(0,0)=u^2(G^{UN})(0,0)=0.$$

The set of positions in the situation associated with Example 2.1.2 consists, therefore, of seven positions, that is,

$$\Gamma \equiv \{G^0,G^I,G^U,G^{IY},G^{IN},G^{UY},G^{UN}\},$$

and the natural inducement correspondence γ is given by:

$$\gamma(\{1\}|G^0,x)=\{G^I,G^U\}, \qquad \text{for all } x \in X(G^0),$$
$$\gamma(\{2\}|G^0,(I,Y))=\gamma(\{2\}|G^0,(I,N))=\{G^{IY},G^{IN}\},$$
$$\gamma(\{2\}|G^0,(U,Y))=\gamma(\{2\}|G^0,(U,N))=\{G^{UY},G^{UN}\},$$

$$\gamma(\{2\}|G^I,x)=\{G^{IY},G^{IN}\}, \qquad \text{for all } x\in X(G^I),$$
$$\gamma(\{2\}|G^U,x)=\{G^{UY},G^{UN}\}, \qquad \text{for all } x\in X(G^U),$$

and, for all $G\in\Gamma$, $S\subset N(G)$, and $x\in X(G)$,

$$\gamma(S|G,x)=\emptyset, \qquad \text{otherwise.}$$

Note that the positions which player 2 can induce from position G^0 depend on the proposed outcome (specifically, on the offer that player 1 makes).

2.2 Standards of behavior

A situation (γ,Γ) describes the social environment. It is totally silent about what outcomes are expected to arise in a particular position G in Γ. It is the role of the particular theory that is employed to predict or suggest the outcomes that might result from the interaction of the players.

Consider a situation (γ,Γ), let G be a position in Γ and x^* be a feasible outcome in G. The inducement correspondence γ informs the players as to what the positions are that a coalition $S\subset N(G)$ can then induce, namely, the subset $\gamma(S|G,x^*)$ of Γ. It provides no answer to the question: Which, if any, of these positions would S want to induce? But this information is required to predict the set of outcomes that the players in $N(G)$ will agree to follow, a set that consists of all the feasible outcomes in $X(G)$ from which no coalition will choose to induce another position.

There is little hope to be able to assert that a particular outcome in $X(G)$ is the only one that is likely to be agreed upon by the players in $N(G)$. In general, we hope to be able to find a subset of the set of outcomes, called a "solution for G," consisting of all those outcomes that are likely to be accepted by the players in $N(G)$. Put differently, the solution for position G is the set of all "sensible" or "reasonable" outcomes in $X(G)$. Outcomes that belong to $X(G)$ but are not in the solution for G are feasible but will be objected to by some players in $N(G)$. These outcomes, therefore, will never actually be reached.

However, at this stage, we have no criterion for deciding which outcomes are "sensible" or "reasonable." (The next sections discuss this issue.) Therefore, and most generally, a solution is defined to be any arbitrary subset of the set of outcomes. In particular, the notion of solution involves no "rationality" or "moral" considerations. Formally, we have Definition 2.2.1.

Definition 2.2.1: *A* ***solution for position G*** *is a subset of* $X(G)$*, denoted* $\sigma(G)$*.*

Notice that although a solution $\sigma(G)$ is, typically, a strict subset of the set of all feasible outcomes, $X(G)$, it is the case that $X(G)$ does affect $\sigma(G)$ and therefore one cannot replace the former set with the latter. In other words, the set $\sigma(G)$ cannot be determined independently of $X(G)$. The mere fact that some outcomes, not necessarily in the solution, could potentially be adopted, may well exclude other outcomes from belonging to the solution. (This point is illustrated by the following story. A newly crowned king asked the "wise man" of his kingdom how to make the people obey him. "Don't ever ask them to do things you know they will refuse to do" was the wise man's reply.)

Let $G \in \Gamma$, $x^* \in X(G)$, and $H \in \gamma(S|G,x^*)$. Should members of S reject x^* and induce H instead? In order to answer this question it is not sufficient for the players to know the set $X(H)$ of potentially feasible outcomes; they must also know the outcomes that are expected to result once position H is induced, namely, the soultion for H. That is, the acceptablity of an outcome x^* in $X(G)$ depends on the outcomes that are (predicted to be) accepted in the positions that can be induced from G when x^* is proposed. It is for this important reason that the concept of a standard of behavior is introduced.

Definition 2.2.2: *Let Γ be a collection of positions. A mapping σ that assigns to each position $G \in \Gamma$ a solution, $\sigma(G)$, is called a* ***standard of behavior (SB) for*** Γ.

Given the description of the social environment as a situation, a standard of behavior specifies the solution to every position in Γ. **A particular theory in the social sciences is delineated by the standard of behavior that it generates.**

It is important to note that no "continuity" or any other assumptions on the mapping σ are imposed. An SB σ for Γ is any arbitrary mapping. Neither ethical nor any other considerations constrain the relations between solutions assigned by σ to positions in Γ.

2.3 Stability

A situation (γ,Γ) describes the social environment, and the standard of behavior σ for this situation specifies for each position $G \in \Gamma$ the set of outcomes that are "reasonable" or "sensible." As was emphasized above, σ can be any arbitrary mapping. But it is clear that "rational" players will not follow a "senseless" standard of behavior. Some restrictions on σ seem necessary if σ is to be adopted. (Recall that players are free to choose to obey or disobey σ.) I shall impose only one restriction on the SB σ, namely, that it be "stable."

To motivate the definition of (internal) stability, consider the SB σ that assigns the outcome "resign" to every player in any configuration of the pieces on the chess board. There are several reasons why this σ is not "sensible.'' One obvious objection to this σ is that if in position $G(c,i)$ player i can checkmate his opponent, then he certainly will not follow the prescription of σ to resign. But there is a more fundamental reason why this SB is ''unreasonable'': It is self-defeating. Indeed, and this is the main contention, even if player i is ''losing,'' he should reject the recommendation of σ because of the following argument: If σ is adopted (by both players), then player i knows that his opponent, j, will resign, no matter what position i will induce, that is, no matter what move i will choose to make (provided only that i is not currently checkmated, in which case he can induce no position). Why, then, should player i resign? More generally,

> the standard of behavior must be free of inner contradictions: No outcome y conforming with the accepted standard of behavior can be upset by another outcome of the same kind (von Neumann and Morgenstern, 1947, p. 41, with minor modifications).

This consistency property of the SB is called ''internal stability.'' More specifically, let (γ,Γ) be a situation, and let σ be an SB for Γ. If all players adopt the recommendations made by σ, it seems reasonable to stipulate that a group of players, S, will reject an outcome, $x^* \in X(G)$, if it can induce a position $H \epsilon \gamma(S|G,x^*)$, whose **solution, $\sigma(H)$, benefits all members of S.**[1] It is important to note that the rejection of x^* must depend only on those outcomes that belong to $\sigma(H)$, not on the entire set of feasible outcomes, $X(H)$. (Recall that if σ is adopted then outcomes that belong to $X(H)\backslash\sigma(H)$ will never be agreed upon by the players in $N(H)$, and therefore cannot be the basis for ''valid objections.'') Indeed,

> if the standard of behavior σ is accepted by the players, then it must impress upon their minds the idea that only outcomes assigned by σ are sound (von Neumann and Morgenstern, 1947, p. 265, with minor modifications).

Let (γ,Γ) be a situation, and let σ be an SB for Γ. We shall say that the SB, σ, is ***internally stable for*** (γ,Γ) if for all $G \in \Gamma$, $x^* \in \sigma(G)$ implies that there exist no coalition $S \subset N(G)$ and position $H \in \gamma(S|G,x^*)$ such that S benefits by rejecting x^* and inducing H, realizing that the solution to H is given by $\sigma(H)$. That is, if σ is internally stable then accepting the

[1] The meaning of the emphasized clause is, however, not entirely clear. What are the utility levels members of S can expect to have, once they induce position H? The difficulty arises when, as is generally the case, $\sigma(H)$ contains several outcomes, some of which may benefit all members of S while other outcomes in $\sigma(H)$ may make some, or even all, members of S worse off than they are under x. It is by no means evident that these players will then be willing to reject x. Two possible ways to resolve this difficulty will be suggested in the next section. Assume, for now, that the expression ''coalition S prefers the set of outcomes $\sigma(H)$ in position H to the outcome x in position G'' is meaningful. Of course, such is the case when $\sigma(H)$ is a singleton, that is, $\sigma(H)=\{y^*\}$ for some $y^* \in X(H)$. See also Section 11.5.

SB σ implies the willingness of all players to follow its recommendations.

I shall now argue that another requirement, in addition to internal stability, should be imposed on the SB. For a dramatic example that illustrates this point, consider the SB σ that assigns the empty set to each position, that is, $\sigma(G)=\emptyset$ for all $G\in\Gamma$. Evidently, as no recommendations are made, no inner contradiction can arise, and hence σ is (trivially) internally stable. [It follows that for every situation (γ,Γ) there exists an internally stable SB.]

Thus, in addition to specifying the set of recommended outcomes, a theory, delineated by the SB σ, should also explain why other feasible outcomes are excluded. That is, the SB σ must account, for every position $G\in\Gamma$, not only for elements in $\sigma(G)$ but also for outcomes in $X(G)\backslash\sigma(G)$. There ought to be a reason why an outcome $x\in X(G)$ does not belong to the solution $\sigma(G)$.

I contend that unless the SB σ is arbitrary, then the only reason for excluding $x\in X(G)$ should be that were it included in $\sigma(G)$, the internal stability of the mapping σ would then be violated. This property is called external stability. More specifically, let (γ,Γ) be a situation, and let σ be an SB for Γ. We shall say that the SB σ is ***externally stable*** if for all $G\in\Gamma$, $x\in X(G)\backslash\sigma(G)$ implies that there exist a coalition $S\subset N(G)$ and a position $H\in\gamma(S|G,x)$ such that S benefits by rejecting x and inducing H, realizing that the solution to H is given by $\sigma(H)$. The appeal of external stability is illustrated by the following quote.

> If the players have accepted σ as the standard of behavior, then the ability to discredit, with the help of σ, any outcome not assigned by σ, is necessary to maintain their faith in σ (von Neumann and Morgenstern, p. 266, with minor modifications).

The overall single consistency requirement that I shall impose on the SB is that it be ***stable,*** that is, that it be both internally and externally stable. Stable standards of behavior are such that

> . . . once they are generally accepted, they overrule everything else and no part of them can be overruled within the limits of the accepted standards. This is clearly how things are in actual social organizations (von Neumann and Morgenstern, 1947, p. 42).

2.4 OSSB and CSSB

Although the motivation behind the requirements of internal and external stability is clear, the expression "members of S prefer (the set) $\sigma(H)$ over the outcome $x\in\sigma(G)$," which appears in the definitions of these terms, is, as noted above, ambiguous. To resolve this difficulty, I shall consider two (extreme) behavioral assumptions: optimistic and conservative. As we shall see, these two extreme assumptions yield many remarkable results. Moreover, many of the situations that we shall analyze (and which yield well-known game-theoretic solution concepts) admit a unique optimistic, which coincides with the unique conservative, stable standard of behavior. But these results should not, of course, discourage the investigation of alternative, and perhaps more plausible, behavioral assumptions. (See Section 11.5.)

The assumption of optimistic behavior entails that members of S prefer $\sigma(H)$ over $x \in X(G)$ if *there exists* an outcome $y \in \sigma(H)$ that all members of S prefer to x. The opposite extreme assumption is that players behave "conservatively," and S will reject a proposed outcome x in position G, and induce, instead, the position $H \in \gamma(S|G,x)$, only if *all* outcomes in $\sigma(H)$ make all members of S better off. Formally, this is expressed by the following definitions.

Definition 2.4.1: *Let σ be an SB for the situation (γ,Γ). We shall say that σ is* ***optimistic internally stable for (γ,Γ)*** *if for all $G \in \Gamma$, $x \in \sigma(G)$ implies that there do not exist a coalition $S \subset N(G)$, a position $H \in \gamma(S|G,x)$, and an outcome $y \in \sigma(H)$ such that for all $i \in S$, $u^i(H)(y) > u^i(G)(x)$.*

Optimistic internal stability requires that no coalition can induce a position whose solution contains an outcome which is more favorable to all its members. The counterpart of optimistic internal stability is the requirement of optimistic external stability, that is, the only reason for excluding an outcome from the solution is that were it included optimistic internal stability would be violated.

Definition 2.4.2: *Let σ be an SB for the situation (γ,Γ). The SB σ is* ***optimistic externally stable for (γ,Γ)*** *if for all $G \in \Gamma$, $x \in X(G) \backslash \sigma(G)$ implies that there exist $S \subset N(G)$, $H \in \gamma(S|G,x)$, and $y \in \sigma(H)$ such that $u^i(H)(y) > u^i(G)(x)$ for all $i \in S$.*

Combining the two stability conditions, we have

Definition 2.4.3: *Let σ be an SB for the situation (γ,Γ). If σ is both optimistic internally and externally stable for (γ,Γ) then σ is an* ***optimistic stable standard of behavior (OSSB) for (γ,Γ).***

If the players behave conservatively, then analogous to Definitions 2.4.1–3, we have the following definitions:

Definition 2.4.4: *Let σ be an SB for the situation (γ,Γ). The SB σ is* ***conservative internally stable for (γ,Γ)*** *if for all $G \in \Gamma$, $x \in \sigma(G)$ implies that there exist no $S \subset N(G)$ and $H \in \gamma(S|G,x)$ such that $\sigma(H) \neq \emptyset$, and for all $y \in \sigma(H)$, $u^i(H)(y) > u^i(G)(x)$ for all $i \in S$.*

Observe that the additional requirement that the induced position H have a nonempty solution is automatically satisfied in Definition 2.4.2; it is guaranteed by the requirement that there exists $y \in \sigma(H)$. One can interpret $\sigma(H)=\emptyset$ to mean that once H is induced, there is no outcome that the players of H might agree upon, that is, H is, according to the SB σ, a "chaotic" position; it contains no "reasonable" outcome. Surely, players who are conservative will avoid such positions.

Definition 2.4.5: *Let σ be an SB for the situation (γ,Γ). The SB σ is* ***conservative externally stable for*** (γ,Γ) *if for all $G \in \Gamma$, $x \in X(G) \setminus \sigma(G)$ implies that there exist $S \subset N(G)$ and $H \in \gamma(S|G,x)$ such that $\sigma(H) \neq \emptyset$, and for all $y \in \sigma(H)$, $u^i(H)(y) > u^i(G)(x)$ for all $i \in S$.*

Definition 2.4.6: *Let σ be an SB for the situation (γ,Γ). If σ is both conservative internally and externally stable for (γ,Γ) then σ is a* ***conservative stable standard of behavior (CSSB) for*** (γ,Γ).

The notions of ODOM and CDOM, introduced below, provide an alternative and most useful way to define OSSB and CSSB. Let (γ,Γ) be a situation, and let σ be an SB for (γ,Γ). For a position $G \in \Gamma$, define the ***optimistic dominion*** of G (relative to the SB σ), denoted ODOM (σ,G), by

$$\mathbf{ODOM}(\sigma,G)=\{x \in X(G) \mid \exists\ S \subset N(G),\ H \in \gamma(S|G,x),\ \text{and } y \in \sigma(H) \text{ such that for all } i \in S,\ u^i(H)(y) > u^i(G)(x)\}.$$

That is, ODOM (σ,G) consists of all outcomes in $X(G)$ which will be rejected by at least one coalition S (whose members behave in an optimistic way). It is easy to see that the following definition coincides with Definitions 2.4.1–3.

Definition 2.4.7: *Let (γ,Γ) be a situation, and let σ be an SB for (γ,Γ). Then, the SB σ is*

i. ***optimistic internally stable*** *if and only if for all $G \in \Gamma$ and $x \in X(G)$, $x \in \sigma(G)$ implies $x \notin ODOM(\sigma,G)$;*
ii. ***optimistic externally stable*** *if and only if for all $G \in \Gamma$ and $x \in X(G)$, $x \notin \sigma(G)$ implies $x \in ODOM(\sigma,G)$; and*
iii. ***optimistic stable*** *if and only if for all $G \in \Gamma$, $\sigma(G)=X(G) \setminus ODOM(\sigma,G)$.*

Similarly, let (γ,Γ) be a situation, and let σ be an SB for (γ,Γ). For a position $G \in \Gamma$, define the ***conservative dominion*** of G (relative to the SB σ), denoted CDOM(σ,G), by

$$\mathbf{CDOM}(\sigma,G)=\{x \in X(G) \mid \exists\ S \subset N(G) \text{ and } H \in \gamma(S|G,x) \text{ such that } \sigma(H) \neq \emptyset, \text{ and for all } y \in \sigma(H) \text{ and } i \in S,\ u^i(H)(y) > u^i(G)(x)\}.$$

That is, CDOM(σ,G) consists of all outcomes in $X(G)$ which will be rejected by at least one coalition S, (whose members behave conservatively). Again, it is easy to see that the following definition coincides with Definitions 2.4.4–2.4.6.

Definition 2.4.8: *Let* (γ,Γ) *be a situation, and let* σ *be an SB for* (γ,Γ). *Then, the SB* σ *is*

i. ***conservative internally stable*** *if and only if for all* $G\in\Gamma$ *and* $x\in X(G)$, $x\in\sigma(G)$ *implies* $x\notin CDOM(\sigma,G)$;
ii. ***conservative externally stable*** *if and only if for all* $G\in\Gamma$ *and* $x\in X(G)$, $x\notin\sigma(G)$ *implies* $x\in CDOM(\sigma,G)$; *and*
iii. ***conservative stable*** *if and only if for all* $G\in\Gamma$, $\sigma(G)=X(G)\setminus CDOM(\sigma,G)$.

Example 2.1.2 can be used to demonstrate the difference between the notions of OSSB and CSSB. Using Definition 2.4.7, the reader can easily verify that the following SB, σ^o, is an OSSB for the situation (γ,Γ) we associated with this example.

$$\sigma^o(G^0)=\{(I,Y)\},\ \sigma^o(G^I)=\{Y,N\},\ \sigma^o(G^U)=\{Y\},\ \sigma^o(G^{IY})=\{(100,0)\},$$
$$\sigma^o(G^{IN})=\{(0,0)\},\ \sigma^o(G^{UY})=\{(0,100)\},\ \sigma^o(G^{UN})=\{(0,0)\}.$$

Similarly, using Definition 2.4.8, the reader can easily verify that the following SB, σ^c, is a CSSB for the situation (γ,Γ) we associated with this example.

$$\sigma^c(G^0)=\{(I,Y),(I,N),(U,Y)\},\ \sigma^c(G^I)=\{Y,N\},\ \sigma^c(G^U)=\{Y\},$$
$$\sigma^c(G^{IY})=\{(100,0)\},\ \sigma^c(G^{IN})=\{(0,0)\},\ \sigma^c(G^{UY})=\{(0,100)\},$$
$$\sigma^c(G^{UN})=\{(0,0)\}.$$

Theorems 5.2.1 and 5.4.1 establish that σ^o and σ^c are, respectively, the unique OSSB and the unique CSSB for (γ,Γ). Observe that these two SBs coincide on all the positions in Γ except for G^0. (For general properties of the unique OSSB and the unique CSSB, and their relationship to subgame perfect equilibria, see Chapter 8, in particular, Corollaries 8.2.3 and 8.3.2.)

Remark 2.4.9: At least at first sight, it might appear that when players behave more conservatively they will be more hesitant to reject outcomes that are proposed to them. One may conclude, therefore, that if σ^o and σ^c are an OSSB and a CSSB, respectively, for a situation (γ,Γ), then for every position $G\in\Gamma$, $\sigma^o(G)$ is a subset of $\sigma^c(G)$. Such a conclusion is, however, erroneous. Indeed, Example 5.4.3 establishes that it is possible that a situation (γ,Γ) admits a unique OSSB, σ^o, and a unique CSSB, σ^c, having the property that there exists a position $G \in \Gamma$ for which $\sigma^o(G)$ is a strict subset of $\sigma^c(G)$, and there exists another position $H \in \Gamma$ for which $\sigma^c(H)$ is a strict subset of $\sigma^o(H)$.

This section concludes the exposition of the theory of social situations. The rest of the book is devoted to further elaborations, analyses, ramifications, and applications of the theory.

2.5 Preliminary observations

This section consists of a collection of observations which are of intrinsic value, and, in addition, will prove useful subsequently.

As noted in Section 2.3, the SB that assigns to every position the empty set is, trivially, both optimistic and conservative internally stable. Indeed, $\sigma(G)=\emptyset$ for all $G \in \Gamma$ implies that $\text{ODOM}(\sigma,G)=\text{CDOM}(\sigma,G)=\emptyset$. But, this SB is neither optimistic nor conservative stable [unless $X(G)=\emptyset$ for all $G \in \Gamma$, a degenerate case that we shall henceforth exclude].

Claim 2.5.1: *Let (γ,Γ) be a situation, and let σ be an OSSB or a CSSB for (γ,Γ). Then, there exists at least one $G \in \Gamma$ such that $\sigma(G) \neq \emptyset$.*

In Chapter 5 we shall establish the existence and uniqueness of OSSB and CSSB for a large class of situations that represent many interesting social environments. But, as the following claims assert, the existence of neither an OSSB nor a CSSB is guaranteed. These claims also demonstrate, as does Remark 2.4.9, that one cannot infer properties of an OSSB from those of a CSSB, or vice versa. (The distinction between these two notions is further highlighted in Chapter 4; see Theorems 4.5 and 4.10.)

Claim 2.5.2: *There exist situations that admit a CSSB but do not admit any OSSB.*

Claim 2.5.3: *There exist situations that admit an OSSB but do not admit any CSSB.*

Claim 2.5.4: *There exist situations that admit neither an OSSB nor a CSSB.*

The ''ideal''case is, of course, when a situation admits a unique OSSB and a unique CSSB, and, moreover, these two SBs coincide, for then both the internal and the external stability conditions are most compelling. Such is the case, for example, in Roemer (1989), which considers the problem of income distribution under the Rawlsian veil of ignorance. Adapting the model of Howe and Roemer (1981), Roemer shows that the Rawlsian maximin allocations constitute the unique OSSB and the unique CSSB for the associated situation. The following two claims will prove useful for identifying another class of such "ideal" situations from which we shall derive several important classical game-theoretic solution concepts.

Claim 2.5.5: *Let* (γ,Γ) *be a situation, and let* σ *be an SB for* Γ. *Assume that for all* $G\in\Gamma$, $i\in N(G)$, *and* $x,y\in\sigma(G)$, $u^i(G)(x)=u^i(G)(y)$. *Then,* σ *is an OSSB for* (γ,Γ) *if and only if it is a CSSB for* (γ,Γ).

Claim 2.5.6 points out another class of situations that share the property that every OSSB (if it exists) is also a CSSB, and vice versa. These situations satisfy the conditon that for every position G in Γ, either G cannot be induced from any of the positions in Γ, or else all outcomes in $X(G)$ yield the same utility levels to the players in G.

Claim 2.5.6: *Let* (γ,Γ) *be a situation such that* Γ *can be partitioned into two sets,* Γ^1 *and* Γ^2, *where if* $G\in\Gamma^1$ *then there is no* $H\in\Gamma$, $S\subset N(H)$, *and* $x\in X(H)$ *for which* $G\in\gamma(S|H,x)$, *and if* $G\in\Gamma^2$ *then for all* $i\in N(G)$ *and* $x,y\in X(G)$, $u^i(G)(x)=u^i(G)(y)$. *Then,*

i. *an OSSB, as well as a CSSB for* (γ,Γ) *is determined by the solutions it assigns to positions in* Γ^2; *and*

ii. *an SB is an OSSB for* (γ,Γ) *if and only if it is a CSSB for* (γ,Γ).

In most of the applications in this book of Claim 2.5.6 the set Γ^1 consists of a single position, and each position in Γ^2 contains a single outcome.

Claim 2.5.7 establishes that the "restriction of a stable SB to a subsituation" remains a stable SB for the "subsituation."

Claim 2.5.7: *Let* (γ,Γ) *be a situation,* σ *be an OSSB (respectively, CSSB) for* (γ,Γ), *and* $\tilde{\Gamma}\subset\Gamma$. *Assume that* $\tilde{\Gamma}$ *together with the restriction of* γ *to* $\tilde{\Gamma}$ *is a situation, denoted* $(\gamma,\tilde{\Gamma})$.[1] *Then, the restriction of* σ *to* $\tilde{\Gamma}$ is an OSSB (respectively, CSSB) for $(\gamma,\tilde{\Gamma})$. *That is, the SB* $\tilde{\sigma}$ *for* $\tilde{\Gamma}$, *defined by* $\tilde{\sigma}(G)=\sigma(G)$ *for all* $G\in\tilde{\Gamma}$, *is an OSSB (respectively, CSSB) for* $(\gamma,\tilde{\Gamma})$.

Remark 2.5.8: The fact that an individual's utility function is allowed to depend on the position to which he belongs is quite important and opens a wide range of applications. Consider, for example, the two positions G and H, where $N(G)=\{1,2\}$, $N(H)=\{2,3\}$, and $X(G)=X(H)=\{x,y\}$. Our formulation allows for player 2, who is present in both positions, to have in position

[1] This slight abuse of notation will be used throughout the book.

G preferences over x and y that differ from the preferences he has in H over these same two outcomes. For example, if x means "having dinner," and y stands for "going to the theater," then it is perfectly possible that 2 prefers x to y with 1 but y to x with 3. In this case, $u^2(G)(x) > u^2(G)(y)$ but $u^2(H)(x) < u^2(H)(y)$. Similarly, a consumer may prefer (buying) beer over (buying) milk when he is single, but reverse his choice when he is a parent.

Remark 2.5.9: Every situation (γ,Γ) can be associated with a situation $(\hat{\gamma},\hat{\Gamma})$ which describes, essentially, the same social environment as (γ,Γ) and has the property that all positions in $\hat{\Gamma}$ have the same set of players but distinct outcomes. That is, for all $\hat{G},\hat{H} \in \hat{\Gamma}$, $N(\hat{G}) = N(\hat{H})$, and if $\hat{G} \neq \hat{H}$ then $X(\hat{G}) \cap X(\hat{H}) = \emptyset$.

Indeed, let (γ,Γ) be a situation. Denote $\boldsymbol{N \equiv \cup\{N(G) | G \in \Gamma\}}$. For $G \in \Gamma$, define the position $\boldsymbol{\hat{G} \equiv \varphi(G)}$ as follows:

$$\boldsymbol{N(\hat{G}) \equiv N,\ X(\hat{G}) \equiv \{(G,x) | x \in X(G)\},}$$

and for $(G,x) \in X(\hat{G})$,

$$\begin{aligned} \boldsymbol{u^i(\hat{G})(G,x)} &\boldsymbol{\equiv u^i(G)(x),} && \textbf{if } \boldsymbol{i \in N(G),} \\ &\boldsymbol{\equiv 0,} && \textbf{if } \boldsymbol{i \in N \backslash N(G).} \end{aligned}$$

The situation $(\hat{\gamma},\hat{\Gamma})$ which describes essentially the same social environment as (γ,Γ) is given by:

$$\boldsymbol{\hat{\Gamma} \equiv \{\hat{G} | \textbf{there exists } G \in \Gamma \textbf{ such that } \hat{G} = \varphi(G)\},}$$

and for $\hat{G} = \varphi(G)$ and $\hat{H} = \varphi(H)$, where $G,H \in \Gamma$,

$$\boldsymbol{\hat{G} \in \hat{\gamma}(S | \hat{H},(H,x)) \textbf{ if and only if } G \in \gamma(S | H,x).}$$

However, this transformation is artificial and in many contexts makes the analysis unnecessarily complex and cumbersome. [For example, although, for all $G \in \Gamma$, $N(G)$ might be a finite set, the set $N(\hat{G}) = N$ might contain an infinite number of elements.]

2.6 ϵ-stability

As previously emphasized, it is evident that there are interesting behavioral assumptions other than the two extremes of optimistic and conservative. The study of the resulting stable SBs for such behavioral assumptions will most likely prove to be worthwhile. However, in view of the abundance of the results obtained by employing the two notions of OSSB and CSSB, I shall not pursue this possibility. Instead, I shall now offer a modification, not of the behavioral assumptions, but of the concept of stability.

Suppose (as is often the case) that the act of inducing a position is costly.

Specifically, assume that each member of the inducing coalition has to pay ϵ, $\epsilon \geq 0$, units of his "utils." Then, a coalition will reject an outcome and induce another position only if after the inducement, that is, after "paying" ϵ units of utils, each of its members is made better off.

The analogs of ODOM(σ,G) and CDOM(σ,G), for a given ϵ, become, respectively,

$$\mathbf{ODOM}^{\epsilon}(\boldsymbol{\sigma},\boldsymbol{G}) \equiv \{\boldsymbol{x} \in \boldsymbol{X}(\boldsymbol{G}) \mid \exists\, \boldsymbol{S} \subset \boldsymbol{N}(\boldsymbol{G}),\ \boldsymbol{H} \in \boldsymbol{\gamma}(\boldsymbol{S} \mid \boldsymbol{G},\boldsymbol{x}),\ \textbf{and}\ \boldsymbol{y} \in \boldsymbol{\sigma}(\boldsymbol{H})\ \textbf{such that for all}\ \boldsymbol{i} \in \boldsymbol{S},\ \boldsymbol{u}^{i}(\boldsymbol{H})(\boldsymbol{y}) > \boldsymbol{u}^{i}(\boldsymbol{G})(\boldsymbol{x}) + \boldsymbol{\epsilon}\},$$

and

$$\mathbf{CDOM}^{\epsilon}(\boldsymbol{\sigma},\boldsymbol{G}) \equiv \{\boldsymbol{x} \in \boldsymbol{X}(\boldsymbol{G}) \mid \exists\, \boldsymbol{S} \subset \boldsymbol{N}(\boldsymbol{G})\ \textbf{and}\ \boldsymbol{H} \in \boldsymbol{\gamma}(\boldsymbol{S} \mid \boldsymbol{G},\boldsymbol{x}),\ \textbf{such that}\ \boldsymbol{\sigma}(\boldsymbol{H}) \neq \emptyset,\ \textbf{and for all}\ \boldsymbol{i} \in \boldsymbol{S},\ \textbf{and all}\ \boldsymbol{y} \in \boldsymbol{\sigma}(\boldsymbol{H}),\ \boldsymbol{u}^{i}(\boldsymbol{H})(\boldsymbol{y}) > \boldsymbol{u}^{i}(\boldsymbol{G})(\boldsymbol{x}) + \boldsymbol{\epsilon}\}.$$

Observe that for $\epsilon = 0$, ODOM$^{\epsilon}$(σ,G) coincides with ODOM(σ,G), and CDOM$^{\epsilon}$(σ,G) coincides with CDOM(σ,G). The following two definitions, therefore, generalize Definitions 2.4.7 and 2.4.8, respectively.

Definition 2.6.1: *Let* (γ,Γ) *be a situation, and let* σ *be an SB for* (γ,Γ). *Then, the SB* σ *is*

i. ***ε-optimistic internally stable*** *if for all* $G \in \Gamma$ *and* $x \in X(G)$, $x \in \sigma(G)$ *implies* $x \notin ODOM^{\epsilon}(\sigma,G)$;

ii. ***ε-optimistic externally stable*** *if for all* $G \in \Gamma$ *and* $x \in X(G)$, $x \notin \sigma(G)$ *implies* $x \in ODOM^{\epsilon}(\sigma,G)$; *and*

iii. ***ε-OSSB*** *if for all* $G \in \Gamma$, $\sigma(G) = X(G) \backslash ODOM^{\epsilon}(\sigma,G)$.

Definition 2.6.2: *Let* (γ,Γ) *be a situation, and let* σ *be an SB for* (γ,Γ). *Then, the SB* σ *is*

i. ***ε-conservative internally stable*** *if for all* $G \in \Gamma$ *and* $x \in X(G)$, $x \in \sigma(G)$ *implies* $x \notin CDOM^{\epsilon}(\sigma,G)$;

ii. ***ε-conservative externally stable*** *if for all* $G \in \Gamma$ *and* $x \in X(G)$, $x \notin \sigma(G)$ *implies* $x \in CDOM^{\epsilon}(\sigma,G)$; *and*

iii. ***ε-CSSB*** *if for all* $G \in \Gamma$, $\sigma(G) = X(G) \backslash CDOM^{\epsilon}(\sigma,G)$.

The notion of ϵ-stability, in addition to its intuitive appeal, proves fruitful. For example, Asheim (1989) proved that the situation associated with the sequential bargaining game (see Section 8.2) admits infinite OSSBs, but a unique ϵ-OSSB. Moreover, the solutions assigned by this ϵ-OSSB are most attractive. In addition, several social environments that we shall analyze admit a unique ϵ-OSSB and a unique ϵ-CSSB for every $\epsilon > 0$, but admit neither an OSSB nor a CSSB.

Proofs for Chapter 2

Proof of Claim 2.5.1: Let σ be an SB for the situation (γ,Γ). Assume that for all $G\in\Gamma$, $\sigma(G)=\emptyset$. Then, for all $G\in\Gamma$, $\text{ODOM}(\sigma,G)=\text{CDOM}(\sigma,G)=\emptyset$, and, hence, for all $G\in\Gamma$, $X(G)\backslash\text{ODOM}(\sigma,G)=X(G)\backslash\text{CDOM}(\sigma,G)=X(G)$. It follows, by Definitions 2.4.7 and 2.4.8, that if σ is an OSSB or a CSSB, then $\sigma(G)=X(G)$ for all $G\in\Gamma$. But then, $X(G)=\emptyset$ for all $G\in\Gamma$, which is a contradiction. Q.E.D.

Proof of Claim 2.5.2: See Example 3.3. Q.E.D.

Proof of Claim 2.5.3: See Example 3.4. Q.E.D.

Proof of Claim 2.5.4: See Example 3.5. Q.E.D.

Proof of Claim 2.5.5: Let σ be an SB such that for all $G\in\Gamma$, $i\in N(G)$, and $x,y\in\sigma(G)$, $u^i(G)(x)=u^i(G)(y)$. Then, it is easy to see that for all $G\in\Gamma$, $\text{ODOM}(\sigma,G)=\text{CDOM}(\sigma,G)$. Hence, for all $G\in\Gamma$, $X(G)\backslash\text{ODOM}(\sigma,G)=X(G)\backslash\text{CDOM}(\sigma,G)$. Using Definitions 2.4.7 and 2.4.8 we conclude that σ is an OSSB for (γ,Γ) if and only if it is a CSSB for (γ,Γ). Q.E.D.

Proof of Claim 2.5.6: Let σ be an SB for (γ,Γ), and let $G\in\Gamma^1$. By the definition of Γ^1 we can write ODOM and CDOM as follows:

$\text{ODOM}(\sigma,G)=\{x\in X(G)\,|\,$there are no $S\subset N(G)$, $H\in\gamma(S|G,x)$, $H\in\Gamma^2$, and $y\in\sigma(H)$ such that $u^i(H)(y)>u^i(G)(x)$ for all $i\in S\}$.
$\text{CDOM}(\sigma,G)=\{x\in X(G)\,|\,$there are no $S\subset N(G)$ and $H\in\gamma(S|G,x)$, $H\in\Gamma^2$ such that $\sigma(H)\neq\emptyset$ and $u^i(H)(y)>u^i(G)(x)$ for all $i\in S$ and $y\in\sigma(H)\}$.

Hence, both $\text{ODOM}(\sigma,G)$ and $\text{CDOM}(\sigma,G)$ are defined by the solutions σ assigns to positions $H\in\Gamma^2$. Now, if σ is an OSSB for (γ,Γ) then $\sigma(G)=X(G)\backslash\text{ODOM}(\sigma,G)$, and if σ is a CSSB for (γ,Γ) then $\sigma(G)=X(G)\backslash\text{CDOM}(\sigma,G)$. Therefore, (i) is verified.

Turning to (ii), note that the definition of Γ^1 implies that Γ^2 together with the restriction of γ to Γ^2 is a situation, denoted (γ,Γ^2).[1] (That is, Γ^2 is closed under γ.) Hence, if σ is an OSSB (respectively, a CSSB) for (γ,Γ) then (see Proof of Claim 2.5.7) the restriction of σ to Γ^2 is an OSSB (respectively, a CSSB) for (γ,Γ^2). In view of (i), therefore, in order to verify (ii) it suffices to show that σ is an OSSB for (γ,Γ^2) if and only if it is a CSSB for (γ,Γ^2). But this follows from the definition of Γ^2, the fact that $\sigma(G)\subset X(G)$, and Claim 2.5.5. Q.E.D.

[1] This slight abuse of notation will be used throughout the book.

Proof of Claim 2.5.7: Since $(\gamma,\tilde{\Gamma})$ is a situation it follows that for all $G\in\tilde{\Gamma}$, $S\subset N(G)$, and $x\in X(G)$ we have $\gamma(S|G,x)\subset\tilde{\Gamma}$. Therefore, for any SB, $\hat{\sigma}$, for (γ,Γ), the definition of ODOM [CDOM] yields that for all $G\in\tilde{\Gamma}$, ODOM$(\hat{\sigma},G)$ [CDOM$(\hat{\sigma},G)$] for the situation (γ,Γ) coincides with ODOM$(\hat{\sigma},G)$ [CDOM$(\hat{\sigma},G)$] for the situation $(\gamma,\tilde{\Gamma})$. To conclude that the restriction of σ to $(\gamma,\tilde{\Gamma})$ is stable, recall that σ is an OSSB [CSSB] for (γ,Γ) if and only if for all $G\in\Gamma$ (and hence for all $G\in\tilde{\Gamma}$), $\sigma(G)=X(G)\backslash$ODOM(σ,G) [$\sigma(G)=X(G)\backslash$ CDOM(σ,G)].

Q.E.D.

[1] This slight abuse of notation will be used throughout the book.

CHAPTER 3

Examples

Except for Example 3.6, the following examples are provided in order to enhance the familiarity of the reader with the terminology and concepts of the theory of social situations. In addition, some of the examples provided subsequently establish the validity of several claims made in the previous chapter, whereas others will be useful in later chapters. The more interesting implications of the theory of social situations, that is, its application to specific social environments, will be discussed after establishing (in Chapter 5) some existence and uniqueness results of an OSSB and a CSSB for a large class of situations. The main purpose of Example 3.6, where a voting by veto model is cast within the framework of the theory of social situations, is to illustrate both the intuitive appeal and the fruitfulness of the proposed approach. It will become apparent that, as claimed in Chapter 1, the representation of the social environment by means of a situation not only is natural but also forces us to focus on relevant aspects that might otherwise be overlooked.

Example 3.1: Consider the following "game": A player has to choose an integer between 10 and 20. Having stated his choice, say, x, the player receives x dollars, and his utility is linear with money, that is, he gets x units of utils from x dollars. The situation that might be chosen to represent this game is (γ,Γ), where

$$\Gamma=\{G\},\ G=(\{1\},\{10,11,\ldots,20\},u^1)$$

and the utility function u^1: $\{10,11,\ldots,20\}\rightarrow\mathbb{R}$ is given by

$$u^1(x)=x,\ \text{for all}\ x\in\{10,11,\ldots,20\}.$$

Since the player is not obliged to accept any outcome that is recommended to him, but he is free to "reconsider" his choice, the inducement correspondence γ allows the single player, 1, to induce the position G no matter what outcome is proposed to him. That is, for all $x\in\{10,11,\ldots,20\}$,

$$\gamma(\{1\}|G,x)=\{G\}.$$

I claim that:

1. There exists a unique OSSB, σ^o, for (γ,Γ), which is given by $\sigma^o(G)=\{20\}$.

2. The SB σ^c is a CSSB for (γ,Γ) if and only if it is of the form $\boldsymbol{\sigma^c(G)=\{x,x+1,\ldots,20\}}$, where $x\in\{10,11,\ldots,20\}$.

Observe, first, that the SB σ^o is an OSSB for (γ,Γ). Indeed, ODOM$(\sigma^o,G)=\{10,11,\ldots,19\}$. Thus, $\sigma^o(G)=X(G)\setminus$ODOM$(\sigma^o,G)$, that is, σ^o is an OSSB for (γ,Γ). To see that σ^o is the only OSSB for (γ,Γ), let σ be an OSSB for (γ,Γ). We need to show that $\sigma(G)=\sigma^o(G)=\{20\}$.

By Claim 2.5.1, $\sigma(G)\neq\emptyset$. If $\sigma(G)$ contains more than one element, say, $x,y\in\sigma(G)$, then, without loss of generality, $x>y$. Therefore, $y\in$ODOM(σ,G) [since the player can induce G from itself when y is proposed, and there is an outcome, x, in $\sigma(G)$ which he strictly prefers to y]. But then, $y\in$ ODOM$(\sigma,G)\cap\sigma(G)$, contradicting the optimistic (internal) stability of σ. Hence, $\sigma(G)$ contains a single outcome, that is, $\sigma(G)=\{x^*\}$, implying that ODOM$(\sigma,G)=\{10,11,\ldots,x^*-1\}$. Therefore, the optimistic stability of σ yields $\sigma(G)=\{20\}$. Thus, $\sigma\equiv\sigma^o$, as we wished to show. (For a generalization of the uniqueness of OSSB in this example, see Theorem 4.8.)

Turning to the second claim, observe, first, that an SB σ^c of the form $\sigma^c(G)=\{x,x+1,\ldots,20\}$ is a CSSB for (γ,Γ). Indeed, by the definition of CDOM(σ^c,G), since x is the worst outcome in $\sigma^c(G)$, we immediately have that

$$\text{CDOM}(\sigma^c,G)=\{y\in\{10,11,\ldots,20\}\mid y<x\}=\{10,11,\ldots,x-1\}.$$

It therefore follows that $\sigma^c(G)=X(G)\setminus$CDOM$(\sigma^c,G)$, that is, σ^c is a CSSB for (γ,Γ), as we wished to show.

Next, we shall verify that if σ is a CSSB for (γ,Γ), then it is of the form specified in (2). Let σ be a CSSB for (γ,Γ). Then, by Claim 2.5.1, $\sigma(G)$ is not empty. Thus, it is left to be shown that if $x\in\sigma(G)$ then all the integers between x and 20 also belong to $\sigma(G)$. Indeed, if $x\in\sigma(G)$ then $y\notin$CDOM(σ,G) for all $y\in\{x,x+1,\ldots,20\}$. By conservative external stability it follows that if $x\in\sigma(G)$ then $y\in\sigma(G)$ for all $y\in\{10,11,\ldots,20\}$ such that $y\geq x$. This concludes the proof of (2).

Example 3.2: Consider the following continuous version of Example 3.1. A player has to choose a number in the closed interval [10,20]. Having stated his choice, say, x, the player receives x dollars, and his utility is linear with money. The associated situation is (γ,Γ), where

$$\boldsymbol{\Gamma=\{G\},\ G=(\{1\},[10,20],u^1),}$$

the utility function u^1: $[10,20]\to\mathbb{R}$ is given by

$$\boldsymbol{u^1(x)=x,\ \text{for all}\ x\in[10,20],}$$

and for all $x\in[10,20]$ the inducement correspondence is

$$\boldsymbol{\gamma(\{1\}|G,x)=\{G\}.}$$

Similar to the discrete case of Example 3.1, I claim that:

1. There exists a unique OSSB, σ^o, for (γ,Γ), which is given by $\boldsymbol{\sigma^o(G)=\{20\}}$.
2. The SB σ^c is a CSSB for (γ,Γ) if and only if it is either a closed interval of the form $\boldsymbol{\sigma^c(G)=[x,20]}$, or a half open interval of the form $\boldsymbol{\sigma^c(G)=(x,20]}$, where $x\in[10,20]$.

First note that if σ is an OSSB for (γ,Γ) then $20\in\sigma(G)$. Indeed, no outcome $x\in X(G)$ dominates 20. Since $\sigma(G)\subset X(G)$, it follows that no outcome in $\sigma(G)$ dominates 20, that is, $20\notin \text{ODOM}(\sigma,G)$. External stability yields that $20\in\sigma(G)$.

To verify that no element of $X(G)$ other than 20 belongs to $\sigma(G)$, consider $x\in X(G)$, $x\neq 20$. Then, $x<20$, and therefore, since $20\in\sigma(G)$ and $G\in\gamma(\{1\}|G,x)$, we have that $x\in\text{ODOM}(\sigma,G)$. The internal stability of σ implies, therefore, that $x\notin\sigma(G)$. Thus, if σ is an OSSB for (γ,Γ), then $\sigma(G)=\sigma^o(G)$.

Finally, note that $\sigma^o(G)\equiv\{20\}$ satisfies $\sigma^o(G)=X(G)\backslash\text{ODOM}(\sigma^o,G)$, that is, σ^o is an OSSB for (γ,Γ).

The proof of the second claim is similar to the proof of (2) in Example 3.1. Briefly, it is easy to see that if σ^c is of one of the above two forms, then $\sigma^c(G)=X(G)\backslash\text{CDOM}(\sigma^c,G)$, that is, σ^c is a CSSB for (γ,Γ).

To see that if σ is a CSSB for (γ,Γ) then it is of one of the two forms $[x,20]$ or $(x,20]$, note that by Claim 2.5.1 it suffices to verify that if $x\in\sigma(G)$ then all the numbers between x and 20 also belong to $\sigma(G)$. But that such is the case is straightforward: Since $x\in\sigma(G)$, by conservative external stability it follows that $y\in\sigma(G)$ for all $y\in[x,20]$.

The situations in both of the examples admitted an OSSB as well as a CSSB. This is, clearly, not the general case. Indeed, the following example shows that there are situations that admit no OSSB, but they do admit (infinitely) many CSSBs. This example provides, therefore, a proof of Claim 2.5.2.

Example 3.3: Consider the following slight modification of the last example. A player has to choose a number in the half closed interval $[10,20)$. Having stated his choice, say, x, the player receives x dollars. The situation that represents this game is (γ,Γ), where

$$\boldsymbol{\Gamma=\{G\},\ G=(\{1\},[10,20),u^1),}$$

and the utility function u^1: $[10,20)\rightarrow\mathbb{R}$ is given by

$$\boldsymbol{u^1(x)=x \text{ for all } x\in[10,20).}$$

As before, the inducement correspondence γ allows the single player to induce the position G, no matter what outcome is proposed to him. That is, for all $x\in[10,20)$,

$$\boldsymbol{\gamma(\{1\}|G,x)=\{G\}.}$$

I claim that:

1. There exists no OSSB for (γ,Γ).
2. The SB σ^c is a CSSB for (γ,Γ) if and only if it is either a half open interval of the form $\boldsymbol{\sigma}^c(G) = [x,20)$, or an open interval of the form $\boldsymbol{\sigma}^c(G) = (x,20)$, where $x \in [10,20)$.

The proof of the second claim is identical to the proof of (2) in Example 3.2. We only need to verify the validity of (1). Assume, in negation, that σ is an OSSB for (γ,Γ). First, note that $\sigma(G)$ contains at most a single outcome. Otherwise, there exist $x,y \in \sigma(G)$, $x \neq y$. Without loss of generality, assume that $x > y$. But then, $y \in \mathrm{ODOM}(\sigma,G)$, contradicting our assumption that $y \in \sigma(G)$ and σ is optimistic (internally) stable. Since by Claim 2.5.1, $\sigma(G)$ cannot be empty, it follows that σ contains a single element, that is, $\sigma(G) = \{x^*\}$. Since $x^* \in X(G)$, $x^* < 20$. Therefore, there exists $y \in X(G)$ such that $y > x^*$. As $\sigma(G) = \{x^*\}$, $y \notin \mathrm{ODOM}(\sigma,G)$. But then, by optimistic external stability, $y \in \sigma(G)$. Hence, we have the desired contradiction.

The next example shows that there exist situations that admit an OSSB but do not admit a CSSB. This example provides, therefore, a proof for Claim 2.5.3.

Example 3.4: Let (γ,Γ) be the situation where

$$\boldsymbol{\Gamma = \{G^1, G^2, G^3\},\ X(G^1) = \{0,3\},\ X(G^2) = \{2,4\},\ X(G^3) = \{1,5\},}$$

and for all $G \in \Gamma$ and $x \in X(G)$,

$$\boldsymbol{N(G) = \{1\} \text{ and } u^1(G)(x) = x.}$$

That is, the set of players in all positions $G \in \Gamma$ consists of the single player 1, the set of outcomes in each position contains two outcomes, and the utility function is linear in the outcome. The inducement correspondence is given by

$$\boldsymbol{\gamma(\{1\}|G^1,x) = \{G^2\},\ \gamma(\{1\}|G^2,x) = \{G^3\},\ \gamma(\{1\}|G^3,x) = \{G^1\}.}$$

I claim that:

1. There exists an OSSB for (γ,Γ).
2. There exists no CSSB for (γ,Γ).

Define the SB σ^o as follows:

$$\boldsymbol{\sigma^o(G^1) = \{0,3\},\ \sigma^o(G^2) = \emptyset,\ \sigma^o(G^3) = \{5\}.}$$

To verify that σ^0 is an OSSB, note that $\mathrm{ODOM}(\sigma^o,G^1) = \emptyset$, implying that $\sigma^o(G^1) = X(G^1) \backslash \mathrm{ODOM}(\sigma^o,G^1)$. Similarly, $\mathrm{ODOM}(\sigma^o,G^2) = X(G^2)$, implying that $\sigma^o(G^2) = X(G^2) \backslash \mathrm{ODOM}(\sigma^o,G^2)$. Finally, $\mathrm{ODOM}(\sigma^o,G^3) = \{1\}$, implying that $\sigma^o(G^3) = X(G^3) \backslash \mathrm{ODOM}(\sigma^o,G^3)$. Thus, for all $G \in \Gamma$, $\sigma^o(G) = X(G) \backslash$

ODOM(σ^o,G), that is, σ^o is indeed an OSSB for (γ,Γ). (By Theorem 4.8, σ^o is the unique OSSB for this situation.)

Turning to the second claim, assume, in negation, that there exists a CSSB, σ^c, for (γ,Γ). Consider $\sigma^c(G^3)$. Clearly, $5 \notin$CDOM(σ^c,G^3). Therefore, $5 \in \sigma^c(G^3)$. Distinguish between the following two possibilities:

i. $1 \notin \sigma^c(G^3)$. Then, $\sigma^c(G^3)=\{5\}$, implying that $\sigma^c(G^2)=\emptyset$. Therefore, CDOM(σ^c,G^1)$=\emptyset$, and hence, $\sigma^c(G^1)=X(G^1)=\{0,3\}$. But then, $1 \notin$CDOM(σ^c,G^3). By conservative (external) stability, we have $1 \in \sigma^c(G^3)$, contradicting our assumption that $1 \notin \sigma^c(G^3)$.
ii. $1 \in \sigma^c(G^3)$. Then, $\sigma^c(G^3)=\{1,5\}$, implying that $\sigma^c(G^2)=\{2,4\}$. Therefore, $\sigma^c(G^1)=\{3\}$. But then, $1 \in$CDOM(σ^c,G^3). By conservative (internal) stability, $1 \notin \sigma^c(G^3)$, contradicting our assumption that $1 \in \sigma^c(G^3)$.

The next example demonstrates that there exist situations which admit neither an OSSB nor a CSSB, thereby providing a proof for Claim 2.5.4.

Example 3.5: Let (γ,Γ) be the situation where

$$\Gamma=\{G^1,G^2,G^3\},\ N(G^1)=N(G^2)=N(G^3)=N=\{1,2,3\},$$
$$X(G^1)=\{(1,0,0)\},\ X(G^2)=\{(0,1,0)\},\ X(G^3)=\{(0,0,1)\}.$$

Thus, all positions have the same set of players and the set of outcomes in each position consists of a single outcome. The utility level player i obtains from the outcome x in position G is the ith coordinate of x, that is, for all $G \in \Gamma$, $x \in X(G)$, and $i \in N$,

$$u^i(G)(x)=x_i.$$

The inducement correspondence is given by

$$\gamma(\{2\}|G^1,x)=\{G^2\},\ \gamma(\{3\}|G^2,x)=\{G^3\},\ \gamma(\{1\}|G^3,x)=\{G^1\},$$
$$\gamma(S|G,x)=\emptyset,\ \text{otherwise}.$$

I claim that:

1. There exists no OSSB for (γ,Γ).
2. There exists no CSSB for (γ,Γ).

Assume, in negation, that σ is an OSSB for (γ,Γ). By Claim 2.5.1, σ is not identically empty. In view of the symmetry in (γ,Γ), we may, without loss of generality, assume that $\sigma(G^3)\neq\emptyset$. Thus, $\sigma(G^3)=\{(0,0,1)\}$. Hence, $(0,1,0) \in$ODOM(σ,G^2). The optimistic (internal) stability of σ implies, therefore, that $\sigma(G^2)=\emptyset$. It follows that ODOM(σ,G^1)$=\emptyset$. Because of the (external) optimistic stability of σ we have that $\sigma(G^1)=X(G^1)=\{(1,0,0)\}$, which, together with our assumption that $(0,0,1) \in \sigma(G^3)$, contradicts the optimistic (internal) stability of σ. Thus, (γ,Γ) admits no OSSB. Since every position in Γ contains a single outcome, Claim 2.5.5 yields that (γ,Γ) also admits no CSSB.

The main purpose of the previous examples was to familiarize the reader with the terminology, notations, and concepts (as well as some techniques) of the theory of social situations. In contrast, the prime purpose of the following example, which is a much simplified version of Greenberg and Weg (1987), is to illustrate how the proposed theory can be applied to specific social environments, and the type of (at times counterintuitive) results it yields. In view of the fact that we are only at the early stages of the analysis, the reader may find this example somewhat difficult to fully comprehend on the first reading. I hope that it will, nevertheless, point out some of the advantages of the theory of social situations.

Example 3.6: Consider a **finite set of voters, N,** who have to choose from the **finite set of alternatives A.** The preferences of individual i are represented by the **utility function, u^i,** defined over A, that is, for all $i \in N$, $u^i : A \rightarrow \mathbb{R}$. (The cardinality of the functions $\{u^i\}_{i \in N}$ plays no role in this example.) The "property rights" of the individuals over alternatives in A are given by the ***veto function, Φ,*** which assigns to each individual $i \in N$ a distinct alternative, denoted **$\Phi(i)$,** which "society feels" should not be adopted against i's will. [Our analysis remains valid also for the more general case where $\Phi(i)$ is a subset of A.] If i exercises his veto right and insists that $\Phi(i)$ be excluded, then the modified agenda consists only of outcomes in $A \backslash \Phi(i)$. We shall assume that each voter i, $i \in N$, behaves conservatively, in the sense that he will be willing to veto $\Phi(i)$ only if he prefers every outcome that might consequently result from his veto to $\Phi(i)$.

The quadruple $\Omega \equiv (N, A, \{u^i\}_{i \in N}, \Phi)$ is called ***a society with veto privileges,*** henceforth, simply ***a society.*** The problem of interest here is, of course, which individuals should exercise their veto rights, or, put differently, what is the ***choice set, A^****, consisting of the alternatives in A that are likely to prevail?

When we try to represent the voting by veto model as a situation, we shall realize that the above question cannot be answered without additional information concerning the precise voting process. Indeed, in order for the voters to be able to decide whether or not to cast their vetoes, they need to know, for example, whether successive vetoes are allowed, or coalitions can form and sign binding agreements (concerning the way members will use their veto rights). Such (institutional) information, required for the specification of the inducement correspondence, should, obviously, be part of the description of the model.

By exercising their veto rights voters modify the agendas, that is, the set of remaining alternatives among which the players have to choose. We shall assume that the fact that the agenda "shrinks" has no consequence on either the preferences or the property rights of the individuals over the remaining alternatives. (Although perhaps natural and appealing, it is, nevertheless, an assumption, known as "independence of irrelevant alternatives.") Thus, every agenda, B, $B \subset A$, defines a (sub)society $\mathbf{\Omega}^B = (N, B, \{u^i\}_{i \in N}, \Phi)$, where $\{u^i\}_{i \in N}$ are the restrictions of these functions (defined on A) to the agenda B. It seems natural to associate with Ω^B the position $\mathbf{G}^B = (N, B, \{u^i\}_{i \in N})$. (Since a position captures the current state of affairs, the veto function Φ, which describes the possible evolvement of the voting game, does not appear in G^B.) I therefore define: $\mathbf{\Gamma} \equiv \{G^B | B \subset A\}$.

The inducement correspondence specifies what a coalition, S, of voters can do when the agenda is B and an alternative $b \in B$ is considered. We shall consider three different voting procedures which are of no particular inherent prominence; they merely serve as an illustration of the results and insight provided by the application of the theory of social situations to the model of voting by veto.

The first voting procedure prohibits both successive vetoing and the formation of coalitions: An individual i can exercise his right to exclude the alternative $\Phi(i)$ only if $\Phi(i)$ is currently under consideration and no prior vetoes were cast (that is, the agenda consists of the entire set of alternatives A). This procedure is described by the inducement correspondence γ^1 given by: For every $G^B \in \Gamma$, for each coalition $S \subset N$, and any alternative $b \in B$,

$$\begin{aligned} &\gamma^1(\{i\}|G^B,b) \equiv \emptyset && \text{if } B \neq A,\\ &\gamma^1(\{i\}|G^A,b) \equiv \{G^{A \setminus b}\} && \text{if } \Phi(i) = \{b\},\\ &\gamma^1(S|G^B,b) \equiv \emptyset && \text{otherwise.} \end{aligned}$$

The second voting procedure differs from γ^1 only in that it allows individuals to exercise their veto power even if other individuals did so before, that is, successive vetoing is permitted. Put differently, the process of elimination by vetoes continues until no voter wishes to exercise his veto rights. This procedure is described by the inducement correspondence γ^2 given by: For every $G^B \in \Gamma$, for each coalition $S \subset N$, and any alternative $b \in B$,

$$\begin{aligned} &\gamma^2(\{i\}|G^B,b) \equiv \{G^{B \setminus b}\} && \text{if } \Phi(i) = \{b\},\\ &\gamma^2(S|G^B,b) \equiv \emptyset && \text{otherwise.} \end{aligned}$$

The distinction between the next voting procedure and γ^2 leads to an important observation that comes out of our analysis of the voting by veto model. As stated above, the veto function Φ specifies the alternative which "society feels" that an individual has the right to veto. But individuals might wish to correlate, or unite their vetoes, and form the coalition S, thereby vetoing the alternatives in the set $\cup\{\Phi(i)|\, i \in S\}$. The formation of such coalitions often requires an institution that enforces contracts; that is, binding agreements among individuals can be signed (for otherwise some players may have an incentive to renege on their commitments to veto). The third voting procedure describes societies in which such institutions exist and both successive vetoing and the formation of coalitions are allowed. This procedure is described by the inducement correspondence γ^3 given by: For every $G^B \in \Gamma$, for each coalition $S \subset N$, and any alternative $b \in B$,

$$\gamma^3(S|G^B,b) = \{G^C | C \subset B \backslash \{b\}, \text{ and } B \backslash C \subset [\cup\{\Phi(i) | i \in S\}]\}.$$

That is, coalition S can form and agree to veto any subset of the set of alternatives its members can veto, that is, any subset, D, of $\cup\{\Phi(i)|i \in S\}$ which includes the currently proposed alternative b. The resulting modified agenda becomes $C = B \backslash D$.

Once the voting by veto model is represented as a situation, the conservative[1] stability of the SB determines the choice set, A^*. It can be shown (see Theorem 5.4.1 and Corollary 5.3.3) that each of the three situations (γ^k,Γ), $k=1,2,3$, admits a unique CSSB (as well as a unique OSSB). Let $\boldsymbol{\sigma}^k$ denote the unique CSSB for (γ^k,Γ), $k=1,2,3$. I conclude this chapter by investigating the nature of the choice set A^* that results from the SBs σ^k, $k=1,2,3$, in two particular societies. In the first society, the final choice set expands when successive vetoing is allowed, and in the second society, allowing individuals to sign binding contracts and form coalitions yields a choice set which is completely disjoint from the one that results in the absence of such contracts. The reason for these counterintuitive results is that the theory of social situations requires the players to look ahead, and foresee the (eventual, and not just the immediate) consequences of their actions.

Consider, first, the society $\Omega \equiv (N,A,\{u^i\}_{i \in N},\Phi)$, where

$$N=\{1,2,3\},\ A=\{a,b,c\};$$
$$u^1(a)>u^1(b)>u^1(c),\ u^2(c)>u^2(a)>u^2(b),\ u^3(c)>u^3(a)>u^3(b);$$
$$\Phi(1)=\{c\},\ \Phi(2)=\{b\},\ \Phi(3)=\{a\}.$$

It can be verified (see Theorem 5.4.1) that the unique CSSB, σ^k, for the associated situation (Γ,γ^k), $k=1,2,3$, satisfies:

$$\sigma^1(G^A)=\{a\},\ \sigma^2(G^A)=\{a,b\},\ \sigma^3(G^A)=\emptyset.$$

Recall that the only difference between γ^1 and γ^2 is that the latter allows individuals to exercise their veto power even if other individuals did so before, whereas the former prohibits successive vetoing. And it is this difference that is responsible for the counterintuitive fact that $\sigma^1(G^A)$ is strictly included in $\sigma^2(G^A)$.

A closer look explains this seeming paradox. When the voting procedure is not successive, it is clear that voter 1 will always exercise his right to exclude alternative c, and similarly, voter 2 will always veto alternative b. However,

[1] Recall that voters were assumed to behave conservatively.

when successive vetoing (but not the formation of coalitions) is allowed, player 2 must realize that in the subsociety, $\Omega^{\{a,c\}}$, that results by deleting alternative b, his two co-players have opposing preferences over the remaining agenda, $\{a,c\}$. Moreover, each of the voters 1 and 3 has the right to veto his worst alternative in $\{a,c\}$. Therefore, $\sigma^2(G^{\{a,c\}})$ is empty. Thus, by vetoing alternative b when the voting procedure is γ^2, voter 2 creates "chaos," and he will, therefore, refrain from doing so.

The second society illustrates that increasing the veto power might change altogether the resulting choice set. Consider the society $\Omega \equiv (N,A,\{u^i\}_{i\in N},\Phi)$, where

$$\begin{aligned}
&N=\{1,2,3,4\},\ A=\{a,b,c,d\};\\
&u^1(a)>u^1(b)>u^1(c)>u^1(d),\ u^2(d)>u^2(a)>u^2(b)>u^2(c),\\
&u^3(a)>u^3(d)>u^3(b)>u^3(c),\ u^4(c)>u^4(d)>u^4(b)>u^4(a);\\
&\Phi(1)=\{d\},\ \Phi(2)=\{c\},\ \Phi(3)=\{b\},\ \Phi(4)=\{a\}.
\end{aligned}$$

It can be verified (see Theorem 5.4.1) that the unique CSSB, σ^k, for the associated situation (Γ,γ^k), $k=1,2,3$, satisfies:

$$\sigma^1(G^A)=\{b\},\ \sigma^2(G^A)=\{b\},\ \sigma^3(G^A)=\{a,d\}.$$

Recall that the only difference between γ^2 and γ^3 is that the latter allows binding contracts among individuals to be signed, whereas the former prohibits coalition formation. And it is this difference that is responsible for the fact that $\sigma^2(G^A)\cap\sigma^3(G^A)=\emptyset$; that is, no alternative that is in the choice set that corresponds to the voting procedure γ^2 belongs also to the choice set that corresponds to the voting procedures γ^3, and vice versa. Again, the explanation for this quite unexpected phenomenon lies in the fact that individuals take into account the choice sets in the subsocieties they bring about by exercising their veto rights. I shall show why, for example, alternative d belongs to $\sigma^3(G^A)$ but not to $\sigma^2(G^A)$.

Under γ^2, individual 1 will veto alternative d since in the subsociety Ω^B, in which the agenda is $B\equiv\{a,b,c\}$, we have that $\sigma^2(G^B)\neq\emptyset$. Indeed, $c\in\sigma^2(G^B)$, because player 2 will not veto c, fearing the "chaos" in the resulting subsociety $\Omega^{\{a,b\}}$. [Observe that $\sigma^2(G^{\{a,b\}})=\emptyset$, since player 3 will veto b and player 4 will veto a.] On the other hand, when coalitions are allowed to form, voter 1 will not veto d, since he would thereby induce a "chaotic" subsociety. To realize that $\sigma^3(G^B)$ is, indeed, empty, note that in Ω^B the coalition $\{2,3\}$ would veto the alternatives $\{b,c\}$, yielding the choice set $\sigma^3(G^{\{a\}})=\{a\}$, consisting of the single alternative which is preferred by both players 2 and 3 to any of the two alternatives they vetoed. But, by vetoing alternative a in B, player 4 guarantees that the choice set is $\sigma^3(G^{\{b,c\}})=\{b\}$, and since he prefers b to a, he will certainly cast his veto. Thus, under the voting procedure γ^3, all of the three alternatives in B will be vetoed, and hence, $\sigma^3(G^B)=\emptyset$. Realizing this fact, player 1 will not induce G^B by vetoing alternative d, that is, $d\in\sigma^3(G^A)$.

CHAPTER 4

Abstract stable sets

The reader who is familiar with von Neumann and Morgenstern's (1947) seminal work will immediately recognize that the terms "standards of behavior" and "internal and external stability" are borrowed from their pioneering work. We shall now see that there is more than a semantic similarity between the concept of OSSB, on the one hand, and that of "von Neumann and Morgenstern (vN&M) abstract stable set," on the other hand. (The latter is to be distinguished from the more familiar notion of the "stable set" or "the solution" for cooperative games. See Chapter 6.) Surprisingly, perhaps, no such relationship exists between CSSB and vN&M abstract stable sets.

After presenting the formal definitions, I shall give an example to provide an intuitive feel for the concepts involved.

Definition 4.1: *An* ***(abstract) system*** *is a pair* $(D, \angle)$, *where D is an arbitrary nonempty set, and* $\angle$ is a binary relation on D, called the ***dominance relation.*** *For* $a, b \in D$, $a \angle b$ *is interpreted to mean that b* ***dominates*** *a.*

Definition 4.2: *Let* $(D, \angle)$ *be an abstract system, and let* $a \in D$. *The* ***dominion of a,*** *denoted* $\Delta(a)$, *consists of all elements of D that a dominates, according to the dominance relation* $\angle$. *That is,*

$$\Delta(a) = \{b \in D \mid b \angle a\}.$$

Definition 4.3: *Let* $(D, \angle)$ *be an abstract system, and let* $A \subset D$. *The* ***dominion of A,*** *denoted* $\Delta(A)$, *consists of all elements of D that are dominated, according to the dominance relation* $\angle$, by some element in *A. That is,*

$$\Delta(A) = \cup \{\Delta(a) \mid a \in A\} = \{b \in D \mid \exists\ a \in A \text{ such that } b \angle a\}.$$

Definition 4.4: *Let* $(D, \angle)$ *be an abstract system. The set A,* $A \subset D$, *is called*

- *a* ***vN&M internally stable set*** *if for no two elements* $a, b \in A$ *we have* $b \angle a$, *that is,* $a \in A$ *implies* $a \notin \Delta(A)$;
- *a* ***vN&M externally stable set*** *if* $b \in D \setminus A$ *implies that* $b \angle a$ *for some* $a \in A$, *that is,* $b \in D \setminus A$ *implies* $b \in \Delta(A)$;
- *a* ***vN&M (abstract) stable set*** *for the system* $(D, \angle)$ *if it is both vN&M internally and externally stable, that is,* $A = D \setminus \Delta(A)$.

(a)

(b)

Figure 4.4

The following example might help to understand the above definitions. Let D consist of the sixty-four squares in the chessboard. Let $\Delta(a)$, the dominion of a square $a \in D$, be the set of squares, other than a itself, that are in the same row or in the same column or in the same diagonal as a. That is, $\Delta(a)$ is the set of all squares, different from a, that are covered by a queen that occupies square a. A vN&M (abstract) stable set for this system is a subset A of D with the property that if we place a queen in each of the squares in A then:

i. no queen can capture another queen, and
ii. each of the 64 squares is controlled by at least one of the queens.

[Note that (i) is the requirement that A be an internally stable set, and (ii) is the condition that A is an externally stable set.] This system admits many stable sets. The existence of stable sets containing eight elements corresponds to the solution to Gauss's well-known problem: "Can eight queens be placed on a chessboard so that no queen can capture another queen?"[1] There are 92 such stable sets; one is depicted in Figure 4.4a.

Thus, in general, abstract stable sets, if they exist, need not be unique. Moreover, different abstract stable sets for the same system may contain a different number of elements. For example, as Figure 4.4b demonstrates, there exist stable sets for the system that corresponds to the regular 8×8 chessboard that contain five squares.[2]

[1] Gauss's problem was generalized by Hoffman, Loessi, and Moore (1969). They showed, by construction, that for all $k \geq 4$, it is always possible to place k queens on a $k \times k$ chessboard so that no queen can be taken by any other queen, implying that there exists a vN&M stable set for the corresponding abstract system which contains exactly k elements.

[2] It can be shown that five is the minimum number of queens that can be placed on a chessboard so that each square is controlled by at least one queen.

An important relationship between the OSSB and the vN&M abstract stable set was observed by Shitovitz (private communication). He noticed, as we shall currently verify, that a mapping σ is an OSSB for a situation (γ,Γ) if and only if the graph of σ is a vN&M abstract stable set for the ***associated system*** $(D,\angle)$, defined below. (It is not surprising that the comparison between OSSB and vN&M abstract stable sets has to involve the graph of the SB, since the stability of an SB is imposed on the **mapping,** σ, whereas in vN&M, the stability is required of a **set.**)

The ***abstract system*** $(D,\angle)$ ***associated with a situation*** (γ,Γ) is defined as follows:

$$D \equiv \{(G,x) \mid G \in \Gamma \text{ and } x \in X(G)\}.$$

For (G,x) and (H,y) in D,

$$(G,x) \angle (H,y)$$

if and only if there exists an $S \subset N(G)$ such that $H \in \gamma(S|G,x)$ and for all $i \in S$, $u^i(H)(y) > u^i(G)(x)$.

Denote the graph of the SB σ by C, that is,

$$C \equiv \{(G,x) \mid G \in \Gamma \text{ and } x \in \sigma(G)\}.$$

The following important result is due to Shitovitz (private communication).

Theorem 4.5: *Let* (γ,Γ) *be a situation. The mapping* σ *is an OSSB for* (γ,Γ) *if and only if its graph C is a vN&M abstract stable set for the system* $(D,\angle)$ *that is associated with* (γ,Γ).

In addition to pointing out a formal relationship between OSSB and one of the most important solution concepts in game theory – the abstract stable set – the above theorem enables one to apply results from works on abstract stable sets such as the following theorem due to von Neumann and Morgenstern (1947). To state this theorem, we need an additional definition.

Definition 4.6: *Let* $(D,\angle)$ *be an abstract system. The dominance relation,* $\angle$, *is called* ***acyclic*** *if there is no* ***finite*** *sequence,* $\{a_j\}$, $j=1,2,\ldots,J$, *of elements in D, such that for all* $j=1,2,\ldots,J$, $a_j \angle a_{j+1}$, *where* $a_{J+1}=a_1$. *The dominance relation,* $\angle$, is called ***strictly acyclic*** *if there exists no* ***infinite*** *sequence,* $\{a_j\}$, *of elements in D such that for all j,* $j=1,2,\ldots$, $a_j \angle a_{j+1}$.

That is, if the dominance relation is acyclic, then it is impossible to find a finite set of elements in D that can be arranged in a "cycle" in such a way that each element in the cycle dominates the one to its right. If the dominance relation is strictly acyclic, then it is impossible to find an infinite sequence of elements in the set D such that each element in the sequence dominates the one preceding it. Observe that strict acyclicity implies acyclicity. Indeed, if the dominance relation is not acyclic, then by going around the (finite) cycle infinitely many times we get an infinite sequence, implying that the dominance relation is also not strictly acyclic.

Using mathematical transfinite induction, von Neumann and Morgenstern (1947) proved the following theorem.

Theorem 4.7: *Let $(D, \angle)$ be an abstract system, where the dominance relation $\angle$ is strictly acyclic. Then there exists a unique vN&M (abstract) stable set for the system $(D, \angle)$.*

Using Theorems 4.5 and 4.7, Shitovitz (private communication) proved the following result.

Theorem 4.8: *Let (γ,Γ) be a situation such that Γ contains a finite number of positions, and each position $G \in \Gamma$ contains a finite number of outcomes. Assume, in addition, that the inducement correspondence is such that for all $G,H \in \Gamma$, $x \in X(G)$, and $S \subset N(G)$, if $H \in \gamma(S|G,x)$ then $N(H)=S$. Then, (γ,Γ) admits a unique OSSB.*

Example 3.3 demonstrates that the theorem is not valid if we drop the restriction that for all $G \in \Gamma$, $|X(G)| < \infty$,[1] and Example 3.5 shows that the theorem is not valid if we drop the assumption that if $H \in \gamma(S|G,x)$ then $N(H)=S$. Example 3.4 demonstrates that the analog of Theorem 4.8 for the notion of CSSB is false.

Another important implication of Theorem 4.5 is that it is impossible for one OSSB to "contain" another.

Theorem 4.9: *Let (γ,Γ) be a situation and let σ and $\tilde{\sigma}$ be two OSSBs for (γ,Γ). If for all $G \in \Gamma$, $\sigma(G) \subset \tilde{\sigma}(G)$, then these two OSSBs coincide.*

It is, perhaps, surprising that, as the following theorem shows, in contrast to Theorem 4.5, the notion of CSSB cannot be formally related to a vN&M abstract stable set (see, however, Section 11.8).

Theorem 4.10: *There exists a situation (γ,Γ) such that no abstract system $(D,\angle)$ satisfies the condition that the mapping σ is a CSSB for (γ,Γ) if and only if its graph is a vN&M abstract stable set for $(D,\angle)$.*

The following two theorems extend Theorems 4.5 and 4.10 and show that they are valid for all ϵ-stable SBs.

[1] For a set A, $|A|$ denotes the cardinality of (number of elements in) A.

Theorem 4.11: *Let* (γ,Γ) *be a situation. The SB* σ *is an* ϵ*-OSSB for* (γ,Γ) *if and only if its graph is a vN&M abstract stable set for the system* $(D,\angle^{\epsilon})$, *where*

$$D \equiv \{(G,x) \mid G \in \Gamma \text{ and } x \in X(G)\},$$

and for (G,x) *and* (H,y) *in D,*

$$(G,x) \angle^{\epsilon} (H,y)$$

if and only if there exists $S \subset N(G)$ *such that* $H \in \gamma(S|G,x)$ *and for all* $i \in S$, $u^i(H)(y) > u^i(G)(x) + \epsilon$.

Theorem 4.12: *Let* $\epsilon > 0$*. Then, there exists a situation* (γ,Γ) *such that there is no abstract system* $(D,\angle)$ *with the property that the mapping* σ *is an* ϵ*-CSSB for* (γ,Γ) *if and only if its graph C is a vN&M abstract stable set for* $(D,\angle)$.

The above two theorems should not lead the reader to think that results concerning stability necessarily extend to ϵ-stability or vice versa. For example, as noted in Section 2.6, Asheim (1989) proved that the situation associated with the sequential bargaining game (see Section 8.2) admits infinite OSSBs, but by Theorem 8.3.9, it admits a unique ϵ-OSSB for all $\epsilon > 0$. Moreover, the solutions assigned by this ϵ-OSSB are most appealing.

Example 3.3 shows that there are situations for which an ϵ-OSSB might be discontinuous in ϵ. Recall that the situation (γ,Γ) in Example 3.3 admits no OSSB. In contrast, for every $\epsilon > 0$, an ϵ-OSSB exists. Indeed, as the reader can easily verify, for any $\epsilon > 0$, the SB given by $\sigma(G) \equiv \{x \in [10,20) \mid (20-x) \leq \epsilon\}$, is an ϵ-OSSB for (γ,Γ). By Theorem 4.13, this is the unique ϵ-OSSB for (γ,Γ).

The possible discontinuty of ϵ-CSSB can be demonstrated by Example 3.1. It is easy to verify that due to the discreteness of the set of outcomes $X(G)$, for any SB, σ, and for all ϵ, $0 \leq \epsilon < 1$, $\text{CDOM}(\sigma,G) = \text{CDOM}^{\epsilon}(\sigma,G)$. Hence, for all ϵ, $0 \leq \epsilon < 1$, σ is an ϵ-CSSB for (γ,Γ) if and only if $\sigma(G) = \{x, x+1, \ldots, 20\}$, where $x \in \{10, 11, \ldots, 20\}$. But, if $\epsilon \geq 1$ then an ϵ-CSSB, σ, for (γ,Γ) implies that if $x \in \sigma(G)$ and $x \in \{10, 11, \ldots, 20\}$, then $(x-1) \notin \text{CDOM}^{\epsilon}(\sigma,G)$. By external stability, therefore, $x \in \sigma(G)$ implies that $(x-1) \in \sigma(G)$. Hence if $\epsilon \geq 1$ then the unique ϵ-CSSB is given by $\sigma(G) = X(G)$.

Theorems 4.7 and 4.11 yield the existence of a unique ϵ-OSSB, $\epsilon > 0$, for a large class of situations.

Theorem 4.13: *Let* (γ,Γ) *be a situation that satisfies:*

i. For all $G \in \Gamma$, *if* $H \in \gamma(S|G,x)$ *then* $N(H) = S$; *and ii. There exists a scalar* κ*, such that for all* $G\in\Gamma$*,* $i\in N(G)$*, and* $x\in X(G)$*,* $|u^i(G)(x)|\leq\kappa$*.*

Then, for all $\epsilon>0$*, there exists a unique* ϵ*-OSSB for* (γ,Γ)*.*

Example 3.3 demonstrates that Theorem 4.13, although valid for all $\epsilon>0$, need not be true for $\epsilon=0$.

Proofs of Chapter 4

Proof of Theorem 4.5: Let σ be an SB for Γ, and let C denote its graph. Then, ODOM(σ, G) can be written as:

$$\text{ODOM}(\sigma,G)=\{x\in X(G)|\exists\ S\subset N(G),\ H\in\gamma(S|G,x),\text{ and }(H,y)\in C \text{ such that for all } i\in S,\ u^i(H)(y)>u^i(G)(x)\}.$$

That is, $x\in\text{ODOM}(\sigma,G)$ if and only if there exists $(H,y)\in C$ such that $(G,x)\angle(H,y)$, that is, $x\in\text{ODOM}(\sigma,G)$ if and only if $(G,x)\in\Delta(C)$. Therefore, $x\in X(G)\backslash\text{ODOM}(\sigma,G)$ if and only if $(G,x)\in D\backslash\Delta(C)$. Now, σ is an OSSB if and only if for all $G\in\Gamma$, $\sigma(G)=X(G)\backslash\text{ODOM}(\sigma,G)$, that is, if and only if $C=D\backslash\Delta(C)$. Q.E.D.

Proof of Theorem 4.7: See von Neumann and Morgenstern (1947, p. 597–600). Q.E.D.

Proof of Theorem 4.8: Let (γ,Γ) be a situation that satisfies the conditions of the theorem. In view of Theorems 4.5 and 4.7, it suffices to show that the system $(D,\angle)$ that is associated with (γ,Γ) is strictly acyclic.

Since both Γ and every $X(G)$, $G\in\Gamma$, are finite sets, it follows that D contains only a finite number of elements. Therefore, acyclicity is equivalent to strict acyclicity. Thus, it suffices to show that $\angle$ is acyclic.

Assume, in negation, that $\angle$ is not acyclic. Then, there exists a finite sequence of elements in D, $\{(G_k,x_k)\}$, $k=1,2,\ldots,K$, such that $(G_k,x_k)\angle(G_{k+1},x_{k+1})$ and $(G_{K+1},x_{K+1})=(G_1,x_1)$. Using the definition of $\angle$ and the condition that $H\in\gamma(S|G,x)$ implies $N(H)=S$, we conclude that for all k, $k=1,2,\ldots,K$, $N(G_k)=N(G_1)=N$, and for all $i\in N$, $u^i(G_1)(x_1)>u^i(G_K)(x_K)>\cdots>u^i(G_2)(x_2)>u^i(G_1)(x_1)$. This is a contradiction. Q.E.D.

Proof of Theorem 4.9: First, observe that if A and B are two vN&M abstract stable sets for some abstract system, $(D,\angle)$, then $A\subset B$ implies $A=B$. Indeed, otherwise there is an $a\in B\backslash A$. By external stability of A, there exists a $b\in A$ such that $a\angle b$. Since we assumed that $A\subset B$, it follows that $b\in B$. But then, $a,b\in B$ and $a\angle b$ contradict the internal stability of B.

By Theorem 4.5, therefore, it is impossible to have two OSSBs, σ and $\tilde{\sigma}$, for a situation (γ,Γ), with the property that the graph of $\tilde{\sigma}$ strictly includes the graph of σ. As $\sigma(G)\subset\tilde{\sigma}(G)$ for all $G\in\Gamma$, it follows that the two OSSBs have the same graph, that is, $\tilde{\sigma}\equiv\sigma$. Q.E.D.

Proof of Theorem 4.10: By the proof of Theorem 4.9, it suffices to show that it is possible to have two CSSBs, σ^1 and σ^2, for a situation (γ,Γ), with the property that the graph of σ^1 strictly includes the graph of σ^2. Indeed, consider Example 3.1. Define the two CSSBs $\sigma^1(G)=\{19,20\}$ and $\sigma^2(G)=\{20\}$, yielding the graphs $C^1=\{(G,19),(G,20)\}$ and $C^2=\{(G,20)\}$. Clearly, $C^2\subset C^1$ and $C^2\neq C^1$. Q.E.D.

Proof of Theorem 4.11: This follows, almost exactly, the proof of Theorem 4.5. Let σ be an SB for Γ, and let C denote its graph. Then,

$$\text{ODOM}^{\epsilon}(\sigma,G)=\{x\in X(G)\mid \exists S\subset N(G),\ H\in\gamma(S|G,x),\text{ and }(H,y)\in C \text{ such that for all } i\in S,\ u^i(H)(y)>u^i(G)(x)+\epsilon\}.$$

That is, $x\in\text{ODOM}^{\epsilon}(\sigma,G)$ if and only if there exists $(H,y)\in C$ such that $(G,x)\angle^{\epsilon}(H,y)$, that is, $x\in\text{ODOM}^{\epsilon}(\sigma,G)$ if and only if $(G,x)\in\Delta(C)$. Therefore, $x\in X(G)\setminus\text{ODOM}^{\epsilon}(\sigma,G)$ if and only if $(G,x)\in D\setminus\Delta(C)$. Now, σ is an ϵ-OSSB for (γ,Γ) if and only if for all $G\in\Gamma$, $\sigma(G)=X(G)\setminus\text{ODOM}^{\epsilon}(\sigma,G)$, that is, if and only if $C=D\setminus\Delta(C)$. Q.E.D.

Proof of Theorem 4.12: Let $\epsilon>0$. Define the following situation (γ,Γ) (which is a simplified variant of Example 3.1). $\boldsymbol{\Gamma=\{G\}}$, $\mathbf{G=(\{1\},\{10\epsilon,20\epsilon\},u^1(G))}$**, where** $\boldsymbol{u^1(G)(x)=x}$ **for** $\boldsymbol{x\in X(G)}$**, and** $\boldsymbol{\gamma(\{1\}|G,x)=\{G\}}$. It is easy to see that both $\sigma^1(G)\equiv X(G)$ and $\sigma^2(G)\equiv\{20\epsilon\}$ are ϵ-CSSBs (as well as CSSBs) for (γ,Γ). Thus, the graph of σ^1 strictly includes the graph of σ^2. Therefore, as was established in the proof of Theorem 4.9, these graphs cannot both be abstract stable sets for the same abstract system. Q.E.D.

Proof of Theorem 4.13: Let (γ,Γ) be a situation that satisfies the conditions of Theorem 4.13. First, observe that the abstract system $(D,\angle^{\epsilon})$, which is associated with (γ,Γ), is strictly acyclic. Indeed, assume, in negation, that there exists an infinite sequence (G_j,x_j), $j=1,2,\ldots$, of elements in D such that for all j, $(G_j,x_j)\angle^{\epsilon}(G_{j+1},x_{j+1})$. Let $K=\{1,2,\ldots,J\}$, where J is an integer that satisfies $\boldsymbol{J-1>2\kappa/\epsilon}$. By Condition (i), $\bigcap_{j\in K}N(G_j)\neq\emptyset$, that is, there exists $i\in\bigcap_{j\in K}N(G_j)$. Then, $u^i(G_{j+1})(x_{j+1})>u^i(G_j)(x_j)+\epsilon$, for all j, $j=1,2,\ldots,J$. Condition (ii) together with the fact that $J-1>2\kappa/\epsilon$, imply that $u^i(G_J)(x_J)>u^i(G_1)(x_1)+2\kappa\geq\kappa$, contradicting Condition (ii) for $G=G_J$ and $x=x_J$.

Thus, the system $(D,\angle^{\epsilon})$ is strictly acyclic. By Theorem 4.7, there exists a unique abstract stable set for the system $(D,\angle^{\epsilon})$. Hence, Theorem 4.11 yields Theorem 4.13. Q.E.D.

CHAPTER 5

Existence and uniqueness of OSSB and CSSB

This chapter establishes existence and uniqueness results that will be used extensively in the applications of the theory of social situations in Chapters 6–10. Thus, this chapter is rather technical. The reader may proceed directly to the next chapters and accept statements that refer to this chapter. Alternatively, the reader may wish to familiarize himself (at least in the first reading) only with the definitions and results of this chapter but skip the proofs.

5.1 Hierarchical situations

Interesting social environments are frequently represented by situations said to be "hierarchical," which have a relatively simple structure. For example, the situation in Example 2.1.2, the voting by veto model in Example 3.6, and games in characteristic function, normal, and extensive form (see Chapters 6–10) are naturally associated with hierarchical situations.

An important property of many hierarchical situations is that they admit a unique OSSB and a unique CSSB. Moreover, these two notions can be derived explicitly by the (recursive) formulas that fully characterize them (see Theorems 5.2.1 and 5.4.1).

A situation (γ,Γ) is ***hierarchical*** if there exists a finite "hierarchy" of the positions in Γ such that a position can be induced either from positions of a higher hierarchy than it or else from itself. Moreover, for every $G\in\Gamma$, there is at most one coalition, denoted $S(G)$, that can induce G from itself.

Before stating the formal definition, it should be stressed that the hierarchical structure is only a technical construct that carries no other meaning or interpretation whatsoever. In particular, positions of a higher hierarchy are by no means "superior" or have any "priority" over positions of a lower hierarchy.

Definition 5.1.1: *A situation* (γ,Γ) *is said to be* ***hierarchical*** *if* Γ *can be partitioned into a finite number,* K, *of pairwise disjoint sets of positions,* Γ_1, $\Gamma_2,\ldots,\Gamma_K$, *such that for each* k, $k=1,2,\ldots,K$,

H.1. For each $G \in \Gamma_k$, $(\gamma,(\{G\} \cup \Gamma^{k+1}))$ *is a situation, where* Γ^k *is the set of all positions of hierarchy (weakly) lower than k, that is,* $\mathbf{\Gamma^k \equiv \Gamma_k \cup \Gamma_{k+1} \cup \cdots \cup \Gamma_K}$, ***and*** $\mathbf{\Gamma^{K+1} \equiv \emptyset}$,

and, moreover,

H.2. For every $G \in \Gamma$, *if* $G \in \gamma(S|G,x)$ *for some* $x \in X(G)$, *then* $S = S(G)$.

Condition (H.1) requires that for all k, $k = 1,2,\ldots,K$, if G is a position of hierarchy k, that is, $G \in \Gamma_k$, then the collection of positions $\{G\} \cup \Gamma^{k+1}$, consisting of G and all those positions in Γ whose hierarchies are below k, is closed under the inducement correspondence γ. In particular, it is impossible to induce from any position $H \in \{G\} \cup \Gamma^{k+1}$ a position $\hat{H}$ of hierarchy at least k which differs from G. (Observe that $G \in \Gamma_k$ is of a higher hierarchy the lower that k is, just as grade A is better than B, or "the first" is more highly ranked than "the second.")

Condition (H.2) demands that for every position $G \in \Gamma$, there is at most one coalition, denoted $\mathbf{S(G)}$, that can induce G from itself. Thus, (H.2) requires that if $S(G)$ can induce G from itself when x is proposed, then no coalition other than $S(G)$ can induce G from itself when any outcome, $y \in X(G)$, is proposed. [But (H.2) does not imply that if $S(G)$ can induce G from itself when x is proposed, then it can also do so when another outcome, $y \in X(G)$, is proposed.]

To realize that the situation (γ,Γ) in Example 2.1.2 is hierarchical, define the following partition of Γ:

$$\mathbf{\Gamma_1 \equiv \{G^0\},\ \Gamma_2 \equiv \{G^I, G^U\},\ \Gamma_3 \equiv \{G^{IY}, G^{IN}, G^{UY}, G^{UN}\}.}$$

By the definition of the inducement correspondence, we have that $H \in \gamma(S|G,x)$ implies that H is of a lower hierarchy than G, thus (H.1) holds. Moreover, since for all $G \in \Gamma$, $S \subset N(G)$, and $x \in X(G)$ we have $G \notin \gamma(S|G,x)$, it follows that (H.2) also (trivially) holds.

The three situations associated with the voting by veto model of Example 3.6 are also hierarchical. Indeed, if the position G^C is induced from the position G^D, then it must be the case that agenda D contains strictly more alternatives than C. Therefore, we can define the following hierarchy on Γ: Position G^D is of a higher hierarchy than position G^C if and only if the number of alternatives in D is strictly greater than the number of alternatives that belong to C. This hierarchy leads to the following partition of Γ:

$$\mathbf{\Gamma_1 = \{G^A\},\ \Gamma_2 = \{G^{\{a,b\}}, G^{\{a,c\}}, G^{\{b,c\}}\},\ \Gamma_3 = \{G^{\{a\}}, G^{\{b\}}, G^{\{c\}}\}.}$$

The reader can easily verify that this partition satisfies conditions (H.1) and (H.2).

Notice that for a hierarchical situation (γ,Γ), there may be several different partitions of Γ that satisfy conditions (H.1) and (H.2). For example, in the voting by veto model, the following is another such partition:

$$\tilde{\Gamma}_1=\{G^A\},\ \tilde{\Gamma}_2=\{G^{\{a,b\}}\},\ \tilde{\Gamma}_3=\{G^{\{a,c\}},\ G^{\{b,c\}}\},\ \tilde{\Gamma}_4=\{G^{\{a\}},\ G^{\{b\}}\},\ \tilde{\Gamma}_5=\{G^{\{c\}}\}.$$

Given a hierarchical situation (γ,Γ), let $\boldsymbol{K(\Gamma)}$ denote the number of sets, K, in a partition of Γ which satisfies conditions (H.1) and (H.2). [Notice that, as just demonstrated, $K(\Gamma)$ need not be unique.]

Condition (H.1) implies the weaker condition that the collection of all positions of some hierarchy, k, or lower hierarchy, $k=1,2,\ldots,K(\Gamma)$, is closed under the inducement correspondence γ.

Claim 5.1.2: *If a situation (γ,Γ) satisfies condition (H.1) then it also satisfies*
H.3. For all k, (γ,Γ^k) is a situation.

It is convenient to represent hierarchical situations by graphs. To this end we need the following standard definitions from graph theory (see, e.g., Berge 1962).

Definition 5.1.3: *A* **directed graph** *or* **digraph** *consists of a nonempty (possibly infinite) set V, whose elements are called* **vertices** *or* **nodes,** *together with a collection of ordered pairs, vw, called* **arcs** *or* **edges,** *where v and w are members of V. If vw is an arc, then v is* **adjacent to** *w and w is* **adjacent from** *v. The* **outdegree** *of a vertex v is the number of vertices adjacent from it (i.e., the number of arcs beginning at node v), and the* **indegree** *is the number of vertices adjacent to it (i.e., the number of arcs ending at node v). A vertex v is a* **source** *if its indegree is 0 and it is a* **sink** *if its outdegree is 0.*

A **walk,** *x, is a sequence of vertices $(v_1,v_2,\ldots)$, where, for all j, $j=1,2,\ldots$, v_j is adjacent to v_{j+1}. A* **finite walk** *is a walk $(v_1,v_2,\ldots,v_J)$, where J is a finite number. The* **length of the finite walk** *$(v_1,v_2,\ldots,v_J)$ is $J-1$. A walk with all of its nodes distinct is called a* **path.** *A digraph is* **acyclic** *if every walk is a path. An acyclic digraph where all its walks (paths) have a finite length that does not exceed a finite integer J is called a* **bounded acyclic digraph.** *The* **length of a bounded acyclic digraph** *is the maximal length of its walks (paths).*

If v and w are vertices in V and there is a finite walk $(v_1,v_2,\ldots,v_J)$, where $v_1=v$ and $v_J=w$, we say that w is **reachable** *from v. A* **basis** *of a digraph is a minimal collection of vertices from which all vertices are reachable.*

It is well known, and can easily be proved, that every bounded acyclic digraph has a unique basis consisting of all vertices of indegree 0.

Equipped with the above terminology, we shall now associate a bounded acyclic digraph with a hierarchical situation. Let (γ,Γ) be a situation, and let

$\varphi^*(\gamma,\Gamma)$ be the digraph whose set of vertices are in a one-to-one correspondence with the positions in Γ, and vw is an arc in $\varphi^*(\gamma,\Gamma)$ if and only if the positions G and H that correspond to v and w satisfy the condition that there exist $S \subset N(G)$ and $x \in X(G)$ such that $H \in \gamma(S|G,x)$.

The ***associated digraph*** $\varphi(\gamma,\Gamma)$ is obtained from $\varphi^*(\gamma,\Gamma)$ by deleting edges of the type (v,v). Though $\varphi(\gamma,\Gamma)$ provides only a partial characterization of the situation (γ,Γ) (as it gives no information about whether a position can be induced from itself), we shall see that the associated digraph is useful for the study of hierarchical situations.

Claim 5.1.4: *A situation* (γ,Γ) *satisfies condition (H.1) if and only if its associated digraph* $\varphi(\gamma,\Gamma)$ *is a bounded acyclic digraph.*

Claim 5.1.4 gives a straightforward way to determine whether a situation (γ,Γ) is hierarchical: Draw its associated digraph $\varphi(\gamma,\Gamma)$ and verify whether it is a bounded acyclic digraph.

An important special class of hierarchical situations which, as we shall later see, frequently arise in the applications of the theory of social situations are those whose inducement correspondence is simple, where "simple" is defined as:

Definition 5.1.5: *Let* (γ,Γ) *be a situation. The inducement correspondence* γ *is called* ***simple*** *if for every* $G \in \Gamma$, $x \in X(G)$, *and* $H \in \gamma(S|G,x)$ *we have* $N(H) = S$, *and, if, in addition,* $S = N(G)$, *then* $H = G$.

That is, if γ is simple, then the set of players in any position that a coalition S can induce is the set S itself. [Recall that in general, if $H \in \gamma(S|G,x)$ then $S \subset N(H)$. If γ is simple then the weak inclusion changes to identity.] In addition, if γ is simple, then for every $G \in \Gamma$, the set of all players in G can induce, at most, the position G itself.

The connection between simple inducement correspondences and hierarchical situations is provided by Proposition 5.1.6.

Proposition 5.1.6: *Let* (γ,Γ) *be a situation where* γ *is a simple inducement correspondence. Assume that there exists a finite positive integer M such that the set of players in any position in* Γ *contains no more than M players, that is, for all* $G \in \Gamma$, $|N(G)| \leq M$. *Then,* (γ,Γ) *is a hierarchical situation.*

5.2 Uniqueness of OSSB

One important property of hierarchical situations is that they admit at most a single OSSB. We are now ready to verify this assertion, an assertion that will be used extensively in what follows.

Let (γ,Γ) be a hierarchical situation. For each position $G \in \Gamma$, define, recursively, two subsets of $X(G)$, $\alpha(G)$ and $\beta(G)$, as follows:

For $G \in \Gamma_K$ [recall that $K = K(\Gamma)$ is the lowest hierarchical level],

$$\boldsymbol{\beta(G) \equiv X(G)}$$

and

$$\boldsymbol{\alpha(G) \equiv \{x \in \beta(G) \mid G \in \gamma(S(G) \mid G,x) \text{ and } \exists\, y \in \beta(G) \text{ such that } u^i(G)(y) > u^i(G)(x) \text{ for all } i \in S(G)\}.}$$

That is, for a position G of the lowest hierarchy, K, the set $\beta(G)$ coincides with the set of all feasible outcomes in G. The set $\alpha(G)$ contains all those outcomes x in $\beta(G)$ that have the following two properties:

i. the coalition $S(G)$ can induce G from itself when the outcome x is proposed, and
ii. there exists an outcome $y \in \beta(G)$ which every member of $S(G)$ prefers to x. That is, x is **$S(G)$ – Pareto dominated** by an outcome $y \in \beta(G)$.

Assume that $\alpha(G)$ and $\beta(G)$ were defined for all $G \in \Gamma^{m+1}$. For $G \in \Gamma_m$ define

$$\boldsymbol{\beta(G) = \{x \in X(G) \mid \text{there exist no } S \subset N(G),\ H \in \gamma(S \mid G,x),\ H \in \Gamma^{m+1}, \text{ and } y \in \beta(H) \backslash \alpha(H) \text{ such that } u^i(H)(y) > u^i(G)(x) \text{ for all } i \in S\}}$$

and

$$\boldsymbol{\alpha(G) = \{x \in \beta(G) \mid G \in \gamma(S(G) \mid G,x) \text{ and } \exists\, y \in \beta(G) \text{ such that } u^i(G)(y) > u^i(G)(x) \text{ for all } i \in S(G)\}.}$$

Thus, $\beta(G)$ consists of all those outcomes in $X(G)$ that would be accepted by the (optimistic) players in G if they believed that the solution for a position H, of hierarchy lower than that of G, is given by the set $\beta(H) \backslash \alpha(H)$. [Since H is of a lower hierarchy than G, the sets $\alpha(H)$ and $\beta(H)$, and hence $\beta(H) \backslash \alpha(H)$, are assumed to be already defined.] The set $\alpha(G)$ consists of those outcomes in $\beta(G)$ that have properties (i) and (ii). Observe that the mappings α and β are defined without reference to any SB.

Theorem 5.2.1: *Let σ be an OSSB for the hierarchical situation (γ,Γ). Then σ is the unique OSSB for (γ,Γ). Moreover, for $G \in \Gamma$, $\sigma(G)$ is given by the formula:*

$$\boldsymbol{\sigma(G) = \beta(G) \backslash \alpha(G).}$$

Theorem 5.2.1 not only establishes the uniqueness of an OSSB for hierarchical situations, but it also provides an explicit formula for calculating this OSSB. Indeed, the sets $\alpha(G)$ and $\beta(G)$ are constructed recursively, and hence it is possible to explicitly derive the set $\beta(G) \backslash \alpha(G)$, a set which, by Theorem 5.2.1, coincides with the solution that the unique OSSB σ assigns to position G.

Theorem 5.2.1 together with Claim 2.5.7 imply that in a hierarchical situation (γ,Γ), the restriction of the unique OSSB for (γ,Γ) to a situation $(\gamma,\tilde{\Gamma})$, where $\tilde{\Gamma}\subset\Gamma$, yields the unique OSSB for $(\gamma,\tilde{\Gamma})$. It follows that if σ is the unique OSSB for (γ,Γ), then the solution, $\sigma(G)$, for $G\in\Gamma_m$ is independent of the solutions that σ assigns to positions H of hierarchy higher than G. [Recall that $(\gamma,\{G\}\cup\Gamma^{m+1})$ is a hierarchical situation.]

The following three examples show that neither condition (H.1) nor condition (H.2) nor the requirement that Γ is partitioned into a finite number, $K=K(\Gamma)$, of sets of positions is redundant; if one of these three requirements is violated the uniqueness result need not hold.

Example 5.2.2: Suppose that two individuals can divide a dollar between them, and that each can refuse to a given partition by requiring that the allocation of the dollar be "reconsidered." In order to represent this "story" as a situation, let Γ consist of the single position

$$\mathbf{G^1\equiv(N,X(G^1),\{u^i(G^1)\}_{i\in N})},$$

where

$$\mathbf{N\equiv\{1,2\}\;;\;X(G^1)\equiv\{(x_1,x_2)\in\mathbb{R}^2|\,x_1+x_2=1,\;x_1\geq 0,\;\text{and}\;x_2\geq 0\};}$$
$$\mathbf{u^i(G^1)(x)\equiv x_i\;,\;i\in N.}$$

Since every individual can insist on reconsideration, the natural inducement correspondence is, for all $x\in X(G^1)$,

$$\boldsymbol{\gamma(N|G^1,x)\equiv\emptyset\quad\text{and}\quad\gamma(\{i\}|G^1,x)\equiv\{G^1\}\;,\;i=1,2;}$$

this is, each of the two players can induce G^1, no matter what partition of the dollar is proposed.

Since Γ consists of a single position, we have $\Gamma=\Gamma_1=\{G^1\}$. Hence, $K(\Gamma)=1$ and (γ,Γ) satisfies condition (H.1). But condition (H.2) fails to hold, since G^1 can be induced from itself by two different coalitions, $\{1\}$ and $\{2\}$. And it is for this reason that (γ,Γ) admits more than a single OSSB. In fact, as we shall now see, every partition of the dollar, that is, every SB σ of the form

$$\boldsymbol{\sigma(G^1)=\{x\},\;x\in X(G^1),}$$

is an OSSB for (γ,Γ).

Indeed, let $\sigma(G^1)\equiv\{x^*\}$ for some $x^*\in X(G^1)$. Then, since $\sigma(G^1)$ contains a single element, it is clear that σ is optimistic internally stable. To realize that σ is also optimistic externally stable, consider $y\in X(G^1)\backslash\{x^*\}$. Since $y_1+y_2=1$ and $x_1^*+x_2^*=1$ but $y\neq x^*$, there exists $i\in N$ such that $x_i^*>y_i$, that is, $u^i(G^1)(x^*)>u^i(G^1)(y)$. Therefore, $G^1\in\gamma(\{i\}|G^1,y)$ and $x^*\in\sigma(G^1)$ imply that $y\in\text{ODOM}(\sigma,G^1)$. Thus, σ is also optimistic externally stable for (γ,Γ).

Hence, (γ,Γ) admits a continuum of OSSBs. It follows that condition (H.2) is indispensable for Theorem 5.2.1 to hold.

Example 5.2.3: A slight variation of the above example demonstrates that condition (H.1) is also indispensable. Let Γ consist of the two positions G^1 and G^2, where G^1 is as in Example 5.2.2, and

$$G^2 \equiv (N, X(G^2), \{u^i(G^2)\}_{i\in N});$$
$$X(G^2) \equiv \{(x_1,x_2)\in\mathbb{R}^2 | x_1+x_2=2,\ x_1\geq 0, \text{ and } x_2\geq 0\};$$
$$\text{and for } x\in X(G^2),\ u^i(G^2)(x) \equiv (\tfrac{1}{2})x_i,\ i=1,2.$$

The inducement correspondence, for $j=1,2$, is given by:

$$\gamma(N|G^j,x) \equiv \emptyset,\ \gamma(\{1\}|G^j,x) = \{G^1\}, \text{ and } \gamma(\{2\}|G^j,x) = \{G^2\}.$$

That is, player i, $i=1,2$, can induce the position G^i from any position G in Γ, no matter what outcome from $X(G)$ is proposed. Observe that although the positions G^1 and G^2 are different [since $X(G^1)\neq X(G^2)$ and $u^i(G^1)\neq u^i(G^2)$], the sets of attainable utility levels in the two positions coincide.

Clearly condition (H.2) holds, and, as $\Gamma=\{G^1,G^2\}$, it obviously contains only a finite number of positions. Condition (H.1), however, is violated. Indeed, Figure 5.2.3 represents the associated digraph $\varphi(\gamma,\Gamma)$. Since this digraph is not acyclic, it follows, by Claim 5.1.4 that (H.1) fails to hold. And, it is for this reason that (γ,Γ) admits more than a single OSSB. In fact, as we shall now see, every SB σ of the form

$$\sigma(G^1)=\{x\} \text{ and } \sigma(G^2)=\{2x\},\ x\in X(G^1),$$

is an OSSB for (γ,Γ).

Indeed, let $x^*\in X(G^1)$. Then, for the SB σ defined as $\sigma(G^1)\equiv\{x^*\}$ and $\sigma(G^2)=\{2x^*\}$, we have for every $i\in N$, $u^i(G^1)(\sigma(G^1))=u^i(G^2)(\sigma(G^2))=x_i^*$. It follows that σ is optimistic internally stable, since no individual $i\in N$ gains, under σ, by inducing G^i – the only position he can induce. Moreover, since player i can always induce the position G^i, it follows that he can guarantee himself the utility level x_i^*. Now, if for $j\in\{1,2\}$, $y\in X(G^j)$, and $\{y\}\neq\sigma(G^j)$, then, as in Example 5.2.2, there exists $i\in N$ such that $u^i(G^j)(y)<x_i^*$. Since $G^i\in\gamma(\{i\}|G^j,y)$, we conclude that $y\in \text{ODOM}(\sigma,G^j)$. Thus, σ is also optimistic externally stable for (γ,Γ).

Hence, (γ,Γ) admits a continuum of OSSBs. It follows that condition (H.1) is indispensable for Theorem 5.2.1 to hold.

Example 5.2.4: Another slight variation of Example 5.2.2 demonstrates that the requirement that Γ is partitioned into a finite number, $K=K(\Gamma)$, of sets of positions is also indispensable. Let

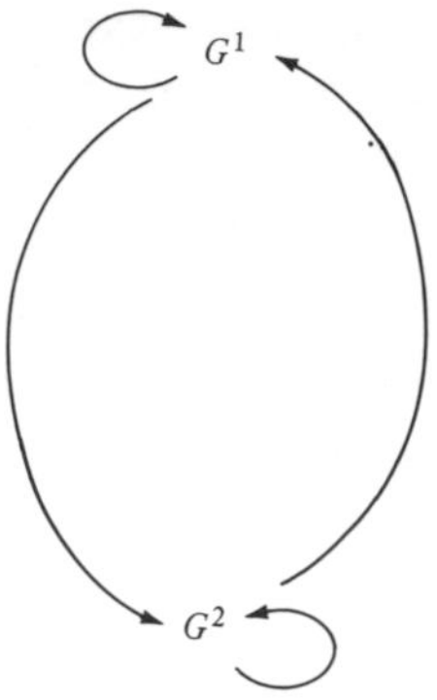

Figure 5.2.3

$$\boldsymbol{\Gamma \equiv \{G^j \mid j=1,2,\ldots\}},$$

where

$$\boldsymbol{G^j = (N, X(G^j), \{u^i(G^j)\}_{i\in N});}$$
$$\boldsymbol{N=\{1,2\}\ ;\ X(G^j)=\{(x_1,x_2)\in\mathbb{R}^2 \mid x_1+x_2=j,\ x_1\geq 0, \text{ and } x_2\geq 0\}\ ;}$$
$$\boldsymbol{u^i(G^j)(x)\equiv({}^1/_j)x_i,\ i=1,2 \text{ and } x\in X(G^j).}$$

The inducement correspondence is given by:

$$\boldsymbol{\gamma(\{1\}|G^j,x)=\{G^j\}} \qquad \textbf{if } j \textbf{ is odd,}$$
$$\boldsymbol{\gamma(\{1\}|G^j,x)=\{G^{j+1}\}} \qquad \textbf{if } j \textbf{ is even,}$$
$$\boldsymbol{\gamma(\{2\}|G^j,x)=\{G^j\}} \qquad \textbf{if } j \textbf{ is even,}$$
$$\boldsymbol{\gamma(\{2\}|G^j,x)=\{G^{j+1}\}} \qquad \textbf{if } j \textbf{ is odd,}$$
$$\boldsymbol{\gamma(N|G^j,x)\equiv\emptyset} \qquad \boldsymbol{j=1,2,\ldots}\ .$$

As in the above two examples, although all the positions in Γ are distinct, they all yield the same set of attainable utility levels for the two players 1 and 2. It is easily verified that both conditions (H.1) and (H.2) are satisfied (for example, let $\Gamma_j\equiv\{G^j\}, j=1,2,\ldots$). But $K(\Gamma)$ is infinite, and it is for this reason that (γ,Γ) admits more than a single OSSB. In fact, as we shall now see, every SB σ of the form

$$\boldsymbol{\sigma(G^j)=\{jx\},\ x\in X(G^1),}$$

is an OSSB for (γ,Γ).

Indeed, let $x^*\in X(G^1)$. Then, for the SB σ defined as $\sigma(G^j)\equiv\{jx^*\}$, we have for $i\in N$, $u^i(G^j)(\sigma(G^j))=x_i^*$. It follows that σ is optimistic internally stable. Moreover, if for some j, $y\in X(G^j)$ and $\{y\}\neq\sigma(G^j)=\{jx^*\}$, then there exists $i\in N$ such that $u^i(G^j)(y)<x_i^*$. Since there exists $H\in\gamma(\{i\}|G^j,y)$ (H is either G^j or G^{j+1}) such that $u^i(H)(\sigma(H))=x_i^*$, we have that $y\in\text{ODOM}(\sigma,G^j)$. Thus, σ is also optimistic externally stable for (γ,Γ).

Hence, (γ,Γ) admits a continuum of OSSBs. It follows that the finiteness of $K(\Gamma)$ is indispensable for Theorem 5.2.1 to hold.

5.3 Existence of a unique OSSB

The fact that a situation is hierarchical does not guarantee the existence of an OSSB for it. Indeed, the situation in Example 3.3 is hierarchical, but, as we saw, it admits no OSSB.

If, however, there exists an OSSB, σ, for the hierarchical situation (γ,Γ), then, by Theorem 5.2.1, it is unique, and is given by $\sigma(G)=\beta(G)\backslash\alpha(G)$, for all $G\in\Gamma$. The problem of existence of an OSSB for a hierarchical situation (γ,Γ), is reduced, therefore, to the question of whether this SB σ is optimistic stable. The following claim characterizes those hierarchical situations for which this is the case.

Claim 5.3.1: *Let (γ,Γ) be a hierarchical situation. The SB σ, where $\sigma(G)=\beta(G)\backslash\alpha(G)$ for all $G\in\Gamma$, is an OSSB for (γ,Γ) if and only if, for all $G\in\Gamma$, $\alpha(G)=\alpha^*(G)$, where, for $G\in\Gamma$,*

$$\boldsymbol{\alpha^*(G)=\{x\in\beta(G)\,|\,G\in\gamma(S(G)|G,x)\text{ and }\exists\ y\in\beta(G)\backslash\alpha(G)\text{ such that }u^i(G)(y)>u^i(G)(x)\text{ for all }i\in S(G)\}.}$$

Recall that the set $\alpha(G)$ contains all those outcomes x in X(G) which satisfy the two properties: (i) The coalition $S(G)$ can induce G from itself when the outcome x is proposed, and (ii) x is $S(G)$-Pareto dominated by an outcome $y\in\beta(G)$. The set $\alpha^*(G)$, on the other hand, consists of all those outcomes x in $X(G)$ that possess property (i) as well as the following property:

iii. x is $S(G)$-Pareto dominated by an outcome $y\in\beta(G)\backslash\alpha(G)$.

Since the set β(G)\\α(G) is included in $\beta(G)$, it follows that condition (iii) is stronger than (ii); for all positions G in Γ, $\alpha^*(G)$ is always included in $\alpha(G)$. The reverse inclusion, for all $G\in\Gamma$, is, as stated in Claim 5.3.1, a necessary and sufficient condition for the hierarchical situation to admit a (unique) OSSB.

Since $\alpha(G)$ always includes $\alpha^*(G)$, it follows that if $\alpha(G)$ is empty then so is $\alpha^*(G)$. In particular, in such cases the two sets (trivially) coincide. This immediate observation leads to the definition of an important class of hierarchical situations, called strictly hierarchical. A strictly hierarchical situation is a hierarchical situation, (γ,Γ), such that no position can be induced from itself; that is, if $H\in\gamma(S|G,x)$ for some $G\in\Gamma$, $S\subset N(G)$, and $x\in X(G)$, then $H\neq G$. Alternatively, a hierarchical situation is strictly hierarchical if, and only if, $\varphi(\gamma,\Gamma)=\varphi^*(\gamma,\Gamma)$.

Definition 5.3.2: *A situation* (γ,Γ) *is* ***strictly hierarchical*** *if it is hierarchical and, in addition, for all* $G\in\Gamma$, $S\subset N(G)$, *and* $x\in X(G)$, $G\notin\gamma(S|G,x)$.

The reader can easily verify that the situations in Examples 2.1.2 and 3.6 are both strictly hierarchical. We shall see in the next section that a strictly hierarchical situation admits a unique CSSB. As the following corollary asserts, the same is true for OSSB.

Corollary 5.3.3: *Let* (γ,Γ) *be a strictly hierarchical situation. Then there exists a unique OSSB for* (γ,Γ).

Clearly, not all social environments give rise to strictly hierarchical situations. In order to assure that an OSSB exists for hierarchical situations which include positions that can be self-induced (and hence are not strictly hierarchical), additional assumptions are necessary. Consider the following two standard assumptions which are likely to be met in many of the applications of the theory of social situations to concrete models:

A.1. For all $G\in\Gamma$, $X(G)$ is a topological compact set.
A.2. For all $G\in\Gamma$ and for all $i\in N(G)$, $u^i(G)$ is a continuous function [according to the topology of (A.1)].

But, as the following example shows, these two assumptions do not guarantee the existence of an OSSB.

Example 5.3.4: Consider the hierarchical situation (γ,Γ), where

$$\Gamma=\{G^1,G^2\}\ ,\ G^1=(\{1\},[10,20],u^1(G^1))\ ,$$
$$G^2=(\{1\},\{100\},u^1(G^2)),$$

and for all $G\in\Gamma$ and $x\in X(G)$,

$$u^1(G)(x)=x.$$

The inducement correspondence is given by:

$$\gamma(\{1\}|G^1,x)=\{G^1\} \qquad \text{if } x<20,$$
$$\gamma(\{1\}|G^1,x)=\{G^1,G^2\} \qquad \text{if } x=20,$$
$$\gamma(\{1\}|G^2,100)=\emptyset.$$

The situation (γ,Γ) represents the social environment in which a single individual is asked to state a number from the closed interval [10,20]. Stating any number in [10,20] allows the player to reconsider his choice, and if he wishes, he can state another number from [10,20]. If he states the number 20, then he can, in turn, also state the number 100. Once the player sticks to the number he chooses, he receives an amount of utils equal to that number.

Observe that both (A.1) and (A.2) are satisfied. Indeed, since $X(G^1)$ is a closed interval and $X(G^2)$ consists of a single outcome, assumption (A.1) obviously holds. It is equally evident that the functions $u^1(G^1)$ and $u^1(G^2)$ are continuous, that is, (A.2) also holds. Nevertheless, (γ,Γ) admits no OSSB.

Indeed, assume, in negation, that σ is an OSSB for (γ,Γ). By Theorem 5.2.1 we have that $\sigma(G)=\beta(G)\backslash\alpha(G)$ for all $G\in\Gamma$. It is easy to see that $\alpha(G^2)=\emptyset$, and, hence, by Theorem 5.2.1, $\sigma(G^2)=\{100\}$. Since $G^2\in\gamma(\{1\}|G^1,20)$ and $\sigma(G^2)=\{100\}$, it follows that $20\in ODOM(\sigma,G^1)$. The optimistic (internal) stability of σ implies, therefore, that $20\notin\sigma(G^1)$.

Assume, next, that $\sigma(G^1)\neq\emptyset$. Then, there exists $x\in[10,20)\cap\sigma(G^1)$. Distinguish between the two cases:

i. $\sigma(G^1)\cap(x,20)\neq\emptyset$. Then, there exists $y\in\sigma(G^1)$ with $y>x$. As $G^1\in\gamma(\{1\}|G^1,x)$, $x\in ODOM(\sigma,G^1)$, which contradicts the optimistic stability of σ.

ii. $\sigma(G^1)\cap(x,20)=\emptyset$. Then, for $y\in(x,20)$, $y\notin ODOM(\sigma,G^1)$. By the optimistic (external) stability of σ, $y\in\sigma(G^1)$. This is a contradiction.

We must, therefore, conclude that $\sigma(G^1)=\emptyset$. But then, $x\notin ODOM(\sigma,G^1)$ for all $x\in[10,20)$. By (external) stability, therefore, $[10,20)\subset\sigma(G^1)$, contradicting $\sigma(G^1)=\emptyset$. Thus, there exists no OSSB for (γ,Γ).

Whereas assumptions (A.1) and (A.2) do not guarantee the existence of an OSSB, it is possible to establish the existence of a unique OSSB for hierarchical situations if (A.1) is replaced by:

A.3. For all $G\in\Gamma$, $\beta(G)$ is a compact set.

Theorem 5.3.5: *Let (γ,Γ) be a hierarchical situation which satisfies assumptions (A.2) and (A.3). Then, there exists a unique OSSB for (γ,Γ).*

A disadvantage of assumption (A.3) is that it concerns the sets $\beta(G)$, $G\in\Gamma$, which are derived from the more "primitive" or "basic" data – the set of positions Γ and the inducement correspondence γ. Unfortunately, as we saw in Example 5.3.4, the more appealing assumption, (A.1), cannot be substituted for (A.3) in Theorem 5.3.5. There are, however, two immediate corollaries of Theorem 5.3.5 that consider situations where the compactness of the sets $\beta(G)$ is easily verified.

Corollary 5.3.6: Let (γ,Γ) be a hierarchical situation such that for all $G\in\Gamma$, $X(G)$ contains a finite number of outcomes. Then, there exists a unique OSSB for (γ,Γ).

Corollary 5.3.7: *Let* (γ,Γ) *be a hierarchical situation which satisfies (A.1) and (A.2). Assume, in addition, that the inducement correspondence* γ *is independent of the proposed outcome, and that the set of players in any position in* Γ *is finite.* [*That is, for all* $G\in\Gamma$, $x,y\in X(G)$, and $S\subset N(G)$, *we have* $\gamma(S|G,x)=\gamma(S|G,y)$, *and* $|N(G)|<\infty$.] *Then, there exists a unique OSSB for* (γ,Γ).

5.4 Existence and uniqueness of CSSB

In the previous sections we established that:

i. If a hierarchical situation possesses an OSSB, then it is the unique one (Theorem 5.3.5).
ii. There need not exist an OSSB for a hierarchical situation (Example 3.3).

Neither (i) nor (ii) is true for the notion of CSSB. The situation in Example 3.2 has a continuum of CSSBs, and hence the analog of (i) fails to hold for CSSB. Theorem 5.4.2 asserts that every hierarchical situation necessarily possesses at least one CSSB, that is, the analog of (ii) also fails to hold.

It is useful to first consider the class of strictly hierarchical situations and verify the validity of the analog of Corollary 5.3.3, for the notion of CSSB. Let (γ,Γ) be a hierarchical situation. Define, recursively, the mapping η as follows: For positions of the lowest hierarchy, that is, for $G\in\Gamma_K$,

$$\eta(G)\equiv X(G).$$

Assume that η is defined for all positions in Γ^{k+1}. For $G\in\Gamma_k$, define,

$$\eta(G)\equiv\{x\in X(G)|\text{there is no } S\subset N(G) \text{ and } H\in\gamma(S|G,x),\ H\in\Gamma^{k+1}, \text{ such that } \eta(H)\neq\emptyset, \text{ and for all } i\in S \text{ and } y\in\eta(H),\ u^i(H)(y)>u^i(G)(x)\}.$$

The set $\eta(G)$ consists of all those outcomes in $X(G)$ that would not be rejected by conservative players if they believed that the solution for a position H of a hierarchy lower than G is $\eta(H)$. It follows that the SB which coincides with η is a natural candidate to be a CSSB for (γ,Γ). This is formalized by the following theorem which is due to Eythan Weg (private communication).

Theorem 5.4.1: *Let* (γ,Γ) *be a strictly hierarchical situation. Then there exists a unique CSSB for* (γ,Γ). *Moreover, this unique CSSB is given by the SB* η.

Theorems 5.2.1 and 5.4.1 together with Corollary 5.3.3 establish that strictly hierarchical situations admit a unique OSSB and a unique CSSB, and more-

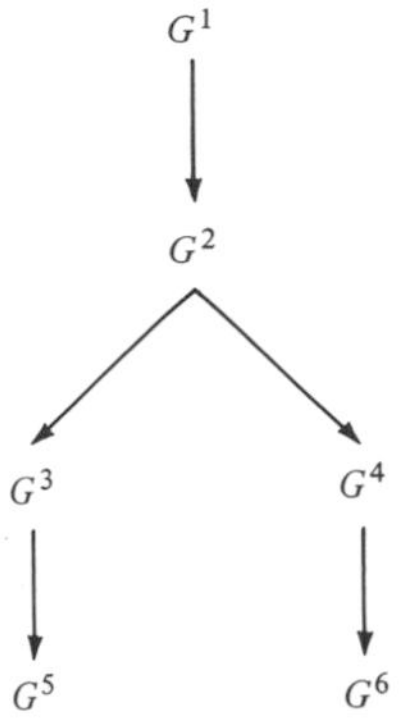

Figure 5.4.3

over, they provide the explicit formula to calculate these two (possibly distinct) SBs.

Theorem 5.4.1 together with Claim 2.5.7 implies that in a strictly hierarchical situation (γ,Γ), the restriction of the unique CSSB, σ, for (γ,Γ), to a situation $(\gamma,\tilde{\Gamma})$, where $\tilde{\Gamma}\subset\Gamma$, yields the unique CSSB for $(\gamma,\tilde{\Gamma})$. It follows that if σ is the unique CSSB for (γ,Γ) then the solution, $\sigma(G)$, for $G\in\Gamma_m$ is independent of the solutions that σ assigns to positions H of hierarchy higher than m. [Recall that $(\gamma,\{G\}\cup\Gamma^{m+1})$ is a strictly hierarchical situation.]

Another implication of Theorem 5.4.1 is that, in contrast to the possible nonexistence of an OSSB, we have the following result.

Theorem 5.4.2: *Every hierarchical situation (γ,Γ) admits at least one CSSB. Moreover, a maximal*[1] *CSSB for (γ,Γ) is given by the mapping η.*

The proof of Theorem 5.4.2 shows that it can be strengthened: Condition (H.2) is not necessary for the theorem to hold. But, as Example 5.2.2 demonstrates, condition (H.2) is indispensable for the existence of an OSSB.

Using Theorems 5.3.5 and 5.4.1, I can now show, as promised in Chapter 2, that a "CSSB need not contain an OSSB." Indeed, the following example exhibits a strictly hierarchical situation (γ,Γ) in which, for some position $G\in\Gamma$, $\sigma^o(G)$ strictly includes $\sigma^c(G)$, whereas for other positions the reverse strict inclusion holds, where σ^o is the unique OSSB, and σ^c is the unique CSSB, for (γ,Γ).

Example 5.4.3: Figure 5.4.3 represents the graph $\varphi^*(\gamma,\Gamma)$ of the strictly hierarchical situation (γ,Γ), where Γ consists of six positions G^k, $k=1,2,\ldots,6$, given by:

[1] With respect to set inclusion; that is, $\sigma<\tilde{\sigma}$ if for all $G\in\Gamma$, $\sigma(G)\subset\tilde{\sigma}(G)$ and $\sigma\neq\tilde{\sigma}$.

$$\mathbf{N(G^1)=N(G^2)=\{1,2\}\ ,\ N(G^3)=N(G^5)=\{1\},\ N(G^4)=N(G^6)=\{2\}\ ;}$$
$$\mathbf{X(G^1)=[6,8]\times[6,8]\ ,\ X(G^2)=\{(7,7)\}\ ,}$$
$$\mathbf{X(G^3)=X(G^4)=[6,8]\ ,\ X(G^5)=X(G^6)=[5,8]\ ;}$$
$$\mathbf{u^i(G^k)(x)=x_i\ ,\ i=1,2,\ k=1,2,\ldots,6.}$$

The inducement correspondence γ is

$$\gamma(\{i\}|G^1,x)=\{G^2\},\ \text{for } i=1,2\ ,\ \gamma(\{1\}|G^2,x)=\{G^3\}\ ,$$
$$\gamma(\{2\}|G^2,x)=\{G^4\}\ ,\ \gamma(\{1\}|G^3,x)=\{G^5\}\ ,\ \gamma(\{2\}|G^4,x)=\{G^6\}\ ,$$
$$\text{and, otherwise, } \gamma(S|G,x)=\emptyset.$$

Since (γ,Γ) is a strictly hierarchical situation, Corollary 5.3.3 and Theorem 5.4.1 yield that there exist a unique OSSB, σ^o, and a unique CSSB, σ^c, for (γ,Γ). Using the recursive formula provided in Theorem 5.2.1, it is easy to derive σ^o: Since $\gamma(S|G^5,x)=\gamma(S|G^6,x)=\emptyset$, we have that

$$\sigma^o(G^5)=X(G^5)=[5,8] \text{ and } \sigma^o(G^6)=X(G^6)=[5,8].$$

Therefore,

$$\sigma^o(G^3)=\{8\},\ \sigma^o(G^4)=\{8\},\ \sigma^o(G^2)=\emptyset,\ \text{and } \sigma^o(G^1)=X(G^1).$$

The recursive formula in Theorem 5.4.1 yields that the unique CSSB σ^c is given by:

$$\sigma^c(G^5)=X(G^5),\ \sigma^c(G^6)=X(G^6)\ ,\ \sigma^c(G^3)=X(G^3),\ \sigma^c(G^4)=X(G^4),$$
$$\sigma^c(G^2)=X(G^2),\ \text{and } \sigma^c(G^1)=[7,8]\times[7,8].$$

In particular, we have that the solution assigned to position G^3 by the unique OSSB is strictly included by the solution assigned to position G^3 by the unique CSSB, and the reversed strict inclusion holds for the solution to position G^1. Both SBs assign the same solution to position G^5. Indeed,

$$\sigma^o(G^5)=\sigma^c(G^5)=[5,8],\ \sigma^o(G^3)=\{8\} \text{ and } \sigma^c(G^3)=[6,8]\ ,$$
$$\sigma^o(G^1)=[6,8]\times[6,8] \text{ and } \sigma^c(G^1)=[7,8]\times[7,8].$$

Thus, all of the three possible inclusion relationships between the solutions assigned by the unique OSSB, σ^o, and the unique CSSB, σ^c, are possible.

There are, however, situations in which, conforming with intuition, the OSSB is indeed included in the CSSB. Such is the case with all strictly hierarchical situations for which the OSSB assigns a nonempty set to each position that the CSSB assigns a nonempty set. [Observe that this condition is violated in Example 5.4.3, since $\sigma^c(G^2)=X(G^2)$ but $\sigma^o(G^2)=\emptyset$.] In particular, therefore, the OSSB is included in the CSSB of a strictly hierarchical situation whose OSSB is nonempty valued (implying that its CSSB also assigns a nonempty set to each position).

Theorem 5.4.4: *Let (γ,Γ) be a strictly hierarchical situation, and let σ^o and σ^c denote its unique OSSB and CSSB, respectively. Assume that for all $G\in\Gamma$, $\sigma^c(G)\neq\emptyset$ implies $\sigma^o(G)\neq\emptyset$. Then, $\sigma^o(G)\subset\sigma^c(G)$ for all $G\in\Gamma$.*

Proofs for Chapter 5

Proof of Claim 5.1.2: Note that for all $k=1,\ldots,K$, Γ^k is the union of $(\{G\}\cup\Gamma^{k+1})$ over all $G\in\Gamma_k$. By (H.1), for each $G\in\Gamma_k$, $(\{G\}\cup\Gamma^{k+1})$ is closed under γ. Hence, Γ^k is also closed under γ, that is, (H.3) is satisfied.

Q.E.D

Proof of Claim 5.1.4: Let $\varphi(\gamma,\Gamma)$ be a bounded acyclic digraph of length J. To see that (γ,Γ) satisfies (H.1), define Γ_1 to be the set of all those positions in Γ that correspond to the vertices in $\varphi(\gamma,\Gamma)$ whose indegree is 0, that is, to the basis of $\varphi(\gamma,\Gamma)$. It is easy to see that $\varphi(\gamma,\Gamma\backslash\Gamma_1)$ is also a bounded acyclic digraph of length $J-1$. Define Γ_2 to be the set of positions that correspond to the basis of $\varphi(\gamma,\Gamma\backslash\Gamma_1)$. Continuing inductively, define Γ_{k+1} to be the set of positions that correspond to the basis of the bounded acyclic digraph $\varphi(\gamma,\Gamma\backslash\{G\in\Gamma|G\in\Gamma_j$ for some j, $j\leq k\})$. Note that the length of this acyclic digraph does not exceed $J-k+1$. Therefore, this process yields a partition of Γ that contains no more than J elements. By construction, for all k and all $G\in\Gamma_k$, the indegree, in $\varphi(\gamma,\Gamma^k)$, of the vertex $v\in V$ that corresponds to $G\in\Gamma_k$, is 0. Thus, the collection $(\{G\}\cup\Gamma^{k+1})$ is closed under γ, that is, condition (H.1) is satisfied.

To verify the other direction, we need to show that for any situation (γ,Γ) that satisfies (H.1), $\varphi(\gamma,\Gamma)$ is a bounded acyclic digraph. The proof is by induction on $K=K(\Gamma)$. For $K=1$, by condition (H.1), for all $G\in\Gamma$, $(\gamma,\{G\})$ is a situation, implying that $\varphi(\gamma,\Gamma)$ consists of isolated vertices, and, hence, clearly it is a bounded acyclic digraph.

Assume the validity of the claim for all situations with $K=K(\Gamma)<q$, $q>1$, and consider a situation (γ,Γ) where $K(\Gamma)=q$. By Claim 5.1.2, (γ,Γ^2) is a situation, and it obviously satisfies (H.1). Since $K(\Gamma^2)=q-1<q$, the induction hypothesis yields that $\varphi(\gamma,\Gamma^2)$ is a bounded acyclic digraph. Since the indegree of every vertex in $\varphi(\gamma,\Gamma)$ that corresponds to a position $G\in\Gamma_1$ is 0, it follows that $\varphi(\gamma,\Gamma)$ is a bounded acyclic digraph. Q.E.D.

Proof of Proposition 5.1.6: Define the following partition of Γ into M subsets:

$$\Gamma_j=\{G\in\Gamma\,|\,|N(G)|=M-j+1\},\quad j=1,2,\ldots,M.$$

That is, $G\in\Gamma_j$ if and only if its set of players, $N(G)$, contains exactly $M-j+1$ players. Since γ is a simple inducement correspondence, if $H\in\gamma(S|G,x)$ then

$N(H)=S\subset N(G)$. Therefore, if $H\in\gamma(S|G,x)$ and $H\in\Gamma_k$ then $G\in\Gamma_j$, with $j\leq k$, and, if, in addition, $N(H)=N(G)$, then $H=G$. Hence, the associated digraph $\varphi(\gamma,\Gamma)$ is bounded and acyclic. By Claim 5.1.4 it follows that condition (H.1) is satisfied. To see that condition (H.2) also holds, note that, by the simplicity of γ, if $G\in\gamma(S|G,x)$, then $N(G)=S=S(G)$. Q.E.D.

Proof of Theorem 5.2.1: We need to show that if σ is an OSSB for the hierarchical situation (γ,Γ), then for all $G\in\Gamma$, $\sigma(G)=\beta(G)\backslash\alpha(G)$. We shall first prove that this equality holds for all positions of the lowest hierarchy, that is, for all $G\in\Gamma_K$.

i. **For $G\in\Gamma_K$, ODOM$(\sigma,G)\subset\alpha(G)$:** Since $G\in\Gamma_K$, for all $x\in X(G)$, $\gamma(S|G,x)=\emptyset$ for all $S\neq S(G)$, and $\gamma(S(G)|G,x)$ is either G itself or else it is empty. Hence,

   ODOM$(\sigma,G)=\{x\in X(G)|G\in\gamma(S(G)|G,x)$ and $\exists\ y\in\sigma(G)$ such that $u^i(G)(y)>u^i(G)(x)$ for all $i\in S(G)\}$.

   Since $\sigma(G)\subset X(G)$ and $\beta(G)=X(G)$, we have, by the definition of $\alpha(G)$, that ODOM$(\sigma,G)\subset\alpha(G)$.

ii. **For $G\in\Gamma_K$, $\alpha(G)\subset$ ODOM(σ,G):** Assume, in negation, that there exists $z\in\alpha(G)\backslash$ODOM(σ,G). By definition, $z\in\alpha(G)$ means that $G\in\gamma(S(G)|G,z)$, and there is an outcome $y\in\beta(G)$ with $u^i(G)(y)>u^i(G)(z)$ for all $i\in S(G)$. Since $z\in X(G)\backslash$ODOM(σ,G) and σ is optimistic (externally) stable, $z\in\sigma(G)$. Therefore, the internal stability of σ yields that $y\notin\sigma(G)$. Using again the external stability of σ, it follows that $y\in$ODOM(σ,G). As $G\in\Gamma_K$, it follows that there exists $x\in\sigma(G)$ with $u^i(G)(x)>u^i(G)(y)$ for all $i\in S(G)$. Recalling that $u^i(G)(y)>u^i(G)(z)$ for all $i\in S(G)$, we have that $u^i(G)(x)>u^i(G)(z)$ for all $i\in S(G)$. But then, $x\in\sigma(G)$ and $G\in\gamma(S(G)|G,z)$ imply that $z\in$ODOM(σ,G). Hence, we have a contradiction.

By (i) and (ii) we have that for all $G\in\Gamma_K$, $\alpha(G)=$ ODOM(σ,G). By the optimistic stability of σ, $\sigma(G)=X(G)\backslash$ODOM(σ,G). But for $G\in\Gamma_K$, $\beta(G)=X(G)$, and, therefore, for $G\in\Gamma_K$, $\sigma(G)=\beta(G)\backslash\alpha(G)$.

To conclude the proof of the theorem we need to show that this equality holds not only for positions of the lowest hierarchy, but also for every position $G\in\Gamma$. The proof is by induction on the hierarchy of the position.

Assume that for all positions $H\in\Gamma^{m+1}$, $\sigma(H)=\beta(H)\backslash\alpha(H)$. Let $\boldsymbol{G\in\Gamma_m}$, $\boldsymbol{m<K}$. By the induction hypothesis we can write $\beta(G)$ as

$\beta(G)=\{x\in X(G)|$ there are no $S\subset N(G)$, $H\in\gamma(S|G,x)$, $H\in\Gamma^{m+1}$, and $y\in\sigma(H)=\beta(H)\backslash\alpha(H)$ such that $u^i(H)(y)>u^i(G)(x)$ for all $i\in S\}$.

Hence, $\beta(G) \supset [X(G) \setminus \text{ODOM}(\sigma,G)]$, which, by the stability of σ, implies that $\sigma(G) \subset \beta(G)$ and $x \in \beta(G) \setminus \sigma(G)$ implies $x \in \alpha(G)$, or, equivalently, $x \in \beta(G) \setminus \alpha(G)$ implies $x \in \sigma(G)$. That is, we established that $\sigma(G) \supset [\beta(G) \setminus \alpha(G)]$.

To conclude the proof of the theorem it remains to be shown that if $x \in \sigma(G)$ then $x \in \beta(G) \setminus \alpha(G)$. A straightforward modification of the proof of (ii) yields this implication. Specifically, assume, in negation, that there exists a $z \in \sigma(G) \cap \alpha(G)$. [Recall that both $\alpha(G)$ and $\sigma(G)$ are subsets of $\beta(G)$.] By definition, $z \in \alpha(G)$ means that $G \in \gamma(S(G)|G,z)$, and there is an outcome $y \in \beta(G)$ with $u^i(G)(y) > u^i(G)(z)$ for all $i \in S(G)$. As $z \in \sigma(G)$, the internal stability of σ yields that $y \notin \sigma(G)$. By the external stability of σ, $y \in \text{ODOM}(\sigma,G)$. Since $y \in \beta(G)$, it follows that there exists $x \in \sigma(G)$ with $u^i(G)(x) > u^i(G)(y)$ for all $i \in S(G)$. Recalling that $u^i(G)(y) > u^i(G)(z)$ for all $i \in S(G)$, we have that $u^i(G)(x) > u^i(G)(z)$ for all $i \in S(G)$. But then, $x \in \sigma(G)$ and $G \in \gamma(S(G)|G,z)$ imply that $z \in \text{ODOM}(\sigma,G)$. This is a contradiction.

Hence, if σ is an OSSB for the hierarchical situation (γ,Γ), then for all $G \in \Gamma$, $\sigma(G) = \beta(G) \setminus \alpha(G)$. Q.E.D.

Proof of Claim 5.3.1: Since (γ,Γ) is hierarchical, we can rewrite $\text{ODOM}(\sigma,G)$, for $G \in \Gamma_k$, as the union of the two sets:

$$\{x \in X(G) |\ \exists\ S \subset N(G),\ H \in \gamma(S|G,x),\ H \in \Gamma^{k+1}, \text{ and } y \in \sigma(H) \text{ such that } u^i(H)(y) > u^i(G)(x) \text{ for all } i \in S\}$$

and

$$\{x \in X(G) |\ G \in \gamma(S(G)|G,x) \text{ and } \exists\ y \in \sigma(G) \text{ such that } u^i(G)(y) > u^i(G)(x) \text{ for all } i \in S(G)\}.$$

Since $\sigma(G) = \beta(G) \setminus \alpha(G)$, the definition of β implies that

$$\text{ODOM}(\sigma,G) = [X(G) \setminus \beta(G)] \cup \alpha^*(G).$$

Since $\alpha^*(G) \subset \beta(G)$, it follows that

$$X(G) \setminus \text{ODOM}(\sigma,G) = \beta(G) \setminus \alpha^*(G).$$

Now, σ is an OSSB if, and only if, for all $G \in \Gamma$, $\sigma(G) = X(G) \setminus \text{ODOM}(\sigma,G)$. Thus, σ is an OSSB if, and only if, for all $G \in \Gamma$, $\beta(G) \setminus \alpha(G) = \beta(G) \setminus \alpha^*(G)$. That is, σ is OSSB if, and only if, for all $G \in \Gamma$, $\alpha(G) = \alpha^*(G)$. Q.E.D.

Proof of Corollary 5.3.3: Since (γ,Γ) is hierarchical, by Theorem 5.2.1 it admits at most one OSSB, σ. By Claim 5.3.1, it therefore suffices to show that for all $G \in \Gamma$, $\alpha(G) = \alpha^*(G)$. Indeed, since no position can be induced from itself, we have that for all $G \in \Gamma$, $\alpha(G) = \alpha^*(G) = \emptyset$. Q.E.D.

Proof of Theorem 5.3.5: By Theorem 5.2.1 and Claim 5.3.1, we need to show that for all $G \in \Gamma$, $\alpha(G) = \alpha^*(G)$. As it is always the case that $\alpha^*(G) \subset \alpha(G)$, we need to verify that the reverse inclusion also holds. Let $z \in \alpha(G)$, that is, $G \in \gamma(S(G)|G,z)$ and $u^i(G)(y) > u^i(G)(z)$ for all $i \in S(G)$, for some $y \in \beta(G)$. Since $\beta(G)$ is a compact set, (A.2) implies that there exists $\tilde{y} \in \beta(G)$ such that $u^i(G)(\tilde{y}) \geq u^i(G)(y)$ for all $i \in S(G)$, and there is no $x \in \beta(G)$ with $u^i(G)(x) > u^i(G)(\tilde{y})$ for all $i \in S(G)$. Therefore, $\tilde{y} \notin \alpha(G)$, that is, $\tilde{y} \in \beta(G) \backslash \alpha(G)$. Hence, $z \in \alpha^*(G)$. Q.E.D.

Proof of Corollary 5.3.6: Let (γ,Γ) satisfy the conditions of the corollary. Endow $X(G)$, $G \in \Gamma$, with the discrete topology. Then (γ,Γ) satisfies assumptions (A.1) and (A.2), and, clearly, $\beta(G)$, being a subset of the finite set $X(G)$, is a compact set (in the discrete topology). To conclude the proof, apply Theorem 5.3.5. Q.E.D.

Proof of Corollary 5.3.7: In view of Theorem 5.3.5, it suffices to show that for all $G \in \Gamma$, the set $\beta(G)$ is a compact set. Since by (A.1), $X(G)$ is compact, and $\beta(G) \subset X(G)$, it suffices to show that $\beta(G)$ is closed. Let $\{y_j\}$ be a sequence (or a net) of outcomes in $\beta(G)$ with $y_j \to y$. We need to show that $y \in \beta(G)$.

Otherwise, there exist $S \subset N(G)$, $H \in \gamma(S|G,y)$, $H \in \Gamma^{m+1}$, and $z \in \beta(H) \backslash \alpha(H)$ such that for all $i \in S$, $u^i(G)(y) < u^i(H)(z)$. Since $|N(G)| < \infty$, we have that $|S| < \infty$. Therefore, assumption (A.2) yields that there exists J such that for all $j \geq J$, $u^i(G)(y_j) < u^i(H)(z)$ for all $i \in S$. Moreover, the fact that γ is independent of the proposed outcome implies that for all j, $H \in \gamma(S|G,y_j)$. But then, $z \in \beta(H) \backslash \alpha(H)$ contradicts the fact that $y_j \in \beta(G)$. Q.E.D.

Proof of Theorem 5.4.1: First, note that the SB η is a CSSB for (γ,Γ). Indeed, since (γ,Γ) is strictly hierarchical, we have that for all $G \in \Gamma$, $\text{CDOM}(\eta,G) = X(G) \backslash \eta(G)$.

To conclude the proof of the theorem, we need to show that if σ is a CSSB for (γ,Γ), then for all $G \in \Gamma$, $\sigma(G) = \eta(G)$.

Consider, first, positions of the lowest hierarchy, $K = K(\Gamma)$. Since (γ,Γ) is strictly hierarchical, then for all $G \in \Gamma_K$, $S \subset N(G)$, and $x \in X(G)$, we have $\gamma(S|G,x) = \emptyset$. Therefore, for any SB $\hat{\sigma}$, $\text{CDOM}(\hat{\sigma},G) = \emptyset$ for all $G \in \Gamma_K$. Thus, if σ is a CSSB, then for all $G \in \Gamma_K$, $\sigma(G) = X(G) = \eta(G)$.

Assume now that σ and η coincide for all positions in Γ^k for some k, $k \leq K$. If $k = 1$, we are done. Otherwise, let $G \in \Gamma_{k-1}$. Then, since (γ,Γ) is strictly hierarchical, and σ and η coincide for all positions in Γ^k, we have that $\text{CDOM}(\sigma,G) = \text{CDOM}(\eta,G)$. The stability of these SBs yields, therefore, that for all $G \in \Gamma_{k-1}$, $\sigma(G) = \eta(G)$. Continuing in this manner, we conclude that σ and η coincide for all $G \in \Gamma$. Q.E.D.

Proof of Theorem 5.4.2: Let (γ,Γ) be a hierarchical situation. Using the definitions of CDOM and η, it is easily verified that for all $G\in\Gamma$, $\eta(G)=X(G)\backslash\text{CDOM}(\eta,G)$, that is, η is a CSSB for (γ,Γ). It remains to be shown that if σ is a CSSB for (γ,Γ) such that for all $G\in\Gamma$, $\sigma(G)\supset\eta(G)$, then $\sigma=\eta$.

The proof is by induction on the hierarchy of G. For $G\in\Gamma_K$, $\eta(G)=X(G)$, and hence $\sigma(G)\supset\eta(G)$ implies $\eta(G)=\sigma(G)$. Assume the validity of the induction hypothesis for all $H\in\Gamma^{m+1}$, and let $G\in\Gamma_m$. Since for all $H\in\Gamma^{m+1}$, $\sigma(H)=\eta(H)$ and (γ,Γ) is hierarchical, the definition of η implies that $\text{CDOM}(\eta,G)\subset\text{CDOM}(\sigma,G)$. Therefore, $\sigma(G)=X(G)\backslash\text{CDOM}(\sigma,G)\subset X(G)\backslash\text{CDOM}(\eta,G)=\eta(G)$. But, for all $G\in\Gamma$, $\sigma(G)\supset\eta(G)$. Therefore, $\sigma(G)=\eta(G)$. Q.E.D.

Proof of Theorem 5.4.4: This proof proceeds by induction on the hierarchy of the position. For $G\in\Gamma_K$, $\sigma^o(G)=\sigma^c(G)=X(G)$. Assume, now, the validity of the theorem for all $H\in\Gamma^{k+1}$, and let $G\in\Gamma_k$. We need to show that $\sigma^o(G)\subset\sigma^c(G)$, or, alternatively, that $X(G)\backslash\sigma^o(G)\supset X(G)\backslash\sigma^c(G)$, which, by the stability of the two standards of behavior, is equivalent to $\text{ODOM}(\sigma^o,G)\supset\text{CDOM}(\sigma^c,G)$.

Let $x\in\text{CDOM}(\sigma^c,G)$. Then, there exist $S\subset N(G)$ and $H\in\gamma(S|G,x)$ such that $\sigma^c(H)\neq\emptyset$ and for all $i\in S$, $u^i(H)(y)>u^i(G)(x)$, for all $y\in\sigma^c(H)$. Since (γ,Γ) is strictly hierarchical, $H\in\Gamma^{k+1}$. Therefore, by the induction hypothesis, $\sigma^o(H)\subset\sigma^c(H)$. Moreover, since $\sigma^c(H)\neq\emptyset$ we have that $\sigma^o(H)\neq\emptyset$, and it follows that there exists $y^*\in\sigma^o(H)$ such that for all $i\in S$, $u^i(H)(y^*)>u^i(G)(x)$. Thus, $x\in\text{ODOM}(\sigma^o,G)$. Q.E.D.

CHAPTER 6

Characteristic function form games

In this chapter the theory of social situations is applied to the simplest of the three types of games – games in characteristic function form (known also as cooperative games). Several possible ways to represent such games as situations will be suggested. As in the procedural voting-by-veto model (Example 3.6), this demonstrates that the description of a social environment as a cooperative game is incomplete. It omits some essential information. I shall argue that a cooperative game specifies the power coalitions have if and when they form, but it is totally silent on the crucial issue of how exactly this power can be used. (As every card player knows, the distribution of the cards does not, in itself, suffice to determine the course of the game; it is important to know how the "hands" are played.)

The representation of a cooperative game as a situation forces us to address, among other issues, the following two fundamental questions in the theory of coalition formation:

C.1. What, in fact, is the meaning of forming a coalition – is it a binding commitment of the players to remain and never leave a coalition once it forms, or is it merely a "declaration of intentions" which can be revised?

C.2. Do players first form a coalition and only then discuss their payoff there, or are the two decisions made simultaneously?

We shall see that two of the most important game-theoretic solution concepts for cooperative games – the core and the vN&M solution – can be regarded as stemming from the way (C.1) and (C.2) are answered. More specifically, the stability of the standard of behavior for the situation which describes negotiations where "threats" are, in fact, commitments that must actually be carried out leads to the core, whereas the stable SB for the situation which describes negotiations that allow for contingent "tender threats," that is, when players are allowed to "renegotiate" freely among themselves, leads to the vN&M solution.

We shall also analyze another negotiation process where each player updates his "reservation price" according to the last tender offer that was made to him. The stability of the standard of behavior for the corresponding situation yields the new concept of the ***stable bargaining set.*** This concept ammends the following deficiency in the various notions of the bargaining set: For a threat to be "justified" it has to be immune against all counter threats, including those which are themselves not justified. (The application of the theory of social situations to cooperative games points out a similar problem in the definition of the core: A payoff for the grand coalition has to be immune against all threats, including those which, in turn, can themselves be countered. It turns out, however, that the core of finite cooperative games does not suffer from this deficiency.)

In view of Theorem 4.5, some of the results of this chapter can be cast in the terminology of classical game theory. In particular, the core, the vN&M solution, and the stable bargaining set can all be derived from vN&M abstract stable sets for the corresponding abstract systems.

Remark 6.0.1: Another central solution concept for cooperative games is the "Shapley value" (Shapley 1953). Its plausibility was recently contested by several scholars who provided examples in which the Shapley value yields a payoff that, it was argued, "is inconsistent with the hypothesis that players are rational utility maximizers" (see, e.g., Roth 1980, Shafer 1980, and Beja and Gilboa 1987). But the Shapley value is derived from a set of axioms that, presumably, represent some social desiderata. It should not, therefore, surprise us if it lacks strategic considerations – and these are the basis for the contesters. This entire debate would not arise were the Shapley value derived from a stable standard of behavior for some "Shapley situation" that is associated with the cooperative game. For if such were the case, then the rationale behind this concept, and, in particular, the reason that rational individuals might agree to follow it, would have been clear. Unfortunately, such a "Shapley situation" has not, as yet, been formulated.

Let N be a nonempty (possibly infinite) set, and let $\mathbb{R}$ be the set of all real numbers. For a coalition[1] $S \subset N$, $\mathbb{R}^S$ denotes the set of all functions from S to $\mathbb{R}$. (Thus, when S is finite, $\mathbb{R}^S$ can be identified with the S-dimensional Euclidean space.) If $x \in \mathbb{R}^N$ and S is a coalition, then x^S denotes the restriction of x on S. [When S is a singleton, that is, $S=\{i\}$ for some $i \in N$, we shall use $x(i)$ and x^i interchangeably.] Let S be a coalition and let $x^S, y^S \in \mathbb{R}^S$. Then, $x^S \geq y^S$ if $x(i) \geq y(i)$ for all $i \in S$; $x^S > y^S$ if $x^S \geq y^S$ but $x^S \neq y^S$; and $x^S >> y^S$ if $x(i) > y(i)$ for all $i \in S$.

Definition 6.0.2: *A **game in characteristic function form**, or a **cooperative game** is a pair **(N,v)**, where N is the nonempty (possibly infinite) **set of players** and v is the **characteristic function** which assigns to every coalition $S \subset N$, a nonempty subset of $\mathbb{R}^S$, denoted $v(S)$.*

[1] Recall that a coalition is a *nonempty* subset of N.

A function $y \in v(S)$ is interpreted to mean that if and when coalition S forms, its members can take joint actions that result in player $i \in S$ enjoying a utility level of $y(i)$. Thus, the characteristic function v specifies the set of combinations of utility levels, or ***payoffs,*** that are available to members of S, if and when they act on their own.

Definition 6.0.3: *An* ***n-person (finite) game in characteristic function form,*** *or an* ***n-person (finite) cooperative game,*** *is a cooperative game (N,v), where N is a finite set, $N=\{1,2,\ldots,n\}$, and for every coalition S, $v(S)$ is a* **compact** *nonempty subset of (the Euclidean space) $\mathbb{R}^S$. If, in addition, for all $S \subset N$ there exists a nonnegative scalar, $\mu(S)$, such that $v(S)$ is given by*

$$v(S)=\{x \in \mathbb{R}^S_+ \mid \Sigma_{i \in S} x^i \leq \mu(S)\},$$

then the game (N,v) is called a ***game with side payments.***

Unless explicitly specified, the unqualified terms "cooperative games" and "games in characteristic function form" will stand for games where the set of players is possibly infinite.

The central question in the theory of cooperative games (in fact, in game theory in general) is:

Q. What is the appropriate (game-theoretic) solution concept for a cooperative game, that is, what are the payoffs in the set $v(N)$ which should be recommended to the players?

Game theory offers an abundance of answers to (Q). I shall argue, however, and this is one of the main purposes of this chapter, that the description of a social environment as a cooperative game is incomplete in order for (Q) to be answered. It fails to specify in exactly what way S can use the payoffs in the set $v(S)$. In contrast, when (N,v) is represented as a situation, this specification is provided by the inducement correspondence.

6.1 The core situation

One natural situation that might be associated with the game (N,v) is the ***core situation*** (γ,Γ) defined as follows: For $S \subset N$, define the position

$$G^S \equiv (S, v(S), \{u^i(G^S)\}_{i \in S}),$$

where for all $i \in S$ and all $x \in v(S)$,

$$u^i(G^S)(x) \equiv x(i).$$

That is, the players in position G^S are members of the coalition S; the set of feasible outcomes is the set of utility levels that are feasible for that coalition if it acts on its own, that is, $X(G^S) = v(S)$; and the utility level player i derives from a feasible outcome $x \in v(S)$ is $x(i)$ – the amount (of utils) assigned to him by the function x.

Let Γ consist of all the positions of the above form, that is,

$$\Gamma \equiv \{G^S | S \subset N\}.$$

The inducement correspondence γ in the core situation is given by: For all $G^S \in \Gamma$, $T \subset N(G^S) = S$, and $x \in X(G^S) = v(S)$,

$$\gamma(T | G^S, x) = \{G^T\}.$$

As I have repeatedly emphasized, one advantage of the theory of social situations is that it (at least implicitly) specifies the exact negotiation process. Indeed, consider the inducement correspondence γ of the core situation. Suppose that the grand coalition is offered some feasible payoff $x \in v(N)$. What can coalition S do? According to γ, members of S can decide to operate on their own and abandon the players in $N \backslash S$. Coalition T, **which is a subset of S,** has then the right to continue this process. That is, if members of T are not satisfied with the payoff proposed by S, they may, in turn, decide to establish their own coalition. This process can then continue by the formation of a subset of T and so on.

Observe that the inducement correspondence in the core situation (γ, Γ) associated with a finite cooperative game is simple (Definition 5.1.5), hence, (γ, Γ) is hierarchical. As we shall presently see, for such games, the unique OSSB for the core situation (γ, Γ) yields the well-known concept of the core of the game.

Definition 6.1.1: *Let* (N, v) *be a game in characteristic function form. Coalition S* ***blocks*** *the payoff* $x \in v(N)$ *if there exists a payoff* $z \in v(S)$ *with* $z >> x^S$. *The* ***core of the game*** (N, v), *denoted* **Core(N, v)**, *is the set of all unblocked payoffs, that is,*

$$\text{Core}(N, v) \equiv \{x \in v(N) | \text{ there are no } S \subset N \text{ and } z \in v(S) \text{ such that } z >> x^S\}.$$

That is, a payoff $x \in v(N)$ belongs to the core of the game (N, v) if and only if by acting on its own, no coalition can guarantee each of its members a utility level higher than the one he receives under x.

In order to characterize the unique OSSB for the core situation we need the following definition.

Definition 6.1.2: *Let* (N, v) *be a game in characteristic function form, and let* $S \subset N$ *be a coalition. The* ***subgame*** (S, v_S) *is the cooperative game, where*

$$v_S(T) \equiv v(T) \qquad \text{for all } T \subset S.$$

Thus, the set of players in the subgame (S,v_S) is S. [It follows that in this (sub)game no coalition can include members from $N \backslash S$.] The characteristic function v_S is such that a coalition in the game (S,v_S), that is, a subset T of S, can guarantee its members exactly those payoffs that T could guarantee its members in the original game (N,v).

We are now ready to state the main result of this section, namely, that for finite cooperative games the solution assigned by the unique OSSB for the core situation to the position that corresponds to the original game is the core of that game.

Theorem 6.1.3: *Let (N,v) be a finite cooperative game, and let (γ,Γ) be its associated core situation. Then, there exists a unique OSSB, σ, for (γ,Γ). Moreover, this unique OSSB is given by*

$$\boldsymbol{\sigma(G^S) = Core(S,v_S)} \quad \textit{for every } G^S \in \Gamma.$$

In particular, $\sigma(G^N) = Core(N,v)$.

Theorem 6.1.3 fully characterizes the core of finite games: The core correspondence is the only standard of behavior that is both optimistic internally and externally stable for the core situation (γ,Γ). Put differently, for a finite cooperative game (N,v), a payoff vector $x \epsilon v(N)$ belongs to the Core(N,v) if and only if it cannot be blocked by any coalition S, **using a payoff vector in the core of the subgame (S,v_S).** But this is a stronger condition than the one given in Definition 6.1.1, where S could block x **using any payoff vector in $v(S)$.**

Thus, Theorem 6.1.3 points out a lack of symmetry in the definition of the core. Indeed, according to the original definition of the core (Definition 6.1.1), a coalition S is allowed to block an outcome $x \in v(N)$ by using any payoff y, $y \in v(S)$, even if y itself can, in turn, be blocked, that is, even if $y \in v(S) \backslash$Core(S,v_S). But if we require that x be immune against being blocked, then the same should be required of y. There seems to be no reason for the payoff used for blocking to have a different status from the payoff that is being blocked. An implication of Theorem 6.1.3 is that, for finite games, modifying Definition 6.1.1 by insisting that blocking must be done through payoffs that are themselves unblocked does not change the resulting set, that is, the modified definition coincides with Definition 6.1.1.

Proposition 6.1.4: *Let (N,v) be a finite cooperative game and let $x \in v(N)$. If $x \notin Core(N,v)$ then there exist a coalition $S \subset N$ and a payoff $z \in Core(S,v_S)$ such that $z >> x^S$.*

Remark 6.1.5: A variant of Proposition 6.1.4 was proved by Debraj Ray (1983). Specifically, Ray defines recursively the notion of "credible coalitions'' as follows: Singleton coalitions are credible. A coalition S of size k, $1 \leq k \leq n$, is ***credible*** if there exists $x \in v(S)$ that is not blocked by any credible subcoalition of S. The ***modified core*** is the set of all payoffs that are not blocked by a credible coalition. Ray shows that the core for an n-person cooperative game coincides with the modified core.

The restriction of Theorem 6.1.3 to finite games is essential. For infinite games only the following partial version of Theorem 6.1.3 is valid.

Theorem 6.1.6: *Let (N,v) be a cooperative game (possibly with an infinite number of players) and let (γ,Γ) be its associated core situation. If σ is an OSSB for (γ,Γ), then for every $G^S \in \Gamma$, $\sigma(G^S)$ coincides with the core of the game (S,v_S). In particular, $\sigma(G^N) = Core(N,v)$.*

Observe that Theorem 6.1.6 is weaker than Theorem 6.1.3; it does not state that the SB, σ, $\sigma(G^S) \equiv \text{Core}(S,v_S)$, is an OSSB. Indeed, as the following examples show, when the set N is either infinitely countable or a continuum, the core correspondence need not be an OSSB for (γ,Γ), in which case, by Theorem 6.1.6, there exists no OSSB for (γ,Γ).

Example 6.1.7: Consider the cooperative game (with side payments) with a countable number of agents $\mathbf{N=\{1,2,3,\ldots,\ldots\}}$, where each coalition $S \subset N$ containing an infinite number of players can divide two dollars among its members. That is, **for an infinite coalition S, $v(S)$** consists of all functions, x, from S to $\mathbb{R}_+$ such that $\Sigma_{i \in S}\, \mathbf{x(i) \leq 2}$. If **$S$ is finite, then $v(S) = \{0\}$**, that is, $v(S)$ consists of the function that assigns 0 to every member of S. Then, the core situation associated with this game admits no OSSB. (See verification in the proof section.)

Example 6.1.8: A similar example can be given for games with a continuum of players. Specifically, let the set of agents be the unit interval, that is, $\mathbf{N \equiv [0,1]}$, and assume that for every measurable coalition $S \subset N$, whose Lebesgue measure **$\lambda(S)$ is positive,** the characteristic function v assigns a single payoff, namely, $\mathbf{v(S) \equiv \{\chi^S\}}$, where $\chi^S(i) \equiv 2 - \lambda(S)$ for all $i \in S$. **Otherwise,** $\mathbf{v(S) \equiv \{0\}}$. That is, if $\lambda(S) > 0$ then each member of S receives a utility level equal to 2 minus the size of S. Every other coalition (that is, a nonmeasurable or a null coalition) can guarantee its members the payoff 0. Then, the core situation associated with this game admits no OSSB. (See verification in the proof section.)

In view of the above examples it might be interesting to investigate cooperative games with an infinite number of players whose associated core situations admit a unique OSSB, which, by Theorem 6.1.6, coincides with the core correspondence. It turns out that one such class of games are "market games" derived from exchange economies with a continuum of traders. (For the precise model, see, e.g., Aumann 1964.)

Theorem 6.1.9: *For market games whose set of traders is an atomless measure space, the core situation admits a unique OSSB which coincides with the core correspondence.*

Using Aumann's well-known "core equivalence theorem," Theorem 6.1.9 can be restated as follows: In atomless exchange economies, a feasible allocation is not competitive if and only if it can be blocked by a competitive allocation in a subeconomy, as per the results of Mas-Colell (1985).

Let us go back and examine, once again, the core situation. A close scrutiny yields that it addresses the two fundamental questions in the theory of coalition formation (C.1) and (C.2) mentioned at the beginning of this chapter. Specifically, the core situation describes a negotiation process where forming a coalition S implies that:

a. Members of S commit to never negotiate with players in $N \setminus S$.
b. Members of S are allowed to renegotiate among themselves and to form subcoalitions.
c. The payoff that S will adopt is left undetermined.[1] That is, individuals form a coalition prior to agreeing on the particular payoff that will prevail there.

The two fundamental issues (C.1) and (C.2) can, of course, be answered in many interesting ways other than (a)–(c), giving rise to solution concepts other than the core (see the next sections). But, as we shall presently see, the notion of the core is quite robust with respect to the negotiation process; it emerges as the unique OSSB and the unique CSSB also for situations in which (b) and (c) are drastically changed.

Consider, first, the negotiation process where once a coalition forms it will never break again, and moreover, when forming a coalition its members sign a binding contract saying, "We form and adopt the payoff x." This process, which is most closely related to Definition 6.1.1, is captured by the following situation. For $S \subset N$ and $x \in v(S)$, let $\boldsymbol{G_x^S}$ denote the position where the set of players is S, the set of outcomes $X(G_x^S)$ consists of the single outcome x, and the utility level a player $i \in S$ derives from the payoff x is the ith coordinate of x. That is,

[1] Even if the players realize that the payoff will be S-Pareto optimal or in Core(S, v_S), still, the exact payoff is undetermined.

$$G_x^S = (S,\{x\},\{u^i(G_x^S)\}_{i\in S}),$$

where $u^i(G_x^S)(x) \equiv x^i$.

Recall that $G^N = (N, v(N), \{u^i(G^N)\}_{i\in N})$. Let the set of positions be

$$\tilde{\Gamma} \equiv \{G^N\} \cup \{G_x^S \mid S \subset N \text{ and } x \in v(S)\}.$$

According to the above negotiation process, once S forms it commits to some payoff $y \in v(S)$. The associated inducement correspondence, γ^1, is, therefore, given by: For all $G \in \tilde{\Gamma}$, $x \in X(G)$, and $S \subset N(G)$,

$$\begin{aligned} \gamma^1(S|G^N,x) &= \{G_y^S | y \in v(S)\}, \\ \gamma^1(S|G,x) &= \emptyset \quad \text{if } G \neq G^N. \end{aligned}$$

The situation $(\gamma^1,\tilde{\Gamma})$ describes a negotiation process where the two fundamental issues in the theory of coalition formation (C.1) and (C.2) are answered as follows:

a. Members of S commit to never negotiate with players in $N \backslash S$.
d. Members of S are *not* allowed to negotiate among themselves or to form subcoalitions.
e. S has to specify the particular payoff $x \in v(S)$ it intends to adopt.

Observe that (d) and (e) are the negations of (b) and (c), respectively. Nevertheless, the core remains the unique stable solution.

Theorem 6.1.10: *Let (N,v) be a cooperative game (possibly with an infinite number of players). The situation $(\gamma^1,\tilde{\Gamma})$ admits a unique OSSB and a unique CSSB. Moreover, these two SBs coincide. Let σ^1 denote this SB. Then, $\sigma^1(G^N) = Core(N,v)$.*

Another negotiation process which is of interest is one where forming a coalition is partially binding, but, as in the core situation, the resulting payoff need not be fully determined. That is, when considering the formation of S, its members sign a binding contract saying: "If we form S, then we adopt the payoff x, unless we all agree on a different payoff." This process is captured by the situation $(\gamma^2,\tilde{\Gamma})$, where $\tilde{\Gamma}$ is defined above, and the inducement correspondence γ^2 is given by: For all $G \in \tilde{\Gamma}$, $x \in X(G)$, and $S \subset N(G)$,

$$\gamma^2(S|G,x) = \{G_y^S \mid y \in v(S)\}.$$

Note that this third negotiation process is "in between" the previous two; it is characterized by (a), (b), and (e). As the following theorem states, for finite cooperative games this situation also gives rise to the core.

Theorem 6.1.11: *Let (N,v) be a finite cooperative game. The situation $(\gamma^2,\tilde{\Gamma})$ admits a unique OSSB and a unique CSSB. Moreover, these two SBs coincide. Let σ^2 denote this SB. Then, $\sigma^2(G^N)=Core(N,v)$.*

The fact that the three different negotiation processes, captured by the core situation (γ,Γ) and the two situations $(\gamma^1,\tilde{\Gamma})$ and $(\gamma^2,\tilde{\Gamma})$, yield the same solution concept, namely, the core, is quite remarkable. (This is certainly not the case with other solution concepts; see, e.g., Theorems 6.2.3 and 6.2.4).

6.2 The vN&M situation

Since the characteristic function does not provide all the relevant information concerning the negotiation process, situations other than the above three situations may be adequate descriptions of the social environment that corresponds to a cooperative game (N,v). In particular, we may want to allow coalitions to make "tender threats" which other coalitions can, in turn, counter by other tender threats. Thus, in contrast to the three situations in the previous section, members of $N\backslash S$ can still be active in the negotiation process, and respond to a tender threat that S makes. Heuristically, one can view the negotiation process implicit in the three situations in Section 6.1 to be such that once members of S object to a proposed outcome, its members "leave the room" and will never negotiate again with players in $N\backslash S$.

In contrast, we may wish to consider the negotiation process where all individuals are "locked in a room" and every offer that is being made can be objected to by some coalition which offers a new payoff in $v(N)$. This payoff, in turn, can be objected to by any other coalition, and so on. The situation that describes this "tender threats" negotiation process for the cooperative game (N,v), denoted $(\hat{\gamma}, \hat{\Gamma})$, is defined as follows: For each $S\subset N$, define the position

$$\hat{G}^s = (N,\hat{v}(S),\{u^i(\hat{G}^S)\}_{i\in N}),$$

where

$$\hat{v}(S) = \{x\in v(N) | x^S \in v(S)\},$$

and for all $i\in N$ and $x\in\hat{v}(S)$,

$$u^i(\hat{G}^S)(x) = x^i.$$

That is, the set of players in position $\hat{G}^S$ is the set N, and the set of outcomes, $\hat{v}(S)$, in that position contains all those payoffs that are feasible for the grand coalition N, and whose projection on S yields a payoff that is feasible also for coalition S.[1] Observe that $\hat{v}(N)=v(N)$ and $\hat{G}^N=G^N$.

The situation $(\hat{\gamma},\hat{\Gamma})$ is given by

$$\hat{\Gamma}=\{\hat{G}^S|\ S\subset N\}$$

and, for all $\hat{G}^S\in\hat{\Gamma}$, $x\in X(\hat{G}^S)$, and $T\subset N$,

$$\hat{\gamma}(T|\hat{G}^S,x)=\{\hat{G}^T\}.$$

That is, no matter what the currently proposed payoff, x, is and which coalition proposes it, coalition T, $T\subset N$, can counter propose the payoff y, $y\in\hat{v}(T)$.

It is remarkable that, as we shall see shortly, the negotiation process that uses "tender threats," as delineated by the situation $(\hat{\gamma},\hat{\Gamma})$, gives rise to the vN&M solution, which is the original (and more sophisticated) answer to (Q), provided by the founders of game theory – von Neumann and Morgenstern. For this reason we shall call $(\hat{\gamma},\hat{\Gamma})$ the ***vN&M situation***.

Definition 6.2.1: *A **stable set,** or a **vN&M solution,** for the cooperative game* (N,v) *is a set A which is a subset of* $v(N)$ *and satisfies the following:* $y\in v(N)\backslash A$ *if and only if there exist a coalition* $S\subset N$ *and a payoff* $x\in A$ *such that* $x^S\in v(S)$ and $x^S>>y^S$.

That is, if A, $A\subset v(N)$, is a vN&M solution and $x\in A$, then there exists no coalition that can block x using a payoff that belongs to A. In addition, for any payoff that is feasible for the grand coalition N but does not belong to A, there exists a coalition that can block it by using a payoff in A.

The following straightforward claim provides an alternative definition for the vN&M solution.

Claim 6.2.2: *The set A is a vN&M solution for the cooperative game* (N,v) *if and only if A is a vN&M abstract stable set for the abstract system* $(\mathbf{D},\angle)$, *where* $\mathbf{D}\equiv\mathbf{v(N)}$ *and, for* $x,y\in v(N)$, $\mathbf{x}\angle\mathbf{y}$ *if and only if there exists a coalition* S such that $y^S\in v(S)$ and $y^S>>x^S$.

Peter DeMarzo (1986) has established the following relationship between an OSSB for the vN&M situation $(\hat{\gamma},\hat{\Gamma})$, and a vN&M solution for the game (N,v).

[1] Note (the inconsequential technical observation) that it is possible that two different coalitions, S and T, are associated with the same situation, that is, it is possible that $S\neq T$ and yet $\hat{G}^S=\hat{G}^T$. The reason is that $S\neq T$ does not imply $\hat{v}(S)\neq\hat{v}(T)$.

Theorem 6.2.3: *Let (N,v) be a cooperative game (possibly with an infinite number of players). The SB σ is an OSSB for $(\hat{\gamma},\hat{\Gamma})$ if and only if $\sigma(\hat{G}^N)\equiv\sigma(G^N)\equiv A$, where A is a vN&M solution for the game (N,v), and for all $\hat{G}^S\in\hat{\Gamma}$, $\sigma(\hat{G}^S)\equiv A\cap\hat{v}(S)$.*

Observe that the situation $(\hat{\gamma},\hat{\Gamma})$ is not hierarchical. Hence, it is possible that $(\hat{\gamma}, \hat{\Gamma})$ admits no, or alternatively, several OSSBs. And, as is well known, a cooperative game may admit several, or no, stable sets.

A close examination of the vN&M situation yields that it describes a negotiation process where forming a coalition S implies that:

f. Members of S are allowed to renegotiate with *all* other players and to form any coalition they wish.
c. The payoff that S will adopt is left undetermined. That is, individuals form a coalition prior to agreeing on the particular payoff that will prevail there.

It might be interesting to study the analogs of the situations $(\gamma^1,\tilde{\Gamma})$ and $(\gamma^2,\tilde{\Gamma})$ of the previous section [that is, the effects of modifying (c)]. To this end, define, for $x\in\hat{v}(N)$, the position G_x where the set of players is N, the set of outcomes consists of the single outcome x, and the utility level a player $i\in N$ derives from payoff x is the ith coordinate of x. That is, for $x\in\hat{v}(N)$,

$$G_x=(N,\{x\},\{u^i(G_x)\}_{i\in N}),$$

where $u^i(G_x)(x)\equiv x^i$. Define the situation $(\hat{\gamma}^1,\overline{\Gamma})$ as follows:

$$\overline{\Gamma}\equiv\{G^N\}\cup\{G_x|\ x\in v(N)\},$$

and the inducement correspondence $\hat{\gamma}^1$ is given by: For all $G\in\overline{\Gamma}$, $x\in X(G)$, and $S\subset N$,

$$\begin{aligned}\hat{\gamma}^1(S|G^N,x) &= \{G_y|y\in\hat{v}(S)\},\\ \hat{\gamma}^1(S|G,x) &= \emptyset \quad \text{if } G\neq G^N.\end{aligned}$$

That is, $(\hat{\gamma}^1,\overline{\Gamma})$ describes the negotiation process where once a coalition forms it will never break again and, moreover, when forming a coalition, S, its members sign a binding contract saying: "We form S, and commit ourselves to the payoff $x\in\hat{v}(S)$."

Recall that the OSSB of both the core situation (γ,Γ) and the situation $(\gamma^1,\tilde{\Gamma})$ assigned the same solution to G^N, namely, the core of (N,v) (see Theorems 6.1.6 and 6.1.10). In contrast, as the following theorem asserts, the solution assigned to G^N by an OSSB for the vN&M situation $(\hat{\gamma},\hat{\Gamma})$ differs from that assigned to G^N by the unique OSSB (or the unique CSSB) for the situation $(\hat{\gamma}^1,\overline{\Gamma})$.

Theorem 6.2.4: *Let (N,v) be a cooperative game (possibly with an infinite number of players). The situation $(\hat{\gamma}^1,\bar{\Gamma})$ admits a unique OSSB and a unique CSSB. Moreover, these two SBs coincide. Let $\hat{\sigma}^1$ denote this SB. Then, $\hat{\sigma}^1(G^N) = Core(N,w)$, where, for $S \subset N$, $w(S)$ is the projection of $\hat{v}(S)$ on $\mathbb{R}^S$.*

Theorems 6.2.3 and 6.2.4 suggest that the ability to "renegotiate" is essential for a vN&M solution to arise. Indeed, as Theorem 6.2.5 asserts, a vN&M solution is reached when all players may continue to negotiate with other players, even if [unlike $(\hat{\gamma}^1,\bar{\Gamma})$] each coalition, upon its formation, has to announce the payoff it intends to propose for the entire society to adopt. This latter negotiation process is captured by the situation $(\hat{\gamma}^2,\bar{\Gamma})$, which is the analog of $(\gamma^2,\bar{\Gamma})$ of the previous section. The set of positions $\bar{\Gamma}$ is defined above, and the inducement correspondence $\hat{\gamma}^2$ is given by: For all $G \in \bar{\Gamma}$, $x \in X(G)$, and $S \subset N$,

$$\hat{\gamma}^2(S|G,x) = \{G_y | y \in \hat{v}(S)\}.$$

That is, $(\hat{\gamma}^2,\bar{\Gamma})$ describes the negotiation process where each coalition announces the payoff (for all players) it will propose if and when it forms. The coalition is committed to propose this declared payoff unless all its members unanimously agree to change it.

Theorem 6.2.5: *Let (N,v) be a cooperative game (possibly with an infinite number of players). The SB σ is an OSSB for the situation $(\hat{\gamma}^2,\bar{\Gamma})$ if and only if it is a CSSB for $(\hat{\gamma}^2,\bar{\Gamma})$. Moreover, σ is an OSSB (or a CSSB) for $(\hat{\gamma}^2,\bar{\Gamma})$ if and only if $\sigma(G^N) = A$, where A is a vN&M solution for (N,v), and for all $G \in \bar{\Gamma}$, $\sigma(G) = A \cap X(G)$.*

6.3 The core and the vN&M solution

As mentioned at the beginning of this chapter, in view of Theorem 4.5, we can state Theorems 6.1.3 and 6.2.3 using the terminology of classical game theory, without explicitly referring to notions such as situation, OSSB, or CSSB.

Let (N,v) be a cooperative game with a finite number of players. In order to facilitate the notation, assume that the game (N,v) is such that every vector of utility levels that members of S can attain when they act on their own may also be attained by the grand coalition, N. Formally, assume that (N,v) is ***monotonic relative to N,*** that is, for all $S \subset N$, if $y \in v(S)$ then there exists $x \in v(N)$ such that $y = x^S$. Put differently, the game (N,v) is monotonic relative to N if for all $S \subset N$, $v(S)$ is the projection of $\hat{v}(S)$ on S [recall that

$\hat{v}(S) \equiv \{x \in v(N) | x^S \in v(S)\}$]. Define the following two abstract systems $(D, \angle^1)$ and $(D, \angle^2)$:

$$\mathbf{D \equiv \{(S,x) | S \subset N \text{ and } x \in \hat{v}(S)\},}$$

and for (S,x) and (T,y) in D,

$$\mathbf{(S,x) \angle^1 (T,y) \text{ if and only if } y^T >> x^T ,}$$
$$\mathbf{(S,x) \angle^2 (T,y) \text{ if and only if } T \subset S \text{ and } y^T >> x^T.}$$

Theorem 6.1.3 can be restated as follows:

Theorem 6.3.1: *Let (N,v) be a cooperative game with a finite number of players which is monotonic relative to N. Then, K is an abstract stable set for the system $(D, \angle^2)$ if and only if the set $A \equiv \{x | (N,x) \in K\}$ is the core of the game (N,v), and, moreover, for all $S \subset N$, $K^S \equiv \{x^S | (S,x) \in K\}$ is the core of the subgame (S, v_S).*

Theorem 6.2.3 also can be restated in s similar manner.

Theorem 6.3.2: *Let (N,v) be a cooperative game which is monotonic relative to N. Then, K is an abstract stable set for the system $(D, \angle^1)$ if and only if the set $A \equiv \{x | (N,x) \in K\}$ is a vN&M solution for (N,v), and, moreover, for all $S \subset N$, $(S,x) \in K$ if and only if $x \in \hat{v}(S)$ and $(N,x) \in K$.*

The two dominance relations $\angle^1$ and $\angle^2$ have the following interpretation: Let (N,v) be a finite cooperative game (which, for simplicity, is assumed to be monotonic relative to N). Suppose that a payoff vector $x \in v(N)$ is proposed. It seems reasonable to require that a coalition S can object to x only if members of S can counter propose a payoff $y \in v(N)$ such that each $i \in S$ is better off under y than under x, that is, that $y^S >> x^S$, and, at the same time, if S were to act on its own, it could indeed guarantee to every $i \in S$ the utility level of y^i, that is, that $y^S \in v(S)$. The chain reaction that the counter proposal, y, made by S, might engender is that y will be objected to by some other coalition, T. One can interpret the difference between the two dominance relations $\angle^1$ and $\angle^2$ as stemming from the sets of coalitions that are allowed to counter object to an objection of S. Specifically, according to $\angle^1$ **every coalition** T, $T \subset N$, can counter object, whereas $\angle^2$ restricts the counter objections to **subsets** of the objecting coalition S.

Which of these two dominance relations is more appropriate depends, of course, on the particular negotiation process that is adopted in the specific context that is being studied. As was emphasized above, the theory of cooperative games is silent on this essential issue.

6.4 The ϵ-Core

The application of the theory of social situations to cooperative games demonstrates also the distinction between OSSB and ϵ-OSSB for $\epsilon>0$. Furthermore, as Theorem 6.4.2 asserts, for a large class of cooperative games, the core situation admits a unique ϵ-OSSB. Moreover, this ϵ-OSSB yields the game-theoretic concept of the **ϵ-Core.** Recall that a payoff $x \in v(N)$ belongs to the ϵ-Core(N,v) if and only if no coalition, by acting on its own, can guarantee each of its members a utility level which is greater, by at least ϵ, than that which the member enjoys under the payoff x. That is,

$$\boldsymbol{\epsilon\text{-Core}(N,v) \equiv \{x \in v(N) \mid \text{there is no } S \subset N \text{ and } z \in v(S) \text{ such that } z >> x^S + \epsilon\},}$$

where $z>>x^S+\epsilon$ means that for all $i \in S$, $z(i)>x(i)+\epsilon$.

Definition 6.4.1: *A cooperative game* (N,v), *is* ***bounded*** *if there exists a scalar* κ, *such that for all* $S \subset N$, *if* $x \in v(S)$ *then* $|x(i)| \leq \kappa$, *for all* $i \in S$.

That is, (N,v) is bounded if no player can receive in any of the coalitions to which he belongs a utility level that exceeds the fixed scalar κ. This boundedness condition is trivially satisfied by all cooperative games with a finite number of players, since we required in Definition 6.0.3 that in such games $v(S)$ is a compact set for all $S \subset N$.

That the core situation (γ,Γ) associated with a bounded cooperative game need not admit any OSSB is demonstrated by Examples 6.1.7 and 6.1.8. (In both examples the bound κ can be chosen to be the scalar 2.) On the other hand, Theorem 6.4.2 establishes that for every $\epsilon>0$, an ϵ-OSSB for (γ,Γ) exists.

Theorem 6.4.2: *Let* (N,v) *be a bounded cooperative game (possibly with an infinite number of players), and let* (γ,Γ) *be its associated core situation. For any* $\epsilon>0$, *there exists a unique* ϵ-*OSSB*, σ^ϵ, *for* (γ,Γ). *Moreover, this* ϵ-*OSSB is given by: For all* $G^S \in \Gamma$, $\sigma^\epsilon(G^S) = \epsilon\text{-Core}(S,v_S)$. *In particular,* $\sigma^\epsilon(G^N) = \epsilon\text{-Core}(N,v)$.

6.5 The stable bargaining set situation

Evidently, there are many negotiation processes that can be employed by players in a characteristic function form game, (N,v). Thus, many situations describing these negotiation processes can be associated with (N,v). I conclude this chapter by considering a bargaining procedure where each player updates his reservation price according to the last tender offer that was made to him. More specifically, assume that a payoff x is offered. As in the previous sections, coalition S can object to x if there is an S-feasible payoff $y^S \in v(S)$ which makes each member strictly better off, that is, $y^S >> x^S$. Assume further that the payoff y^S is required to be S-Pareto optimal in $v(S)$. The new modified offer then becomes $y \equiv (y^S, x^{N \setminus S})$. Now, another coalition, T, may object to y, again, on the basis that there is a T-Pareto optimal payoff $z^T \in v(T)$ such that each member of T is strictly better off under z^T than under y, that is, $z^T >> y^T$. The resulting new modified offer is then $z \equiv (z^T, y^{N \setminus T})$, and the bargaining process continues in the same manner. Observe that in contrast to the vN&M situation where each tender offer had to be feasible, that is, belong to $v(N)$, the bargaining procedure described here is such that modified offers need no longer be feasible.

The above procedure is described by the following situation (γ, Γ). Let (N, v) be a finite game. Let $v^*(S)$ denote the set of all S-Pareto optimal payoffs in $v(S)$, that is,

$$\boldsymbol{v^*(S) = \{x \in v(S) \mid \text{there is no } y \in v(S) \text{ such that } y^i > x^i \text{ for all } i \in S\}.}$$

The compactness of $v(S)$ (see Definition 6.0.3) implies that $v^*(S)$ is nonempty, and, in addition, that there exists a compact cube Q, $Q \subset \mathbb{R}^N$, such that for all $S \subset N$, $v(S)$ is contained in the interior of the projection of Q on $\mathbb{R}^S$. For $x \in Q$, let G_x be the position given by

$$\boldsymbol{G_x \equiv (N, \{x\}, \{u^i(G_x)\}_{i \in N}),}$$

where for all $i \in N$,

$$\boldsymbol{u^i(G_x)(x) = x^i.}$$

The ***stable bargaining set situation*** is the situation (γ, Γ) where

$$\boldsymbol{\Gamma \equiv \{G^N\} \cup \{G_x \mid x \in Q\},}$$

and for all $S \subset N$, $G \in \Gamma$, and $x \in X(G)$,

$$\boldsymbol{\gamma(S \mid G, x) = \{G_y \mid y^S \in v^*(S) \text{ and } y^{N \setminus S} = x^{N \setminus S}\}.}$$

Notice that the inducement correspondence γ depends on the proposed payoff (which determines the reservation prices of players not in S). Note also that (essentially) the only difference between (γ, Γ) and the situation $(\hat{\gamma}^2, \overline{\Gamma})$ (see Section 6.2) is that here a coalition S does not have to offer a payoff that is feasible for the entire society, that is, a payoff that belongs to $\hat{v}(S)$, but, as in the core situation, only a payoff that is S-feasible. But, in contrast to the core situation, every coalition, and not only subsets of S, can respond to the new modified payoff.

Theorem 6.5.1: *Let (N,v) be a finite cooperative game. Then, its associated stable bargaining set situation admits a unique OSSB and a unique CSSB. Moreover, these two SBs coincide. Let σ denote this unique stable SB. Then $\sigma(G^N)$ is independent of the choice of the cube Q.*

Let σ denote the unique OSSB (and the unique CSSB) for the stable bargaining set situation. Then, as we shall presently see, $\sigma(G^N)$ is closely related to the concept of the bargaining set, originally introduced by Aumann and Maschler (1964). Aumann and Maschler, who considered games with side payments, allowed only single players to make objections to a proposed payoff, and, moreover, they insisted that an objection be directed toward one and only one player. Recently, Mas-Colell (1989) modified the bargaining set in two ways. First, every coalition can make objections, and second, an objection is not directed to a particular coalition, but rather, can be countered by any coalition. The following definition of the bargaining set is a variant of Mas-Colell's.

Definition 6.5.2: *Let (N,v) be a game. A pair (S,y) is an **objection** to $x \in v(N)$ if $S \subset N$, $y \in \mathbb{R}^N$, $y^S \in v^*(S)$, $y^i > x^i$ for all $i \in S$, and $y^i = x^i$ for all $i \in N \setminus S$. Let (S,y) be an objection to x. (T,z) is a **counter objection** to (S,y) if $T \subset N$, $z \in \mathbb{R}^N$, $z^T \in v^*(T)$, $z^i > y^i$ for all $i \in T$, and $z^i = y^i$ for all $i \in N \setminus T$. An objection (S,y) is **justified** if there does not exist any counter objection to (S,y). The **modified bargaining set, MBS(N,v),** consists of all payoffs in $v(N)$ for which there exists no justified objection.*

The definitions of MBS(N,v), as well as Aumann and Maschler's and Mas-Colell's bargaining set, involve difficulties similar to those present in the definition of the core (see Proposition 6.1.2 and Remark 6.1.3). That is, in contrast to objections, counter objections are not required to be immune against "counter counter objections." As the following definition shows, Theorem 6.5.1 can be used to resolve this deficiency (see also Section 11.6).

Definition 6.5.3: *Let (N,v) be a finite cooperative game and let σ be the unique OSSB (and the unique CSSB) for the associated stable bargaining set situation. The **stable bargaining set (SBS)** of (N,v) is the set*

$$\mathbf{SBS}(N,v) \equiv \sigma(G^N).$$

The following theorem relates the notions of the modified and the stable bargaining set.

Theorem 6.5.4. *Let* (N,v) *be a finite cooperative game. Then,*

$$Core(N,v) \subset SBS(N,v) \subset MBS(N,v).$$

The following well-known "three-person majority rule game" demonstrates that both of the inclusions in the statement of Theorem 6.5.4 can be strict. Moreover, this example shows that the notion of SBS yields very appealing outcomes.

Example 6.5.5: There are three players. Every coalition that has a (simple) majority, that is, every coalition consisting of two or more players, can distribute among its members 2 dollars. The utilities of the three players are linear with money. The characteristic function form game (with side payments) that describes this social environment is given by

$$N=\{1,2,3\},\ \mu(S)=2 \text{ if } |S| \geq 2, \text{ and for } i \in N,\ \mu(\{i\})=0.$$

Alternatively,

$$v(S) = \begin{cases} \{x \in \mathbb{R}^S_+ \mid \Sigma_{i \in S} x^i \leq 2\} & \text{if } |S| > 1, \\ \{0\} & \text{otherwise.} \end{cases}$$

Then, (see verification in the proof section),

$$\text{Core}(N,v) = \emptyset,$$
$$\text{SBS}(N,v) = \{(1,1,0),(1,0,1),(0,1,1)\},$$

and

$$\text{MBS}(N,v) = \{x \in v(N) | x^i < 1,\ i \in N\} \cup \text{SBS}(N,v).$$

Thus, the core of this game is empty, and the modified bargaining set includes almost all of $v(N)$ (it excludes only those payoffs $x \in v(N)$ such that one player gets 1 dollar, and the other two get positive amounts of the other dollar). In contrast, the stable bargaining set consists of the three outcomes that stem from two players forming a coalition and distributing the 2 dollars evenly between them!

Clearly, a general and systematic analysis of the notion of the stable bargaining set is called for. Such is also the case with many of the other new solution concepts that are offered in this book. (Recall that my main purpose in this book is to whet the appetite of the reader by demonstrating the scope of the theory of social situations.) Example 6.5.5 suggests that such research may well prove to be worthwhile, and the following theorem shows that it is also feasible. For a large class of finite cooperative games the stable bargaining set (hence, by Theorem 6.5.4, the modified bargaining set) is nonempty.

Theorem 6.5.6: *Let (N,v) be a finite game in characteristic function form such that there exists $\xi \in v(N)$ with the property that for all $S \subset N$, $x \in v(S)$ implies $(x,\xi^{N \setminus S}) \in v(N)$, where $y=(x,\xi^{N \setminus S})$ is given by: $y^i = x^i$ if $i \in S$ and $y^i = \xi^i$ if $i \notin S$. Then, $SBS(N,v) \neq \emptyset$.*

In view of Theorem 4.5, and since the position $G_x \in \Gamma$ is fully characterized by $x \in Q$, the stable bargaining set can be defined using the notion of vN&M abstract stable sets, without explicit reference to the terminology of the theory of social situations.

Theorem 6.5.7: *Let (N,v) be a finite game. Define the abstract system $(D,\angle)$, where $\mathbf{D} \equiv \mathbf{Q}$, and for $x,y \in Q$, $\mathbf{x} \angle \mathbf{y}$ if and only if there exists $S \subset N$* such that *$y^S \in v^*(S)$, $y^S >> x^S$, and $y^{N \setminus S} = x^{N \setminus S}$. Then, $(D,\angle)$ admits a unique vN&M abstract stable set, K. Moreover, $SBS(N,v) = v(N) \cap K$.*

Proofs for Chapter 6

Proof of Theorem 6.1.3: Since γ is a simple inducement correspondence, and N is a finite set, Proposition 5.1.6 yields that the associated core situation (γ,Γ) is hierarchical. Therefore, by Theorem 5.2.1, it suffices to show that the core correspondence, σ, defined in the theorem, is an OSSB for (γ,Γ).

By definition, $x \in \text{Core}(T,v_T)$ if and only if $x \in v(T)$ and there is no $S \subset T$ and $y \in v(S)$ with $y >> x^S$. Since $\sigma(G^S) = \text{Core}(S,v_S) \subset v(S)$, it follows that if $x \in \sigma(G^T)$ for some $G^T \in \Gamma$, then there is no $S \subset T$ and $y \in \sigma(G^S)$ with $y >> x^S$, that is, σ is optimistic internally stable.

To conclude the proof we need to show that σ is also optimistic externally stable, that is, if $x \notin \text{Core}(T,v_T)$ then there exist a coalition $S \subset T$ and $y \in \text{Core}(S,v_S)$ with $y >> x^S$. But this is the content of Proposition 6.1.4. Q.E.D.

Proof of Proposition 6.1.4: By definition, $x \notin \text{Core}(N,v)$ implies that there exist as least one coalition $T \subset N$ and a payoff $y \in v(T)$ such that $y >> x^T$. Since N is a finite set, there exists a coalition S which is a minimal (under the ordering of set inclusion) among the coalitions that block x. That is, S satisfies the following two conditions:

i. There exists $y \in v(S)$ such that $y >> x^S$.
ii. There is no $T \subset S$, $T \neq S$, and $z \in v(T)$ such that $z >> x^T$.

Choose y^* on the boundary of $v(S)$ such that $y^* \geq y$, where y is given in (i), and there is no $\tilde{y} \in v(S)$ with $\tilde{y} >> y^*$. [Since $v(S)$ is a compact set, such a y^* exists.] By definition, for all $T \subset S$, $v_S(T) = v(T)$, and, therefore, (ii) yields that $y^* \in \text{Core}(S,v_S)$. Q.E.D.

Proof of Theorem 6.1.6: By definition of an SB, for all $G \in \Gamma$, $\sigma(G) \subset X(G)$. Therefore, the definition of Core(S, v_S) yields that for any SB, σ, for (γ, Γ), if $x \in$ Core(S, v_S) then $x \notin$ ODOM(σ, G^S). Thus, if σ is an OSSB for (γ, Γ), then for all $G^S \in \Gamma$, Core$(S, v_S) \subset \sigma(G^S)$.

To see that the reverse inequality also holds, assume, in negation, that there exists $x \in \sigma(G^S) \setminus$Core$(S, v_S)$. Since $x \notin$ Core(S, v_S), there exist $T \subset S$ and $y \in X(G^T)$ such that $y >> x^T$. Since $x \in \sigma(G^S)$, the optimistic internal stability of σ implies that $y \notin \sigma(G^T)$. The optimistic external stability of σ yields, therefore, that $y \in$ ODOM(σ, G^T), that is, there exist $Q \subset T$ and $z \in \sigma(G^Q)$ such that $z >> y^Q$. Since, $Q \subset T \subset S$, $G^Q \in \gamma(Q | G^S, x)$, and $z >> y^Q >> x^Q$, it follows that $x \in \sigma(G^S)$ and $z \in \sigma(G^Q)$ contradict the optimistic internal stability of σ. Q.E.D.

Verification of Example 6.1.7:

i. **Core(S, v_S) is empty whenever the cardinality of S is infinite:** Assume, in negation, that there exists an $x \in$ Core(S, v_S) for some S that contains an infinite number of players. Then, since $x \in$ Core(S, v_S) implies that $\Sigma_{i \in S} x(i) = 2$, there exists a player $r \in S$ for whom $x(\mathrm{r}) > 0$. But then, the coalition T, $T \equiv S \setminus \{r\}$, blocks x, using, for example, the payoff z, where, for all $i \in T$, $z(i) \equiv x(i) + [x(r)/2^i]$. This contradicts our assumption that $x \in$ Core(S, v_S).

ii. **The SB σ, $\sigma(G^S) \equiv$ Core(S, v_S), is not an OSSB for the associated core situation (γ, Γ):** By (i), Core(N, v) is empty. In particular, therefore, the payoff x^*, where for all $i \in N$, $x^*(i) \equiv 1/2^i$, belongs to $v(N)$ but does not belong to Core(N, v), that is, $x^* \notin \sigma(G^N)$. Using (i) again, together with the fact that for a finite coalition S, $v(S) = \{0\}$, we have that there is no coalition S and $y \in \sigma(G^S)$ such that $y(i) > x^*(i)$ for all $i \in S$. Thus, $x^* \notin$ ODOM(σ, G^N). As $x^* \notin \sigma(G^N)$, it follows that σ is not optimistic externally stable.

iii. **The associated core situation (γ, Γ) admits no OSSB:** Otherwise, by Theorem 6.1.6, the OSSB, σ, for (γ, Γ) is given by $\sigma(G^S) \equiv$ Core(S, v_S). By (ii), this SB is not optimistic stable.

Verification of Example 6.1.8:

i. **For all coalitions S of positive measure, Core(S, v_S) is empty:** Clearly, if $x \in$ Core(S, v_S) then $x = \chi^S$. But this is blocked by every coalition T, $T \subset S$, that has a smaller, but positive, measure, that is, by every measurable T, $T \subset S$, that satisfies $0 < \lambda(T) < \lambda(S)$. Indeed, for such a coalition T, we have that $\chi^T \in v(T)$ and for all $i \in T$, $\chi^T(i) > \chi^S(i)$.

ii. **The SB σ, where $\sigma(G^S) \equiv$ Core(S, v_S), is not an OSSB for the core situation (γ, Γ):** Since $N = [0,1]$ is a measurable set of positive Lebesgue measure, by (i) Core(N,v) is empty. In particular, $\chi^N \notin \sigma(G^N)$. But, by (i) and the definition of the characteristic function v, there exist no coalition S and $y \in \sigma(G^S)$ such that for all $i \in S$, $y(i) > \chi^N(i) = 2-1=1$. Hence, $x \notin \text{ODOM}(\sigma, G^N)$, which, together with the fact that $x \notin \sigma(G^N)$, implies that σ is not optimistic externally stable.

iii. **The associated core situation (γ,Γ) admits no OSSB:** Otherwise, by Theorem 6.1.6, the OSSB σ for (γ,Γ) is given by $\sigma(G^S) \equiv \text{Core}(S, v_S)$. By (ii), this SB is not optimistic stable.

Proof of Theorem 6.1.9: Mas-Colell (1985, p. 269) proved that in such economies any noncompetitive allocation can be blocked by a coalition that uses a competitive allocation in its exchange subeconomy. By Aumann's (1964) equivalence theorem, in each subeconomy, the core and the set of competitive allocations coincide. Thus, the SB for the associated core situation (γ,Γ), which assigns to each position $G \in \Gamma$ the core of the subeconomy to which G corresponds, is optimistic externally stable. As was shown in the proof of Theorem 6.1.6, this SB is always optimistic internally stable, hence it is an OSSB. By Theorem 6.1.6, it is the unique OSSB for the core situation (γ,Γ). Q.E.D.

Proof of Theorem 6.1.10: Note first that $(\gamma^1,\tilde{\Gamma})$ is strictly hierarchical (e.g., let $\tilde{\Gamma}_1 = \{G^N\}$ and $\tilde{\Gamma}_2 = \tilde{\Gamma} \setminus \{G^N\}$). Theorem 5.4.1 implies, therefore, that $(\gamma^1,\tilde{\Gamma})$ admits a unique CSSB. By Claim 2.5.6, σ is an OSSB for $(\gamma^1,\tilde{\Gamma})$ if and only if it is also a CSSB for $(\gamma^1,\tilde{\Gamma})$. Hence the first part of the theorem is verified.

It is left to be shown that $\sigma^1(G^N) = \text{Core}(N,v)$. Using Theorem 5.4.1 again, we have that $\sigma^1 \equiv \eta$. Thus, for all $G^S_x \in \tilde{\Gamma}$:

$$\boldsymbol{\sigma}^1(G^S_x) = \boldsymbol{\eta}(G^S_x) = X(G^S_x) = \{x\},$$

and, by Definition 6.1.1,

$$\boldsymbol{\sigma}^1(G^N) = \boldsymbol{\eta}(G^N) = \textbf{Core}(N,v). \qquad \text{Q.E.D.}$$

Proof of Theorem 6.1.11: Define $\tilde{\Gamma}_1 = \{G^N\}$ and $\tilde{\Gamma}_2 = \tilde{\Gamma} \setminus \{G^N\}$. Then, by Claim 2.5.6, σ is an OSSB for $(\gamma^2,\tilde{\Gamma})$ if and only if it is also a CSSB for $(\gamma^2,\tilde{\Gamma})$. To complete the proof of the theorem, we shall now establish that the following SB, σ^2, is the unique OSSB for $(\gamma^2,\tilde{\Gamma})$, where

$$\boldsymbol{\sigma}^2(G^N) = \textbf{Core}(N,v),$$

and for all $G^S_x \in \tilde{\Gamma}$,

$$\begin{aligned} \boldsymbol{\sigma}^2(G^S_x) &= X(G^S_x) = \{x\} && \textbf{if } x \in \textbf{Core}(S,v_S), \\ &= \emptyset && \textbf{if } x \notin \textbf{Core}(S,v_S). \end{aligned}$$

i. **σ^2 is an OSSB for $(\gamma^2,\tilde{\Gamma})$:** Since $x \in \text{Core}(S,v_S)$ implies that $x \notin \text{ODOM}(\sigma,G_x^S)$ for any SB, σ, for $(\gamma^2,\tilde{\Gamma})$, it follows that σ^2 is (optimistic) internally stable. The (optimistic) external stability of σ^2 follows from Proposition 6.1.4.

ii. **σ^2 is the unique OSSB for $(\gamma^2,\tilde{\Gamma})$:** Let σ be an OSSB for $(\gamma^2,\tilde{\Gamma})$. In view of Theorem 4.9, it suffices to show that for all $G \in \tilde{\Gamma}$, $\sigma^2(G) \subset \sigma(G)$. Indeed, $x \in \text{Core}(S,v_S)$ implies that $x \notin \text{ODOM}(\sigma,G_x^S)$. Therefore, by the (optimistic) external stability of σ, $x \in \sigma(G_x^S)$. Similarly, $x \in \text{Core}(N,v)$ implies that $x \in \sigma(G^N)$. Hence, for all $G \in \tilde{\Gamma}$, $\sigma^2(G) \subset \sigma(G)$.

Q.E.D.

Proof of Claim 6.2.2: By Definition 4.4, A is a vN&M abstract stable set for the system $(D,\angle)$ defined in the claim if and only if

$A = D \setminus \Delta(A) \Leftrightarrow A = \{x \in v(N) \mid$ there is no $z \in A$ such that $x \angle z\} \Leftrightarrow A = \{x \in v(N) \mid$ there is no $z \in A$ and $S \subset N$ such that $z^S \in v(S)$ and $z^S >> x^S\}$. Q.E.D.

Proof of Theorem 6.2.3:

i. Let A be a vN&M solution for (N,v). Define the SB for the vN&M situation $(\hat{\gamma},\hat{\Gamma})$ as follows. **For all $\hat{G}^S \in \hat{\Gamma}$, $\sigma(\hat{G}^S) \equiv A \cap \hat{v}(S)$.** We need to show that this SB is an OSSB for $(\hat{\gamma},\hat{\Gamma})$, that is, that for all $\hat{G}^S \in \hat{\Gamma}$, $\sigma(\hat{G}^S) = \hat{v}(S) \setminus \text{ODOM}(\sigma,\hat{G}^S)$. Since A is a vN&M solution, we have

$x \in A \Leftrightarrow$ there is no $T \subset N$ and $y \in A \cap \hat{v}(T)$ with $y^T >> x^T$.

Therefore,

$x \in \sigma(\hat{G}^S) \Leftrightarrow x \in A \cap \hat{v}(S) \Leftrightarrow x \in \hat{v}(S)$ and there is no $T \subset N$ and $y \in A \cap \hat{v}(T)$ with $y^T >> x^T$.

By the definitions of ODOM, $\hat{\gamma}$, and σ,

$\text{ODOM}(\sigma,\hat{G}^S) = \{x \in \hat{v}(S) \mid \exists\, T \subset N$ and $y \in A \cap \hat{v}(T)$ with $y^T >> x^T\}$.

Therefore, $x \in \sigma(\hat{G}^S) \Leftrightarrow x \in \hat{v}(S) \setminus \text{ODOM}(\sigma,\hat{G}^S)$, that is, σ is an OSSB for $(\hat{\gamma},\hat{\Gamma})$.

ii. Let σ be an OSSB for the vN&M situation $(\hat{\gamma},\hat{\Gamma})$. Denote **$A \equiv \sigma(\hat{G}^N)$.** We need to show: (1) For all $\hat{G}^S \in \hat{\Gamma}$, $\sigma(\hat{G}^S) \equiv A \cap \hat{v}(S)$, and (2) A is a vN&M solution for (N,v).
By definition of ODOM and the inducement correspondence $\hat{\gamma}$,

$x \in \text{ODOM}(\sigma,\hat{G}^N) \Leftrightarrow x \in v(N)$ and $\exists\, T \subset N$ and $y \in \sigma(\hat{G}^T)$ with $y^T >> x^T$.

Therefore, for all $S \subset N$,

$x \in \text{ODOM}(\sigma, \hat{G}^S) \Leftrightarrow x \in \hat{v}(S)$ and $x \in \text{ODOM}(\sigma, \hat{G}^N)$.

Since σ is optimistic stable, we have that for all $S \subset N$,

$\sigma(\hat{G}^S) = \hat{v}(S) \backslash \text{ODOM}(\sigma, \hat{G}^S) = \hat{v}(S) \backslash \text{ODOM}(\sigma, \hat{G}^N) = \hat{v}(S) \cap \sigma(\hat{G}^N)$.

Thus, (1) is verified. To show that (2) is also true, note that the stability of σ together with (1) yield that

$x \in A = \sigma(\hat{G}^N) \Leftrightarrow x \in v(N) \backslash \text{ODOM}(\sigma, \hat{G}^N)$
$\Leftrightarrow$ $x \in v(N)$ and there is no $S \subset N$ and $y \in \sigma(\hat{G}^S) = A \cap \hat{v}(S)$ with $y^S >> x^S$. Q.E.D.

Proof of Theorem 6.2.4: Follow the proof of Theorem 6.1.10 with the obvious modifications [such as replacing v by w, $(\tilde{\gamma}^1, \tilde{\Gamma})$ by $(\hat{\gamma}^1, \overline{\Gamma})$, and σ^1 by $\hat{\sigma}^1$]. Q.E.D.

Proof of Theorem 6.2.5: Define $\overline{\Gamma}_1 \equiv \{G^N\}$ and $\overline{\Gamma}_2 \equiv \overline{\Gamma}_1 \backslash \{G^N\}$. Then, by Claim 2.5.6, σ is an OSSB for $(\hat{\gamma}^2, \overline{\Gamma})$ if and only if it is also a CSSB for $(\hat{\gamma}^2, \overline{\Gamma})$. To complete the proof of the theorem, we need to show that σ is an OSSB (or a CSSB) for $(\hat{\gamma}^2, \overline{\Gamma})$ if and only if $\sigma(G^N) = A$, where A is a vN&M solution of (N, v), and for all $G \in \overline{\Gamma}$, $\sigma(G) = A \cap X(G)$.

Let A be a vN&M solution for (N, v). Define the SB σ for $(\hat{\gamma}^2, \overline{\Gamma})$ by: For all $G \in \overline{\Gamma}$, $\boldsymbol{\sigma(G) \equiv A \cap X(G)}$**. That is,** $\boldsymbol{\sigma(G^N) = A}$ and for $G_x \in \overline{\Gamma}_2$, $\boldsymbol{\sigma(G_x) = \{x\}}$ **if** $\boldsymbol{x \in A}$**, and** $\boldsymbol{\sigma(G_x) = \emptyset}$ **if** $\boldsymbol{x \notin A}$**.** Then, the internal (respectively, external) stability of A implies the optimistic internal (respectively, external) stability of σ.

Conversely, let σ be an OSSB for $(\hat{\gamma}^2, \overline{\Gamma})$. Denote $\boldsymbol{\sigma(G^N) = A}$. By the stability of σ we have that $\sigma(G_x) = \emptyset$ if and only if there exist $S \subset N$ and $y \in \hat{v}(S)$ such that $y \in \sigma(G_y)$ and $y^S >> x^S$, that is, if and only if $x \notin A$. Thus, for all $G \in \overline{\Gamma}$, $\sigma(G) = A \cap X(G)$. Therefore, the optimistic internal (respectively, external) stability of σ implies the internal (respectively, external) stability of A. Q.E.D.

Proof of Theorem 6.3.1: Let (N, v) be a monotonic game, and let $(D^*, \angle^*)$ be the abstract system associated with the core situation. The monotonicity of (N, v) implies that for all $T \subset S \subset N$, $x \in \hat{v}(S)$, and $y \in \hat{v}(T)$ we have that $(S, x) \angle^2 (T, y)$ if and only if $(G^S, x^S) \angle^* (G^T, y^T)$. Theorems 4.5 and 6.1.3, yield, therefore, the validity of this theorem. Q.E.D.

Proof of Theorem 6.3.2: Let (N, v) be a monotonic game, and let $(D^*, \angle^*)$ be the abstract system associated with the vN&M situation. The monotonicity of (N, v) implies that for all $x \in \hat{v}(S)$ and $y \in \hat{v}(T)$ we have that $(S, x) \angle^1 (T, y)$ if and only if $(\hat{G}^S, x) \angle^* (\hat{G}^T, y)$. Theorems 4.5 and 6.2.3, yield, therefore, the validity of this theorem. Q.E.D.

Proof of Theorem 6.4.2: By Theorem 4.13 all we need to verify is that the SB σ^ϵ defined in the theorem is indeed an ϵ-OSSB for the core situation (γ,Γ). That is, we need to show that for every $G^S\in\Gamma$, $\sigma^\epsilon(G^S)=X(G^S)\backslash \text{ODOM}^\epsilon(\sigma^\epsilon,G^S)$, that is, that for every $S\subset N$,

$$\epsilon\text{-Core}(S,v_S)=\{x\in v(S)|\text{ there is no } T\subset S \text{ and } y\in\epsilon-\text{Core}(T,v_T) \text{ with } y>>x^T+\epsilon\}.$$

Since, for all $T\subset N$, ϵ-Core$(T,v_T)\subset v(T)$, we have that if there exist $T\subset S$ and $y\in\epsilon$-Core(T,v_T) with $y>>x^T+\epsilon$, then there exist $T\subset S$ and $y\in v(T)$ with $y>>x^T+\epsilon$. To conclude the proof we need to verify also the reverse implication. Let $x\in v(S)$ be such that there exist $T\subset S$ and $y\in v(T)$ with $y>>x^T+\epsilon$. If $y\in\epsilon$-Core(T,v_T) we are done. Otherwise, there exist $Q\subset T$ and $z\in v(Q)$ such that $z>>y^Q+\epsilon>>x^Q+2\epsilon$. Continuing in this manner, the fact that (N,v) is bounded and $\epsilon>0$, yield that there exist $T^*\subset S$ and $y^*\in\epsilon$-Core(T^*,v_T^*), such that $y^*>>x^{T^*}+\epsilon$. Q.E.D.

Proof of Theorem 6.5.1: By Claim 2.5.6, σ is an OSSB for (γ,Γ) if and only if it is a CSSB for (γ,Γ). Therefore, it suffices to show that (γ,Γ) admits a unique OSSB. Since N is finite, the number of coalitions is also finite. The requirement that the payoffs in positions induced by a coalition S be S-Pareto optimal implies, therefore, that the dominance relation in the associated abstract system is strictly acyclic. (In particular, there is no sequence of dominations whose length exceeds 2^n.) By Theorems 4.5 and 4.7, therefore, there exists a unique OSSB for (γ,Γ).

To see that $\sigma(G^N)$ is independent of the choice of the cube Q, let Q_1 and Q_2 be two distinct cubes, $Q_1\subset Q_2$, such that for all $S\subset N$, $v(S)$ is contained in the interior of the projection of Q_1 (hence, of Q_2) on $\mathbb{R}^S$. Let (γ^1,Γ^1) and (γ^2,Γ^2) denote the two associated stable bargaining set situations, and let σ^1 and σ^2 be the corresponding two (unique) OSSBs. Since the restriction of γ^2 to Γ^1 coincides with γ^1, we have, by Claim 2.5.7, that the restriction of σ^2 to Γ^1 is an OSSB for (σ^1,Γ^1). Since (γ^1,Γ^1) admits a unique OSSB, it follows that this restriction coincides with σ^1. But then, $\sigma^1(G^N)=\sigma^2(G^N)$.

Q.E.D.

Proof of Theorem 6.5.4: To verify that Core $(N,v)\subset$ SBS(N,v), let $x\in v(N)\backslash$SBS(N,v). Then $x\in$ODOM(σ,G), where σ is the unique OSSB for the stable bargaining set situation (γ,Γ). By definition of ODOM, it follows that there exists an objection (S,y) to x. Hence, $x\notin$Core(N,v).

Turning to the second inclusion, let $x\in v(N)\backslash$MBS(N,v). We need to show that $x\notin$SBS(N,v). By definition, $x\notin$MBS(N,v) implies that there exists a justified objection (S,y) to x. Therefore, $\sigma(G_y)=\{y\}$, since otherwise, by the external stability of σ, we would have that there exist $T \subset N$ and $z \in \sigma(G_z)$ with $z^T >> y^T$ and $z^{N \setminus T} = y^{N \setminus T}$, implying that (T,z) is a counter objection to (S,y), which contradicts the supposition that (S,y) is justified. But then, by the internal stability of σ we have that $\sigma(G_y) = \{y\}$ implies $x \notin \text{SBS}(N,v)$.

Q.E.D.

Verification of Example 6.5.5:

i. **Core$(N,v) = \emptyset$:** Indeed, let $x \in v(N)$. Then, $S = \{i,j\}$ does not block x if and only if $x^i + x^j \geq 2$. It follows that, for x not to be blocked, x must satisfy: $\Sigma_{i \in N} x^i \geq 3$. But, if $x \in v(N)$, then $\Sigma_{i \in N} x^i \leq 2$. Hence, Core$(N,v) = \emptyset$.

Define the cube Q, $Q = \{x \in \mathbb{R}^3_+ \mid x^i \leq 3,\ i \in N\}$. (Recall that by Theorem 6.5.1, SBS(N,v) is independent of the choice of Q.) Let (γ,Γ) be the stable bargaining set situation associated with the three-person simple majority game (and the cube Q), and let σ be the unique OSSB for (γ,Γ).

ii. **Let $x \in Q$. If for every $\{i,j\} \subset N$, $x^i + x^j \geq 2$, then $x \in \sigma(G_x)$:** Indeed, no coalition S can induce a position G_y where $y^S >> x^S$ and $y^S \in v(S)$.

iii. **Let $x \in Q$ satisfy: $x_i < 1$, $x_j > 1$, $x_k = 1$. Then, $x \notin \sigma(G_x)$:** Indeed, denote: $\epsilon \equiv \text{Min}\{(1 - x_i)/2,\ (x_j - 1)/2\}$ and let $y = (y_1, y_2, y_3)$ where $y_i = 1 - \epsilon > x_i$, $y_j = x_j$, and $y_k = 1 + \epsilon$. Then, $0 < \epsilon \leq 1/2$, and by (ii), $y \in \sigma(G_y)$. Since $G_y \in \gamma(\{i,k\} \mid G_x, x)$, it follows that $x \in \text{ODOM}(\sigma, G_x)$. By the internal stability of σ, we conclude that $x \notin \sigma(G_x)$.

iv. **Let $x \in Q$ satisfy: $x_i = x_j = 1$, $x_k = m$. Then, $x \in \sigma(G_x)$:** Indeed, if $m \geq 1$, then (ii) yields the validity of the assertion. If, on the other hand, $m < 1$, then the only way to block x is by a coalition S that contains player k and uses a vector of the form in (iii). But, as (iii) asserts, no such vector z is in $\sigma(G_z)$. Hence, $x \notin \text{ODOM}(\sigma, G_x)$. By the external stability of σ, we conclude that $x \in \sigma(G_x)$.

v. **If $x \in \sigma(G_x)$, then there exist two players, i and j, such that $x_i \geq 1$ and $x_j \geq 1$:** Otherwise, there exist $\{i,j\} \subset N$ such that $x_i < 1$ and $x_j < 1$. Consider the vector $y = (y_1, y_2, y_3)$ where $y_i = y_j = 1$, and $y_k = x_k$. By (iv), $y \in \sigma(G_y)$. Hence, $x \in \text{ODOM}(\sigma, G_x)$. By the internal stability of σ, we conclude that $x \notin \sigma(G_x)$, contradicting our assumption that $x \in \sigma(G_x)$.

vi. **If $x \in \text{SBS}(N,v)$, then $x_i \leq 1$ for all $i \in N$:** Otherwise, since $x \in v(N)$, there exist two players, i and j, such $x_i < 1$ and $x_j < 1$. But then, since $x \in \text{SBS}(N,v)$ implies $x \in \sigma(G_x)$, we get a contradiction to (v).

Assertions (v) and (vi), together with the fact that SBS$(N,v) \subset v(N)$, yield that **SBS$(N,v) = \{(1,1,0),(1,0,1),(0,1,1)\}$**, as we wished to show.

Let us now turn to the modified bargaining set.

vii. **MBS$(N,v)\supset A \equiv \{x \in v(N) | x_i < 1$, for all $i \in N\}$:** Indeed, every objection (S,y) to $x \in A$ satisfies that there exist i and j such that $y_i \leq 1$ and $y_j = x_j < 1$. Let $\epsilon = (2 - y_i - y_j)/2 > 0$. Then, $(\{i,j\},z)$, where $z_i = y_i + \epsilon$, $z_j = y_j + \epsilon$, and $z_k = y_k$, is a counter objection to (S,y). Hence, $A \subset$ MBS(N,v).

viii. **MBS$(N,v) \subset \{x \in v(N) | x_i \leq 1$, for all $i \in N\}$:** Otherwise, there exists a player k with $x_k > 1$. Then, since $x \in v(N)$, we have that $x_i < 1$ and $x_j < 1$. But then, $(\{i,j\},y)$, where $y_i = y_j = 1$ and $y_k = x_k > 1$, is an objection to x, which cannot be countered, contradicting $x \in$ MBS(N,v).

ix. **MBS$(N,v) = \{x \in v(N) | x_i < 1$, for all $i \in N\} \cup$ SBS(N,v):** Indeed, by Theorem 6.5.4, (vii), and (viii), we need to show that if $x \in$ MBS(N,v) is such that there exists i with $x_i = 1$, then there exists another player j with $x_j = 1$. That is, we need to show that if $x \in v(N)$ satisfies $x_i = 1$, $x_j > 0$, and $x_k > 0$, then $x \notin$ MBS(N,v). Indeed, $(\{j,k\},(1,1,1))$ is an objection to x, which cannot be countered. Hence, $x \notin$ MBS(N,v).

Assertions (i), (v), (vi), and (ix) conclude the verification of Example 6.5.5. Q.E.D.

Proof of Theorem 6.5.6: Let (N,v) be a finite game in characteristic function form that satisfies the condition in the theorem, and let σ be the unique OSSB for the associated stable bargaining set situation. If $\xi \in \sigma(G_\xi)$ then $\xi \in$ SBS(N,v), and thus SBS$(N,v) \neq \emptyset$.

Otherwise, $\xi \in$ ODOM(σ, G_ξ). That is, there exist $S \subset N$ and $x \in v(S)$ such that $y = (x, \xi^{N \setminus S}) \in \sigma(G_y)$ and $x >> \xi^S$. But $x = y^S \in v(S)$ implies $y = (y^S, \xi^{N \setminus S}) \in v(N)$. Therefore, $y \in SBS(N,v)$, and thus SBS$(N,v) \neq \emptyset$. Q.E.D.

Proof of Theorem 6.5.7: Since N is finite, the number of coalitions is also finite. The requirement that the payoffs in positions induced by a coalition S be S-Pareto optimal implies, therefore, that $\angle$ is strictly acyclic. (In particular, there is no sequence of dominations whose length exceeds 2^n.) By Theorem 4.7, therefore, there exists a unique vN&M abstract stable set, K, for $(D,\angle)$, and by Theorem 4.5 and Definition 6.5.3, SBS$(N,v) = K \cap v(N)$. Q.E.D.

CHAPTER 7

Normal form games

The theory of social situations is applied in this chapter to games in normal form. As in the case of cooperative games, I claim that here, too, the description of a social environment as a normal form game is not satisfactory. In particular, it does not provide any information concerning either the beliefs of the players or the availability of the legal institutions that specify, for example, whether self-commitments, communications with other players, or the signing of binding agreements are allowed. Accordingly, a normal form game can be associated with a number of situations.

Stable (both optimistic and conservative) standards of behavior for some of the situations we shall associate with normal form games yield several of the most important game theoretic solution concepts, such as Nash and strong Nash equilibrium. As was the case with cooperative games, this characterization of known solution concepts sheds new light on the negotiation processes, belief structures, and institutional assumptions that underlie them.

In addition, again as in the previous chapter, the proposed approach offers new solution concepts. For example, by representing a normal form game as a situation, it is possible to analyze the consequences of ''open negotiations.'' That is, in contrast to the Nash-type situations where individuals make their moves ''secretly,'' I consider the possibility that players state their decisions openly. (This is in the spirit of the negotiation process delineated by the vN&M situation; see Section 6.2.) I distinguish among four cases, depending on whether it is possible to make ''contingent threats'' or, rather, only ''irrevocable commitments'' and whether coalitions are permitted to form. The optimistic and conservative stable standards of behavior for these situations yield new solution concepts that are of great interest.

As was emphasized before, one advantage of the theory of social situations is that it easily accommodates coalition formation. By mechanically replacing a single player with a coalition, we derive the ''coalition-proof Nash situation'' from the ''Nash situation.'' It turns out that for finite normal form games, the unique stable standard of behavior for this situation yields the game-theoretic solution concept of ''coalition-proof Nash equilibrium'' (CPNE), which was recently introduced by Bernheim, Peleg, and Whinston (1987). It is encouraging that the proposed approach produces ''new'' solution concepts that were independently promoted and are of interest also within the framework of classical game theory. Evidently, the motivations behind this notion, as well as its formal definition, differ in the two formulations. Moreover, the theory of social situations can be used to extend the definition of CPNE to games with an infinite number of players. (The finiteness of the set of players is essential in Bernheim et al.'s recursive definition. See Definition 7.2.2.) This extension has already proved fruitful: Alesina and Rosenthal (1989) study a model with a continuum of voters and use an extension of CPNE to explain the phenomena of "midterm electoral cycle" and "split-ticket voting." Asheim (1988b) used our extension of CPNE to define and study the notion of "renegotiation-proofness in dynamic games."

Furthermore, in view of Theorem 4.5, some of the results of this chapter can be cast in the terminology of classical game theory, without (at least an explicit) reference to the theory of social situations, by using the notion of vN&M abstract stable set.

The normal form game is concerned with a social environment where each player has a set of actions or strategies that is available to him. The utility level of a player depends on the strategies that he, as well as all other players, has chosen.

Definition 7.0.1: *A* ***game in normal, or strategic, form*** *is a triple* $(N,\{Z^i\}_{i\in N},\{u^i\}_{i\in N})$*, where N is the set of players,* Z^i *is a nonempty and compact* ***strategy set of player i****, and* u^i *is player i's continuous* ***payoff function****,* $u^i{:}Z^N\rightarrow\mathbb{R}$*, where, for* $S\subset N$*,* Z^S *denotes the Cartesian product of* Z^i *over* $i\in S$*. If the set N is finite, that is,* $N=\{1,2,\dots,n\}$*, then the game is called a* ***finite, or an n-person game in normal form.***

For $S\subset N$ and $y,z\in Z^N$, we denote by $x=(y^S,z^{N\setminus S})$ **the** N**-tuple of strategies** x**, where for** $i\in S$**,** $x^i=y^i$**, and for** $i\in N\setminus S$**,** $x^i=z^i$**.**

7.1 The Nash situation

Given a game in normal form, the question of interest is, of course, what strategies should be recommended to, or adopted by, the players? The most well-known answer to this question is provided by the notion of Nash equilibrium, where no single player can benefit by unilaterally deviating from the proposed N-tuple of strategies.

Definition 7.1.1: *Let* $(N,\{Z^i\}_{i\in N},\{u^i\}_{i\in N})$ *be a game in normal form. An* N-tuple of strategies, $z\in Z^N$*, is a* ***Nash equilibrium*** *if for all* $i\in N$*,* $u^i(z)\geq u^i(y^i,z^{N\setminus\{i\}})$*, for all* $y^i\in Z^i$*.*

Let $F^N \equiv (N, \{Z^i\}_{i \in N}, \{u^i\}_{i \in N})$ be a game in normal form. Denote the set of all Nash equilibria for F^N by $\mathbf{NE}(F^N)$, that is,

$$\mathbf{NE}(F^N) \equiv \{z \in Z^N \mid \text{there is no } i \in N \text{ and } y^i \in Z^i \text{ such that } u^i(y^i, z^{N \setminus \{i\}}) > u^i(z)\}.$$

Three assumptions characterize the concept of Nash equilibrium:

N.1. Only **single** players are allowed to deviate.
N.2. A deviating individual, i, is free to choose **any strategy** from his strategy set Z^i.
N.3. The deviating player believes that **all other players will stay put** and pursue the same actions they intended to, regardless of the action he chooses.

In view of (N.1), it seems natural that in the associated Nash situation (γ, Γ), the inducement correspondence assigns the empty set to all coalitions with cardinality greater than 1. For a single player $i \in N$, (N.2) and (N.3) imply that γ should assign the position in which i is the only (active) player whose choice set is Z^i (all other players follow their respective proposed strategies), and player i's utility function in this position is the restriction of his original preferences to the restricted set of outcomes in this position. In order to present formally the ***Nash situation***, we first need the following notation. Let $F^N \equiv (N, \{Z^i\}_{i \in N}, \{u^i\}_{i \in N})$ be a game in normal form. The ***position that corresponds to F^N***, denoted by G^N, is given by

$$G^N \equiv (N, Z^N, \{u^i\}_{i \in N}).$$

The (formal) difference between the ***normal form game F^N*** and the ***position G^N*** is that the former specifies the n sets of strategies, Z^i, $i \in N$, whereas the latter provides the (single) set of outcomes, Z^N.

For $i \in N$, and $\zeta \in Z^N$, define the position G^i_ζ in which player i is the only player and he is free to choose any strategy from his strategy set Z^i, assuming that every other player $k \in N$ follows the strategy $\zeta^k \in Z^k$. That is,

$$N(G^i_\zeta) \equiv \{i\} \text{ , } X(G^i_\zeta) \equiv Z^i \times \{\zeta^{N \setminus \{i\}}\},$$

and $u^i(G^i_\zeta)$ is the restriction of u^i to $Z^i \times \{\zeta^{N \setminus \{i\}}\}$.

We are now ready to formally define the ***Nash situation*** (γ, Γ) that is associated with the normal form game $F^N \equiv (N, \{Z^i\}_{i \in N}, \{u^i\}_{i \in N})$. The set of positions is

$$\Gamma \equiv \{G^N\} \cup \{G^i_\zeta \mid i \in N \text{ and } \zeta \in Z^N\},$$

and the inducement correspondence γ is given by: For all $G \in \Gamma$, $\zeta \in X(G)$, and $S \subset N(G)$,

$$\gamma(\{i\}|G,\zeta)=\{G^i_\zeta\},$$
$$\gamma(S|G,\zeta)=\emptyset \qquad \text{if } |S|>1.$$

Let $F^N \equiv (N,\{Z^i\}_{i\in N},\{u^i\}_{i\in N})$ be a normal form game, $i\in N$, and $\zeta\in Z^N$. Denote by $F^i_\zeta \equiv (\{i\},Z^i,\tilde{u}^i)$ the one-person normal form game where, for $\xi^i\in Z^i$, $\tilde{u}^i(\xi^i)\equiv u^i(\xi^i,\zeta^{N\setminus\{i\}})$. Not unexpectedly, we have the following result.

Theorem 7.1.2: *Let $F^N \equiv (N,\{Z^i\}_{i\in N},\{u^i\}_{i\in N})$ be a normal form game, and let (γ,Γ) be its associated Nash situation. Then, there exists a unique OSSB, σ, for (γ,Γ). Moreover, the solution that σ assigns to the position $G^N\in\Gamma$ is the set of Nash equilibria for the original game, that is, $\sigma(G^N)=NE(F^N)$. Furthermore, for each position $G^i_\zeta\in\Gamma$, $\sigma(G^i_\zeta)=\{(\xi^i,\zeta^{N\setminus\{i\}})|\ \xi^i\in NE(F^i_\zeta)\}$.*

Theorem 7.1.2 is certainly not surprising. In fact, it could be rightly claimed that the Nash situation was constructed so as to yield this theorem. Mathematically, the proof is straightforward. It is important to realize, however, that the notion of a Nash equilibrium includes in its definition the beliefs of the players, namely, that a player's deviation will not affect the strategies chosen by the other players. In contrast, the theory of social situations disassociates the notion of an **equilibrium** [which in the framework of the theory of social situations is the (optimistic or conservative) stable standard of behavior] from the **description** of the social environment (which in the framework of the theory of social situations is provided by the associated situation). And it is the latter that must, of course, include the beliefs of the players.

A consequence of this important observation is that the theory of social situations allows for the analysis of equilibria (standards of behavior) that result from sets of beliefs and legal institutions that are different from those underlying the notion of Nash equilibrium.

7.2 The coalition-proof Nash situation

One obvious extension of the notion of Nash equilibrium is to allow coalitions of more than a single player to form. In order to maintain some of the main features of the Nash paradigm, we shall only substitute "coalition S" for "player i" in each of the three characterizing assumptions (N.1)–(N.3). In particular, when contemplating a deviation, coalition S assumes that all nonmembers will not react but will continue to hold their original strategies, no matter what strategies members of S decide to adopt.

Analogous to the position G^i_ζ, define, therefore, for $\zeta\in Z^N$ and $S\subset N$, the position G^S_ζ, where

$$N(G^S_\zeta)=S,\ X(G^S_\zeta)=Z^S\times\{\zeta^{N\setminus S}\},$$

and for all $i\in S$, $u^i(G^S_\zeta)$ is the restriction of u^i to $Z^S\times\{\zeta^{N\setminus S}\}$.

That is, in position G^S_ζ, players in S are free to choose any strategy from their strategy sets (and they believe that every player $i \in N \backslash S$ will continue to follow the strategy $\zeta^i \in Z^i$). Note that G^N coincides with G^N_ζ for all $\zeta \in Z^N$.

The straightforward (almost mechanical) extension of the Nash situation gives rise to the ***coalition-proof Nash (CPN) situation*** (γ, Γ) where coalitions may use correlated deviations. Formally, the CPN situation is (γ, Γ), where

$$\Gamma \equiv \{G^N\} \cup \{G^S_\zeta \mid S \subset N \text{ and } \zeta \in Z^N\}$$

and the inducement correspondence is given by: For all $G \in \Gamma$, $T \subset N(G)$, and $\zeta \in X(G)$,

$$\gamma(T \mid G, \zeta) = \{G^T_\zeta\}.$$

Thus, the coalition-proof Nash situation describes the following negotiation process. When an N-tuple of strategies $\zeta \in Z^N$ is proposed to the N individuals, members of coalition S may decide to deviate from the prescribed S-tuple $\zeta^S \in Z^S$, assuming that members of $N \backslash S$ will follow the proposed $N \backslash S$-tuple of strategies $\zeta^{N \backslash S} \in Z^{N \backslash S}$. Only after the deviation, members of S decide on the S-tuple of strategies they will adopt. A **subset, T, of S,** might then, in turn, decide to deviate from the resulting new N-tuple of strategies, and so on. [The fact that only subsets are allowed to deviate stems from the fact that, as in the core situation, $N(G^S_\zeta) = S$.]

Theorem 7.2.1: *Let $F^N = (N, \{Z^i\}_{i \in N}, \{u^i\}_{i \in N})$ be a finite game in normal form. Then, the associated CPN situation admits at most one OSSB.*

Let $F^N = (N, \{Z^i\}_{i \in N}, \{u^i\}_{i \in N})$ be a finite game in normal form whose associated CPN situation admits a unique OSSB, σ. It turns out that $\sigma(G^N)$ coincides with the concept of "coalition-proof Nash equilibrium" (CPNE) that was recently introduced by Bernheim, Peleg, and Whinston (1987). [This fact accounts for calling (γ, Γ) the CPN situation.] But, in contrast to the mechanical way in which we derived the notion of the CPN situation from the Nash situation, the motivation of Bernheim et al. is to

> . . . introduce a new refinement of the Nash set, the concept of Coalition-Proof Nash Equilibrium, that is designed to capture the notion of an efficient self-enforcing agreement for environments with unlimited, but non-binding, pre-play communication. An agreement is coalition-proof if, and only if, it is Pareto efficient within the class of self-enforcing agreements. In turn, an agreement is self-enforcing if and only if no proper subset (coalition) of players, taking the actions of its complement as fixed, can agree to deviate in a way that makes all of its members better off (p. 4).

The following additional notation is useful for the formal definition of the concept of a CPNE. Let $F^N = (N, \{Z^i\}_{i \in N}, \{u^i\}_{i \in N})$ be a game in normal form. For $S \subset N$ and $\zeta \in Z^N$, define the normal form game

$$\mathbf{F}^S_\zeta \equiv (S, \{Z^i\}_{i\in S}, \{\tilde{u}^i\}_{i\in S}),$$

where, for $\xi^S \in Z^S$ and $i \in S$, $\tilde{u}^i(\xi^S) \equiv u^i(\xi^S, \zeta^{N\setminus S})$.

That is, the set of players in the normal form game F^S_ζ is S, each member of S can choose any strategy from his original strategy set Z^i. The utility function in F^S_ζ of player i in S is derived from the restriction of his original utility function u^i to the subset of strategies $Z^S \times \{\zeta^{N\setminus S}\}$.

The definition of CPNE, due to Bernheim et al. (1987, p. 6), is recursive, and therefore applies only to finite normal form games.

Definition 7.2.2: *Let $F^N = (N, \{Z^i\}_{i\in N}, \{u^i\}_{i\in N})$ be a finite game in normal form.*

> i. *If $n=1$, that is, $N=\{i\}$, then $\xi^i \in Z^i$ is a **CPNE for F^N** if and only if ξ^i maximizes $u^i(\zeta^i)$, over $\zeta^i \in Z^i$.*

Let $n>1$, and assume that a CPNE has been defined for all games with fewer than n players. Then,

> ii. *$\xi \in Z^N$ is **self-enforcing for F^N** if for all $S \subset N$, $S \neq N$, ξ^S is a CPNE for the game F^S_ξ.*
> iii. *$\xi \in Z^N$ is a **CPNE for F^N** if ξ is self-enforcing for F^N and if there does not exist another self-enforcing strategy $\zeta \in Z^N$ for F^N such that $u^i(\zeta) > u^i(\xi)$ for all $i \in N$.*

Quite remarkably, we have the following result.

Theorem 7.2.3: *Let $F^N = (N, \{Z^i\}_{i\in N}, \{u^i\}_{i\in N})$ be a finite game in normal form, and let (γ, Γ) be its associated CPN situation. If σ is an OSSB for (γ, Γ) then for every position $G^S_\zeta \in \Gamma$, the projection of $\sigma(G^S_\zeta)$ on S coincides with the set of CPNE for the game F^S_ζ. In particular, $\sigma(G^N) = CPNE(F^N)$.*

Theorem 7.2.3 reveals the following two appealing properties of the CPNE (which are stated without reference to the theory of social situations). Claim 7.2.4 states that a CPNE cannot be defeated by a CPNE for a "subgame," and Claim 7.2.5 asserts that if the set of self-enforcing strategies for every "subgame" is a compact set then every strategy profile that is not a CPNE can be defeated by a CPNE in some "subgame." For $x, z \in Z^N$ and $S \subset N$, denote $x >_S z$ **if and only if for all $i \in S$, $u^i(x) > u^i(z)$.**

Claim 7.2.4: *Let $F^N = (N, \{Z^i\}_{i\in N}, \{u^i\}_{i\in N})$ be a finite game in normal form. Then, $\zeta \in CPNE(F^N)$ implies that there is no $S \subset N$ and $\xi^S \in CPNE(F^S_\zeta)$ such that $(\xi^S, \zeta^{N\setminus S}) >_S \zeta$.*

Claim 7.2.5: *Let $F^N = (N, \{Z^i\}_{i\in N}, \{u^i\}_{i\in N})$ be a finite game in normal form such that for every F^S_ζ, $S \subset N$, and $\zeta \in Z^N$, the set of self-enforcing strategies for*

F^S_ζ is compact. Then, $\zeta \in Z^N \backslash CPNE(F^N)$ implies that there exist $S \subset N$ and $\xi^S \in CPNE(F^S_\zeta)$ such that $(\xi^S, \zeta^{N \backslash S}) >_S \zeta$.

Claims 7.2.4 and 7.2.5 yield that if the sets of self-enforcing strategies for F^S_ζ, $S \subset N$, $\zeta \in Z^N$, are compact, then the associated CPN situation admits a (unique) OSSB which coincides with the CPNE correspondence. It follows that when the strategy sets Z^i, $i \in N$, are finite, an OSSB exists. However, the sets of self-enforcing strategies need not, in general, be compact. (For examples see Kahn and Mookherjee, 1989.)

Theorem 7.2.3 suggests the following definition of CPNE, which is independent of the number of players. Let $F^N = (N, \{Z^i\}_{i \in N}, \{u^i\}_{i \in N})$ be an arbitrary game in normal form, and let (γ, Γ) be its associated CPN situation. Assume that (γ, Γ) admits a unique OSSB, σ. Then, **the CPNE for F^N is the set $\sigma(G^N)$.** The extension of CPNE to games with an infinite number of players is particularly important since in such games it is often assumed that players are "negligible," that is, do not have an impact on the resulting payoffs, and, therefore, every strategy profile is a Nash equilibrium (but need not be a CPNE).

General conditions on the normal form game, which guarantee the existence and uniqueness of an OSSB for the associated CPN situation, are not, as yet, known. One special class of games for which the above definition of a CPNE is meaningful is when there is a finite number of possible utility levels a player can attain.

Theorem 7.2.6: Let *F^N be a normal form game (possibly with an infinite number of players). Assume that there exists an integer J* such that, for each *$i \in N$, the set $\{u^i(z) \mid z \in Z^N\}$ contains no more than J elements. Then, the associated CPN situation admits a unique OSSB.*

An example when the conditions of Theorem 7.2.6 hold is the following. Let society consist of an infinite number of voters, given by the set N, who have to choose an alternative from the **finite** set Ω. Each voter $i \in N$ has a strategy set Z^i. A ***social choice rule*** is a function F that assigns to every strategy profile $z \in Z^N$ an alternative from Ω. That is, $F: Z^N \rightarrow \Omega$. (See Chapter 10.) The utility functions, $v^i: \Omega \rightarrow \mathbb{R}$, $i \in N$, together with the function F, induce the payoff functions $u^i: Z^N \rightarrow \mathbb{R}$, $i \in$N, defined by: For $z \in Z^N$, $u^i(z) \equiv v^i(F(z))$. Then, for all $i \in N$, the number of elements in the set $\{u^i(z) \mid z \in Z^N\}$ does not exceed that of Ω, which was assumed to be finite. Thus, by Theorem 7.2.6, the CPNE for the normal form game $(N, \{Z^i\}_{i \in N}, \{u^i\}_{i \in N})$ is well defined.

Another extension of CPNE is obtained from the notion of ϵ-OSSB. Let (γ, Γ) be the CPN situation associated with the normal form game $F^N = (N, \{Z^i\}_{i \in N}, \{u^i\}_{i \in N})$. Let $\epsilon > 0$, and assume that (γ, Γ) admits a unique ϵ-OSSB, σ^ϵ. Define the **ϵ-CPNE** for F^N to be **the set $\sigma^\epsilon(G^N)$** for (γ,Γ). The following theorem asserts that ϵ-CPNE is well defined for a large class of games (which includes all finite games).

Theorem 7.2.7: *Let $F^N=(N,\{Z^i\}_{i\in N},\{u^i\}_{i\in N})$ be a normal form game (possibly with an infinite number of players), and let $\epsilon>0$. Assume that the payoff functions, u^i, $i\in N$, are uniformly bounded. Then, there exists a unique ϵ-OSSB for the CPN situation.*

In many ways, the CPN situation is the analog, in normal form games, of the core situation defined for games in characteristic function form. In particular, both situations describe a negotiation process where forming a coalition S implies that:

a. Members of S commit to never negotiate with players in $N\backslash S$.
b. Members of S are allowed to renegotiate among themselves and to form subcoalitions.
c. The actions (strategies) that S will adopt are left undetermined. That is, individuals form a coalition prior to agreeing on the course of action S will take.

As argued at the beginning of Chapter 6, the two fundamental issues (C.1) and (C.2) in the theory of coalition formation can, of course, be answered in many interesting ways other than (a)–(c), giving rise to solution concepts that differ from the CPNE (see the next sections). But, as we shall presently see, the notion of CPNE still emerges from the unique OSSB and the unique CSSB also for situations in which (c) no longer holds.

More specifically, consider the negotiation process where when considering the formation of S, its members sign a binding contract saying: "If we form S, then we will adopt the S-tuple of strategies $\xi^S\in Z^S$, unless we all agree on a different S-tuple."

In order to describe this negotiation process as a situation, more information is needed. The reason is the presence of externalities in normal form games; actions chosen by players not in S do affect the utility levels members of S can attain. Hence, the positions that S can induce depend on the beliefs players in S have concerning the reaction of nonmembers. [This is to be contrasted with cooperative games; see the situation $(\gamma^2,\tilde{\Gamma})$ in Section 6.1.]

One possible set of beliefs was offered by Nash, where members of S assume that every player outside S will continue to follow the strategy that was proposed to him. These beliefs are captured by the following situation. For $S\subset N$ and $\zeta\in Z^N$, let $\tilde{\mathbf{H}}^S_\zeta$ denote the position where the set of players is S, the set of outcomes consists of the **single outcome ζ,** and the utility level a player $i\in S$ derives from the payoff ζ is $u^i(\zeta)$. (Notice the distinction between $\tilde{H}^S_\zeta$ and the position G^S_ζ). That is,

$$\tilde{H}_\zeta^S = (S,\{\zeta\},\{u^i\}_{i\in S}).$$

The foregoing negotiation process together with the Nash-type beliefs is represented by the situation $(\tilde{\gamma},\tilde{\Gamma})$, where

$$\tilde{\Gamma} \equiv \{G^N\} \cup \{\tilde{H}_\zeta^S \mid S \subset N \text{ and } \zeta \in Z^N\}$$

and the inducement correspondence $\tilde{\gamma}$ is given by: For all $G\in\tilde{\Gamma}$, $\zeta\in Z^N$, and $S \subset N(G)$,

$$\tilde{\gamma}(S|G,\zeta) = \{\tilde{H}_\xi^S \mid \xi = (\xi^S,\zeta^{N\setminus S}) \text{ for some } \xi^S \in Z^S\}.$$

Theorem 7.2.8: *Let $F^N = (N,\{Z^i\}_{i\in N},\{u^i\}_{i\in N})$ be a finite game in normal form. The situation $(\tilde{\gamma},\tilde{\Gamma})$ admits at most one OSSB and one CSSB. Moreover, these two SBs (if exist) coincide. Let $\tilde{\sigma}$ denote this SB. Then, $\tilde{\sigma}(G^N) = CPNE(F^N)$.*

Theorems 6.1.3, 6.1.11, 7.2.3, and 7.2.8 suggest that the CPNE in normal form games is the analog of the core in cooperative games. However, this analogy is not complete. The CPNE is less robust under changes in the negotiation process. Thus, the counterpart of Theorem 6.1.10 does not lead to the CPNE but rather to another well-known game-theoretic concept: the strong Nash equilibrium. (See Theorem 7.3.3.)

As in the previous chapter, I conclude this section by showing that by applying Theorem 4.5, it is possible to relate the concepts of vN&M abstract stable set and CPNE without referring to the theory of social situations (see Greenberg 1989a). This observation provides another definition for CPNE, a definition that does not use the finiteness of the set of players. (Recall that Bernheim et al. use a recursive definition.) Furthermore, this new definition suggests a somewhat different, though related, intuitive interpretation of the notion of CPNE.

Let $F^N = (N,\{Z^i\}_{i\in N},\{u^i\}_{i\in N})$ be a game in normal form. Associate with this game the following abstract system $(D,\angle)$:

$$D \equiv \{(S,\zeta) \mid S \subset N \text{ and } \zeta \in Z^N\},$$

and, for (S,ζ) and (T,ξ) in D,

$$(S,\zeta) \angle (T,\xi) \text{ if and only if } T \subset S,\ \zeta^{N\setminus T} = \xi^{N\setminus T}, \text{ and for all } i\in T,\ u^i(\xi) > u^i(\zeta).$$

One can interpret the dominance relation $\angle$ as saying that when an N-tuple of strategies $\zeta\in Z^N$ is proposed, coalition S can **threaten to deviate from ζ** only if members of S can correlate their actions and jointly choose the S-tuple of strategies ξ^S so that the resulting N-tuple of strategies $(\xi^S,\zeta^{N\setminus S})$ makes every member of S better off, that is, $u^i(\xi^S,\zeta^{N\setminus S}) > u^i(\zeta)$ for all $i\in S$. This threat of S is **"credible"** if none of the **subsets** of S can, in turn, credibly threaten to deviate from $(\xi^S,\zeta^{N\setminus S})$. Similar to Bernheim et al.'s motivation, Theorem 7.2.9 might be interpreted as saying that $\zeta\in Z^N$ is a CPNE if and only if every threat to deviate from ζ can be countered by a credible threat to deviate from the resulting new N-tuple of strategies. Moreover, this credible counter threat is made by one of the subsets of the threatening coalition. However, whereas Bernheim et al. define "credibility" (or self-enforcement) recursively, credibility in our framework means "belonging to the abstract stable set for $(D,\angle)$." For finite games, these two credibility notions coincide.

Theorem 7.2.9: *Let $F^N=(N,\{Z^i\}_{i\in N},\{u^i\}_{i\in N})$ be a finite game in normal form, and let $(D,\angle)$ be its associated abstract system. Then, there exists at most one abstract stable set, K, for $(D,\angle)$. Moreover, K satisfies: For all $S\subset N$ and all $\zeta\in Z^N$,*

$$(S,\zeta)\in K \Leftrightarrow \zeta\in Z^N \text{ and } \zeta^S\in CPNE(F^S_\zeta).$$

In particular,

$$A\equiv\{\zeta \mid (N,\zeta)\in K\}=CPNE(F^N).$$

7.3 The strong Nash situation

The first game-theoretic solution concept for games in normal form that involved coalitional considerations was the notion of strong Nash equilibrium (SNE) due to Aumann (1959).

Definition 7.3.1: *Let $F^N=(N,\{Z^i\}_{i\in N},\{u^i\}_{i\in N})$ be a game in normal form. An N-tuple of strategies, $\zeta\in Z^N$, is a **strong Nash equilibrium (SNE)** for F^N if there do not exist $S\subset N$ and $\xi^S\in Z^S$ such that $u^i(\xi^S,\zeta^{N\setminus S})>u^i(\zeta)$ for all $i\in S$.*

Recall that the CPNE required that objections must be **"credible."** That is, an objecting coalition has to take into account the possibility of future objections (by its subsets). In contrast, under the SNE, a coalition S will object to a proposed strategy profile if its members can correlate their strategies in a way that benefits them, without considering the possibility of any further objections.

Definition 7.3.1 suggests that the **strong Nash situation (γ,Γ)** be defined as follows. The set of positions is identical to that in the CPN situation, namely,

$$\Gamma\equiv\{G^N\}\cup\{G^S_\zeta \mid S\subset N \text{ and } \zeta\in Z^N\},$$

and the inducement correspondence is given by: For all $S\subset N$ and $\zeta\in Z^N$,

$$\gamma(S|G^N,\zeta)\equiv\{G^S_\zeta\},$$
$$\gamma(S|G,\zeta)\equiv\emptyset \quad \text{if } G\neq G^N.$$

This inducement correspondence demonstrates clearly the asymmetry, in the definition of SNE, between the grand coalition N and any of its subsets: Every coalition can induce a position from G^N, but no position can be induced by any coalition from any other position in Γ. Not surprisingly, we have the following observation.

Theorem 7.3.2: *Let $F^N = (N,\{Z^i\}_{i\in N},\{u^i\}_{i\in N})$ be a game in normal form, and let (γ,Γ) be its associated strong Nash situation. Then, there exists a unique OSSB, σ, for (γ,Γ). Moreover, σ is given by: $\sigma(G^N)$ is the set of SNE for F^N, and, for all $S\neq N$ and $\zeta\in Z^N$, $\sigma(G^S_\zeta)=X(G^S_\zeta)=Z^S\times\{\zeta^{N\setminus S}\}$.*

As was mentioned in the previous section, the notion of SNE stems also from the analog of the negotiation process described by the situation $(\gamma^1,\bar{\Gamma})$ of Section 6.1, where once coalition S forms it will never break again, and, in addition, its members commit to a particular correlated S-tuple of strategies. Moreover, in the Nash spirit, S assumes that nonmembers will continue to adopt their respective proposed strategies. This process is captured by the situation $(\tilde{\gamma}^1,\tilde{\Gamma})$, defined as follows. Recall, from the previous section, that for $S\subset N$ and $\zeta\in Z^N$, we denote the position $\tilde{H}^S_\zeta \equiv (S,\{\zeta\},\{u^i\}_{i\in S})$ and the set of positions $\tilde{\Gamma}\equiv\{G^N\}\cup\{\tilde{H}^S_\zeta \mid S\subset N \text{ and } \zeta\in Z^N\}$. The inducement correspondence $\tilde{\gamma}^1$ is given by: For all $G\in\tilde{\Gamma}$, $\zeta\in Z^N$, and $S\subset N(G)$,

$$\tilde{\gamma}^1(S|G^N,\zeta)=\{\tilde{H}^S_\xi \mid \xi=(\xi^S,\zeta^{N\setminus S}) \text{ for some } \xi^S\in Z^S\},$$
$$\tilde{\gamma}^1(S|G,\zeta)=\emptyset \qquad \text{if } G\neq G^N.$$

Recall that Theorems 6.1.10 and 6.1.11 establish that in cooperative games both the situation $(\gamma^1,\bar{\Gamma})$ and the situation $(\gamma^2,\bar{\Gamma})$ lead to the same solution concept, namely, the core. In contrast, the stable (both optimistic and conservative) standard of behavior for the situation $(\tilde{\gamma}^1,\tilde{\Gamma})$ does not yield the CPNE, but rather the SNE.

Theorem 7.3.3: *Let $F^N = (N,\{Z^i\}_{i\in N},\{u^i\}_{i\in N})$ be a game in normal form. The situation $(\tilde{\gamma}^1,\tilde{\Gamma})$ admits a unique OSSB and a unique CSSB. Moreover, these two SBs coincide. Let $\tilde{\sigma}^1$ denote this SB. Then, $\tilde{\sigma}^1(G^N)=SNE(F^N)$.*

7.4 Individual contingent threats

Evidently, there are many interesting negotiation processes that are fundamentally different from the Nash situation, or its coalitional variants. In particular, we may want to allow players to **"negotiate openly"** in a way similar to the bargaining scheme delineated by the vN&M situation (see Section 6.2). In the next four sections I shall offer four such situations that might be associated with a normal form game. The stable standards of behavior for these situations give rise to new solution concepts, both for noncooperative environments as well as for environments where coalitions may form. These concepts and their properties are of intrinsic value. They also demonstrate the scope and potential usefulness of the theory of social situations.

Consider the following negotiation process. An n-tuple of strategies, $\zeta \in Z^N$, is proposed to the players. If all individuals **openly** consent to follow ζ, then ζ will be adopted. As in (N.1) (see Section 7.1) objections to ζ can be made only by single players (hence the term "individual"). If individual i objects to the specified choice of ζ^i, he has to **declare that if all other players will stick to the specified N-tuple of strategies ζ** (hence the term "contingent threats"), then he will employ the strategy $\rho^i \in Z^i$ instead of ζ^i. The new revised proposal then becomes $\xi = (\zeta^{N\setminus\{i\}}, \rho^i)$, from which another player, h, can, in turn, threaten to deviate, by stating openly, **"if all other players will stick to the specified N-tuple of strategies ξ, then I shall choose ρ^h instead of ξ^h,"** and the process continues in this manner. Thus, in contrast to the Nash process, under this open negotiation process, a player realizes that **other players are not committed** to the currently proposed strategy, and, therefore, his contingent threats can be countered by other players' contingent threats. In particular, therefore, a player may revise his threat. Indeed, after i threatens to deviate from ζ and proposes the n-tuple of strategies ξ instead, player j may, in turn, threaten to deviate from ξ. Player i can then counter the new proposal made by j.

The foregoing process is described by the following ***individual contingent threats situation*** (γ,Γ), which is the noncooperative version of the situation $(\hat{\gamma}^2,\overline{\Gamma})$ of Section 6.2. For $\zeta \in Z^N$, let G_ζ denote the position where the set of players is N, the set of outcomes consists of the single N-tuple of strategies ζ, and the utility level player $i \in N$ derives from ζ is $u^i(\zeta)$. That is,

$$G_\zeta \equiv (N, \{\zeta\}, \{u^i\}_{i \in N}).$$

The set of positions in the individual contingent threats situation (γ,Γ) is

$$\Gamma \equiv \{G^N\} \cup \{G_\zeta \mid \zeta \in Z^N\},$$

and the inducement correspondence γ is given by: For all $G \in \Gamma$, $\zeta \in Z^N$, and $S \subset N(G)$,

$$\gamma(\{i\} \mid G,\zeta) = \{G_\xi \mid \xi = (\xi^i, \zeta^{N\setminus\{i\}}),\ \xi^i \in Z^i\},$$
$$\gamma(S \mid G,\zeta) = \emptyset \qquad \text{if } |S| > 1.$$

The important feature of the individual contingent threats situation (γ,Γ) is that the set of players in every position $G \in \Gamma$ consists of the entire society, N. Thus, (γ,Γ) is not a hierarchical situation; both (H.1) and (H.2) are violated. Hence, it may admit either no or several OSSBs (respectively, CSSBs). But, as the following theorem asserts, every OSSB is a CSSB for (γ,Γ), and vice versa. Moreover, if σ is an OSSB (or a CSSB) for (γ,Γ), then the solution that σ assigns to the position G^N (which corresponds to the original normal form game F^N) contains the set of Nash equilibria for F^N.

Theorem 7.4.1: *Let F^N be a game in normal form and let (γ,Γ) be its associated individual contingent threats situation. Then, the SB σ is an OSSB for (γ,Γ) if and only if it is a CSSB for (γ,Γ), and, moreover, $\sigma(G^N)\supset NE(F^N)$.*

Observe that Theorem 7.4.1 does not assert that the existence of a Nash equilibrium implies the existence of an OSSB (or a CSSB) for (γ,Γ). Indeed, as Example 7.4.8 demonstrates, such inference is erroneous.

In view of Claim 2.5.6 and Theorem 4.5, an OSSB (hence, a CSSB) for the individual contingent threats situation can be derived from a vN&M abstract stable set for the abstract system $(\boldsymbol{D^*},\angle)$, where $\boldsymbol{D^*}\equiv\boldsymbol{Z^N}$, and for $\zeta,\xi\in Z^N$,

$$\zeta\angle\xi \Leftrightarrow \exists\ i\in N \text{ such that } \zeta^{N\setminus\{i\}}=\xi^{N\setminus\{i\}} \text{ and } u^i(\xi)>u^i(\zeta).$$

That is, an n-tuple of strategies $\xi\in Z^N$ dominates the n-tuple of strategies $\zeta\in Z^N$ if ξ is obtained from ζ by a deviation of a single player and this player is better off under ξ than he is under ζ.

Observation 7.4.2: *Let F^N be a game in normal form and let (γ,Γ) be its associated individual contingent threats situation. The SB σ is an OSSB (or a CSSB) for (γ,Γ) if and only if $\sigma(G^N)=K$, where K is an abstract stable set for the system $(D^*,\angle)$. Moreover, the set of Nash equilibria is the abstract core of $(D^*,\angle)$, that is, $NE(F^N)=D^*\setminus\Delta(D^*)$.*

Since a vN&M abstract stable set for an abstract system always includes its abstract core, Observation 7.4.2 implies the second part of Theorem 7.4.1. This result is particularly useful for normal form games which have no Nash equilibrium (in pure strategies) but whose associated individual contingent threats situation admits an OSSB (or a CSSB), σ, since then, as the following claim asserts, the solution assigned by σ to the position G^N (which corresponds to the original game F^N) is nonempty.

Claim 7.4.3: Let *F^N be a game in normal form and let σ be an OSSB (or a CSSB) for its associated individual contingent threats situation* (γ,Γ). *Then, $\sigma(G^N)\neq\emptyset$. Moreover, for all $G\in\Gamma$, $\sigma(G)=\sigma(G^N)\cap X(G)$.*

But even when both $\sigma(G^N)$ and $\mathrm{NE}(F^N)$ are nonempty, the additional outcomes in $\sigma(G^N)\setminus\mathrm{NE}(F^N)$ might be appealing. The following well-known prisoner's dilemma game illustrates this possibility.

Example 7.4.4: There are two players, 1 and 2, and each has two possible strategies to choose from: Player 1 can choose Up or Down, and player 2 can choose Left or Right. Thus,

$$\boldsymbol{N=\{1,2\},\ Z^1\equiv\{U,D\},\ \text{and}\ Z^2\equiv\{L,R\}.}$$

The utility levels of the players are given by the 2×2 matrix below, where, for example, if player 1 chooses U and player 2 chooses L then the payoff to player 1 is 15 and the payoff to player 2 is 0.

	L	R
U	(15,0)	(5,5)
D	(10,10)	(0,15)

As is easily verified, the unique Nash (in fact, dominant strategy) equilibrium, as well as the unique CPNE for this game is the 2-tuple of strategies **(UR).** Moreover, there exists no strong Nash equilibrium for this game. In contrast, the individual contingent threats situation (γ,Γ) admits a unique OSSB (hence, a unique CSSB), σ, which satisfies $\boldsymbol{\sigma(G^N)=\{UR,DL\}}$. That is, $\sigma(G^N)$ consists of the unique Nash equilibrium as well the unique Pareto outcome. Indeed, let σ be an OSSB for (γ,Γ). Then, by Theorem 7.4.1, $(UR)\in\sigma(G^N)$. Since $\sigma(G)=X(G)\cap\sigma(G^N)$, we have that $(UR)\in\sigma(G_{UR})$, implying that $\sigma(G_{UL})=\sigma(G_{DR})=\emptyset$. Therefore, $(DL)\notin$ODOM(σ,G_{DL}), and hence $(DL)\notin$ ODOM(σ,G^N). Thus, $(DL)\in\sigma(G^N)$.

We shall now establish that the individual contingent threats situation (γ,Γ) associated with any **two-person** normal form game where the set of (pure) strategies is finite (that is, every "matrix game") admits an OSSB (or a CSSB). (Recall that, in contrast, the set of Nash equilibria for such games might be empty.)

Theorem 7.4.5: *Let (γ,Γ) be the individual contingent threats situation associated with the normal form two-person game $(N,\{Z^i\}_{i\in N},\{u^i\}_{i\in N})$ where each player has a finite strategy set. (That is, $N=\{1,2\}$ and for $i\in N$, $|Z^i|<\infty$.) Then. there exists an OSSB (hence, a CSSB) for (γ,Γ).*

In order to establish the existence of an OSSB (or a CSSB) for the individual contingent threats situation associated with a normal form game with an arbitrary number of players, we need to impose the restrictive assumption that no player has more than two strategies to choose from. For such games Claim 7.4.3 and Theorem 7.4.6 imply that the stable standard of behavior assigns a nonempty solution to the position G^N.

Theorem 7.4.6: *Let* $(N,\{Z^i\}_{i\in N},\{u^i\}_{i\in N})$ *be a normal form game where, for each* $i\in N$, $|Z^i|\leq 2$. *Then there exists an OSSB (hence, a CSSB) for the associated individual contingent threats situation.*

The following example, due to Sergiu Hart (private communication), demonstrates that, unfortunately, neither of the previous two theorems can be generalized.

Example 7.4.7: Consider the following three-person game, where player 1 chooses a row, player 2 chooses a column, and player 3 chooses between the following payoff matrices *A* and *B*.

The payoff matrix ***A*** is given by:

	L	*R*
U	1,0,2	0,0,0
C	2,1,0	1,2,0
D	0,0,0	3,1,0

The payoff matrix ***B*** is given by:

	L	*R*
U	0,2,1	4,1,0
C	0,0,0	0,0,0
D	0,0,0	0,0,2

That is, $\boldsymbol{Z^1\equiv\{U,C,D\}}$, $\boldsymbol{Z^2\equiv\{L,R\}}$, and $\boldsymbol{Z^3\equiv\{A,B\}}$ (*U,C,D,L,* and *R* stand for, respectively, Up, Center, Down, Left, and Right). Thus, for example, if player 1 chooses row *D*, player 2 chooses column *R*, and player 3 chooses matrix *A*, then the resulting payoff is (3,1,0).

Let (γ,Γ) be the individual contingent threats situation associated with this game. In order to show that (γ,Γ) admits no OSSB, by Observation 7.4.2, we need to show that there exists no vN&M abstract stable set for the system $(D^*,\angle)$. Indeed, there exists a unique cycle in this system, given by

$$(U,L,A)\angle_1(C,L,A)\angle_2(C,R,A)\angle_1(D,R,A)\angle_3(D,R,B)$$
$$\angle_1(U,R,B)\angle_2(U,L,B)\angle_3(U,L,A),$$

where $\angle_i$ means that the domination is obtained by player *i*'s change in his strategy, while the other two players stay put. Now, a vN&M abstract stable set for the system $(D^*,\angle)$ would have to include exactly half of the seven elements of this cycle. But seven is an odd number, hence no abstract stable set exists for this system.

The following modification of Example 7.4.7 verifies that the existence of a Nash equilibrium does not imply the existence of an OSSB for the individual contingent threats situation. [More generally, the existence of an abstract stable set for an abstract system $(D,\angle)$ does not imply, nor is implied by, the non-emptiness of the abstract core of $(D,\angle)$.]

Example 7.4.8: Consider the same game as the one in Example 7.4.7, where the strategy choices of player 3 are given by the following payoff matrices $\tilde{A}$ and $\tilde{B}$ (instead of A and B).

The payoff matrix $\tilde{A}$ is given by:

	L	M	R
U	1,0,2	0,0,0	0,0,0
C	2,1,0	0,0,0	1,2,0
D	0,0,0	0,0,0	3,1,0
E	0,0,0	1,1,1	0,0,0

The payoff matrix $\tilde{B}$ is given by:

	L	M	R
U	0,2,1	0,0,0	4,1,0
C	0,0,0	0,0,0	0,0,0
D	0,0,0	0,0,0	0,0,2
E	0,0,0	0,0,0	0,0,0

That is, $\boldsymbol{Z^1 \equiv \{U,C,D,E\}}$, $\boldsymbol{Z^2 \equiv \{L,M,R\}}$, and $\boldsymbol{Z^3 \equiv \{\tilde{A},\tilde{B}\}}$. It is easily verified that this game has a unique Nash equilibrium given by $\mathbf{NE} = (\boldsymbol{E,M,\tilde{A}})$. But, because of the cycle mentioned in Example 7.4.7, the associated individual contingent threats situation admits no OSSB (hence, no CSSB).

7.5 Coalitional contingent threats

A modification of the negotiation process delineated by the individual contingent threats situation is obtained by allowing not only single individuals but also coalitions to make contingent threats. That is, when an N-tuple of strategies $\zeta \in Z^N$ is proposed, a coalition S may **declare** that **if all other players will stick to the specified N-tuple of strategies ζ, its members will adopt** $\xi^S \in Z^S$ instead of ζ^S. The new, revised proposal then becomes $\xi = (\zeta^{N \setminus S}, \xi^S)$, from which another coalition may, in turn, threaten to deviate by stating the strategy tuple it will adopt **if all other players will stick to the specified N-tuple of strategies ξ.** The process continues in this manner.

This scheme is described by the following ***coalitional contingent threats situation*** (γ,Γ), which is the exact analog of $(\hat{\gamma}^2,\bar{\Gamma})$ of Section 6.2. Recall that G_ζ denotes the position

$$G_\zeta \equiv (N, \{\zeta\}, \{u^i\}_{i \in N}).$$

The set of positions in the coalitional contingent threats situation is

$$\Gamma \equiv \{G^N\} \cup \{G_\zeta | \; \zeta \in Z^N\},$$

and the inducement correspondence γ is given by: For all $G \in \Gamma$, $\zeta \in Z^N$, and $S \subset N$,

$$\gamma(S|G,\zeta) \equiv \{G_\xi | \; \xi = (\xi^S, \zeta^{N \setminus S}), \; \xi^S \in Z^S\}.$$

The negotiation process described by the coalitional contingent threats situation differs from the one delineated by the CPN situation in two important aspects. First, the objecting coalition realizes that **nonmembers are not committed** to the currently proposed strategies, and, second, **any coalition,** not only a subset of S, is allowed to object to a proposal made by a coalition S. It is because of these features that, unlike the CPN situation, the coalitional contingent threats situation is not hierarchical, and, hence, it may admit either no or several OSSBs or CSSBs.

Analogous to Theorem 7.4.1, we have the following.

Theorem 7.5.1: *Let F^N be a game in normal form and let (γ,Γ) be its associated coalitional contingent threats situation. Then, the SB σ is an OSSB for (γ,Γ) if and only if it is a CSSB for (γ,Γ), and, moreover, $\sigma(G^N) \supset SNE(F^N)$.*

Observe that Theorem 7.5.1 does not assert that the existence of a strong Nash equilibrium implies the existence of an OSSB (or a CSSB) for the coalitional contingent threats situation (γ,Γ). The game in Example 7.4.8 illustrates this assertion. Indeed, since no payoff yields a utility level greater than 1 to more than one player, it follows that allowing coalitions to form does not change the set of possible objections. Hence, the set of strong Nash equilibria coincides with the set of Nash equilibria, which consists of the single strategy profile $(E,M,\tilde{A})$. Moreover, in this example, σ is an OSSB (or a CSSB) for the corresponding coalitional contingent threats situation if and only if it is an

OSSB (or a CSSB) for the corresponding individual contingent threats situation. But, as we saw, the latter admits no OSSB (or CSSB).

As in the previous section, Claim 2.5.6 together with Theorem 4.5 yields that an OSSB (hence, by Theorem 7.5.1, a CSSB) for the coalitional contingent threats situation (γ,Γ) can be characterized by a vN&M abstract stable set for the system $(D^*,\angle^*)$, where $\boldsymbol{D^* \equiv Z^N}$, and for $\zeta,\xi \in Z^N$,

$$\zeta \angle^* \xi \Leftrightarrow \exists\, S \subset N \text{ such that } \zeta^{N\setminus S} = \xi^{N\setminus S} \text{ and for all } i \in S,\ u^i(\xi) > u^i(\zeta).$$

That is, an n-tuple of strategies $\xi \in Z^N$ dominates the n-tuple of strategies $\zeta \in Z^N$ if ξ is obtained from ζ by a deviation of coalition S, whose members are better off under ξ than they are under ζ. Analogous to Observation 7.4.2, we have the following.

Observation 7.5.2: *Let F^N be a game in normal form and let (γ,Γ) be its associated coalitional contingent threats situation. The SB σ is an OSSB (or a CSSB) for (γ,Γ) if and only if $\sigma(G^N) = K$, where K is an abstract stable set for the system $(D^*,\angle^*)$. Moreover, the set of strong Nash equilibria is the abstract core of $(D^*,\angle^*)$, that is, $SNE(F^N) = D^* \setminus \Delta(D^*)$.*

Since a vN&M abstract stable set for an abstract system always includes its abstract core, Observation 7.5.2 implies the second part of Theorem 7.5.1. This result is particularly useful for normal form games which have no strong Nash equilibrium but whose associated coalitional contingent threats situation admits an OSSB (or a CSSB), σ, since then, as the following claim asserts, the solution assigned by σ to the position G^N (which corresponds to the original game F^N) is nonempty. (See Example 7.5.5.) Analogous to Claim 7.4.3, we have the following observation.

Claim 7.5.3: *Let F^N be a game in normal form and let σ be an OSSB (or a CSSB) for its associated coalitional contingent threats situation (γ,Γ). Then, $\sigma(G^N) \neq \emptyset$. Moreover, for all $G \in \Gamma$, $\sigma(G) = \sigma(G^N) \cap X(G)$.*

Clearly, the coalitional contingent threats situation need not admit an OSSB (or a CSSB). In fact, in contrast to Theorem 7.4.5, such may be the case even for a two-person game. Indeed, consider Example 7.4.4, and assume, in negation, that the associated coalitional contingent threats situation admits an OSSB, σ.

i. If the Nash equilibrium (UR) does not belong to $\sigma(G^N)$, then the (external) stability of σ implies that $(UR) \in \text{ODOM}(\sigma,G^N)$. As (UR) is a Nash equilibrium, it follows, again by the (external) stability of σ, that the Pareto outcome (DL) belongs to $\sigma(G^N)$. Hence, Claim

7.5.3 and the (internal) stability of σ imply that $\sigma(G^N)$ does not include either (UL) or (DR). Thus, $\sigma(G^N)=\{DL\}$. But then, $(UL)\notin ODOM(\sigma,G^N)$, contradicting the (external) stability of σ.

ii. If, on the other hand, $(UR)\in\sigma(G^N)$, then by Claim 7.5.3, $(UR)\in\sigma(G_{UR})$, and, hence, by the (internal) stability of σ, $\{UL,DR\}\subset ODOM(\sigma,G^N)$. Therefore, $(DL)\notin ODOM(\sigma,G^N)$, which, by the (external) stability of σ, implies that $(DL)\in\sigma(G^N)$. But then, $(UR)\in ODOM(\sigma,G^N)$, which is a contradiction.

It is certainly interesting to investigate the relationship between the stable standards of behavior for the two situations: the CPN and the coalitional contingent threats. I conclude this section with the following two observations, the first of which is intuitively appealing.

Claim 7.5.4: *Let F^N be a 2×2 matrix game, and let σ be a stable (optimistic or conservative) SB for the associated coalitional contingent threats situation. Then, $\sigma(G^N)\supset CPNE$.*

But, quite unexpectedly, the following example shows that Claim 7.5.4 cannot be generalized. In fact, the CPNE can be completely disjoint from $\sigma(G^N)$. This example also demonstrates that $\sigma(G^N)$ can be nonempty although there exists no strong Nash equilibrium.

Example 7.5.5: Consider the following matrix game:

	L	*M*	*R*
U	0,0	4,8	7,7
C	0,0	9,4	5,5
D	6,6	0,0	0,0

Since, in every two-player game, CPNE consists of the set of Pareto optimal Nash equilibria, we have that **CPNE = NE = (*DL*).** On the other hand, we shall now show that the unique OSSB (or CSSB) for the associated coalitional contingent threats situation is given by $\boldsymbol{\sigma(G^N)=\{(CM),(UR)\}}$.

First, observe that if $\tilde{\sigma}$ is an OSSB, then $(DL)\notin\tilde{\sigma}(G^N)$. Indeed, otherwise, by internal stability, neither (CR) nor (UR) belong to $\sigma(G^N)$, and hence, $\{(CR),(UR)\}\subset ODOM(\tilde{\sigma},G^N)$. It follows that $(UM)\in\tilde{\sigma}(G^N)$, which, by internal stability, implies that $(CM)\notin\tilde{\sigma}(G^N)$. Thus, $\tilde{\sigma}(G^N)=\{(UM),(DL)\}$. But then, $(CM)\notin ODOM(\tilde{\sigma},G^N)$, contradicting the external stability of $\tilde{\sigma}$.

Since $(DL)\notin\tilde{\sigma}(G^N)$, external stability implies that $(UR)\in\sigma(G^N)$. Therefore,

$\{(UM),(CR)\} \subset \text{ODOM}(\tilde{\sigma},G^N)$, yielding that $\tilde{\sigma}(G^N) = \{(CM),(UR)\}$. It is easily verified that this SB is an OSSB.

Notice also that there exists no strong Nash equilibrium in this game. Indeed, the only candidate is the unique Nash equilibrium (DL). But this strategy profile yields the payoff (6,6) which is Pareto dominated by the strategy profile (UR), which yields the payoff (7,7).

7.6 Individual commitments

Consider the following negotiation process, where contingent threats are replaced by firm, irrevocable commitments. More specifically, assume that an n-tuple of strategies $\zeta \in Z^N$ is proposed to the individuals. If all individuals **openly** consent to follow ζ, then ζ will be adopted. As in (N.1), objections to ζ can be made only by single individuals. If individual i **declares** that he objects to follow ζ^i, he has to state what strategy he will adopt instead, that is, he has to specify some $\xi^i \in Z^i$ to which he is **henceforth committed.** The revised proposal then becomes $(\zeta^{N\setminus\{i\}},\xi^i)$, from which another player can deviate by committing himself to a particular strategy from his strategy set, and so on. Thus, in contrast to the Nash process, where an individual believes that ***all other players are committed*** to the proposed strategy and he is the only one who is free to choose any strategy from his strategy set, under the process considered here, a player realizes that other players are not necessarily committed to the proposed strategy and ***it is he who can commit himself*** to a particular strategy.

This negotiation process is represented by the following ***individual commitments situation,*** (γ,Γ). For $S \subset N$ and $\zeta \in Z^N$, define the position H_ζ^S by

$$H_\zeta^S \equiv \{N, Z^S \times \{\zeta^{N\setminus S}\}, \{u^i\}_{i\in N}).$$

The only (but significant) difference between the position G_ζ^S (defined in Section 7.2) and H_ζ^S is that the set of players in the latter is N, rather than S. However, members of $N\setminus S$ in position H_ζ^S are "inactive," or "committed," in the sense that they have no choice of strategies; they must adopt $\zeta^{N\setminus S}$. Observe that for $S=N$, no player is committed, and, therefore, for all $\zeta,\xi \in Z^N$, $H_\zeta^N = H_\xi^N = G^N$. Recall that we use the convention that $S \subset N$ implies $S \neq \emptyset$. Define, therefore, for $\zeta \in Z^N$, the position

$$H_\zeta^\emptyset \equiv \{N, \{\zeta\}, \{u^i\}_{i\in N}).$$

Thus, in $H_\zeta^\emptyset$ (which coincides with the position G_ζ defined in Section 7.4) all players are committed to follow ζ. Let 2^N denote the set of all subsets of N (which includes the empty set). The set of positions in the individual commitments situation is

$$\Gamma \equiv \{H^S_\zeta \mid S \in 2^N \text{ and } \zeta \in Z^N\},$$

and the inducement correspondence, γ, is given by: For all $i \in N$, $H^S_\zeta \in \Gamma$, $\zeta, \xi \in Z^N$, and $T \subset N$,

$$\gamma(\{i\} \mid H^S_\zeta, \xi) \equiv \{H^{S\setminus\{i\}}_\rho \mid \rho^{N\setminus S} = \xi^{N\setminus S}\} \quad \text{if } i \in S,$$
$$\gamma(T \mid H^S_\zeta, \xi) \equiv \emptyset \qquad \text{otherwise.}$$

Thus, γ captures the fact that at each "round" one of the players may decide to commit himself to a particular strategy from his strategy set, Z^i, provided, of course, that he has not done so before.

Claim 7.6.1: *Let F^N be a finite game in normal form and let* (γ,Γ) *be its associated individual commitments situation. Then, there exists a unique OSSB and a unique CSSB for* (γ,Γ).

As was the case with the previous sections, Claim 7.6.1 together with Theorem 4.5 yields that an OSSB for the individual commitments situation (γ,Γ) can be characterized by an abstract stable set for the system $(D,\angle)$, where

$$D \equiv \{(S,\zeta) \mid S \in 2^N \text{ and } \zeta \in Z^N\},$$

and for $\zeta, \xi \in Z^N$, $(S,\zeta) \angle (T,\xi)$ if and only if

$$\exists\ i \in S \text{ such that } T = S\setminus\{i\},\ \zeta^{N\setminus S} = \xi^{N\setminus S}, \text{ and } u^i(\xi) > u^i(\zeta).$$

Analogous to Observation 7.4.2, we have the following.

Observation 7.6.2: *Let F^N be a finite game in normal form and let* (γ,Γ) *be its associated individual commitments situation. Then, there exists a unique abstract stable set, K, for the abstract system* $(D,\angle)$, *which is given by* $K \equiv \{(S,\xi) \mid \xi \in \sigma(H^S_\xi)\}$, *where σ is the unique OSSB for* (γ,Γ).

We now have three different situations that are associated with normal form games where coalitions are not allowed to form, namely, the Nash, the individual contingent threats, and the individual commitments situations. It is interesting to study the relationships among the stable standards of behavior for these situations. The following example is a step in this direction. It shows that the solutions these three situations yield can be distinct.

Example 7.6.3: There are two players, 1 and 2. Player 1 can choose Up, Center, or Down, and player 2 can choose Left or Right. Thus,

$$N = \{1,2\},\ Z^1 \equiv \{U,C,D\}, \text{ and } Z^2 \equiv \{L,R\}.$$

The utility levels of the players are given by the following 3×2 payoff matrix, where, for example, if player 1 chooses C and player 2 chooses L, then their respective payoffs are 8 and 0.

	L	R
U	(0,4)	(5,5)
C	(8,0)	(0,3)
D	(7,7)	(0,6)

Using the recursive formulas of Theorems 5.2.1 and 5.4.2, the reader can easily verify that, in this example, **the unique OSSB, $\boldsymbol{\sigma}$,** for the individual commitments situation (γ,Γ) coincides with **the unique CSSB** for (γ,Γ) and is given by:

$$\begin{aligned}
&\sigma(H^{\emptyset}_{\zeta})=\{\zeta\}, && \zeta\in Z^N;\\
&\sigma(H^{1}_{h,L})=\{(CL)\}, && h\in\{U,C,D\};\\
&\sigma(H^{1}_{h,R})=\{(UR)\}, && h\in\{U,C,D\};\\
&\sigma(H^{2}_{U,h})=\{(UR)\}, && h\in\{L,R\};\\
&\sigma(H^{2}_{C,h})=\{(CR)\}, && h\in\{L,R\};\\
&\sigma(H^{2}_{D,h})=\{(DL)\}, && h\in\{L,R\};
\end{aligned}$$

and

$$\boldsymbol{\sigma(G^N)=\{(DL)\}}.$$

It is straightforward to see that the game in this example admits a unique Nash equilibrium. Specifically,

$$\mathbf{NE}(\boldsymbol{F^N})=\{(\boldsymbol{UR})\}.$$

Thus, $\sigma(G^N)$ is disjoint from the set of Nash equilibria. Finally, let us turn to the stable standards of behavior for the associated individual contingent threats situation, (γ^*,Γ^*). Let σ^* be an OSSB for (γ^*,Γ^*). Then, by Theorem 7.4.1, σ^* is also a CSSB for (γ^*,Γ^*), and $(UR)\in\sigma^*(G^N)$. Hence, Theorem 7.4.3 implies that $\boldsymbol{\sigma^*(G_{UR})=\{(UR)\}}$. By internal stability, therefore, $\boldsymbol{\sigma^*(G_{UL})=\sigma^*(G_{CR})=\sigma^*(G_{DR})=\emptyset}$. It follows that $(CL)\notin\text{ODOM}(\sigma^*,G_{CL})$, and thus $\boldsymbol{\sigma^*(G_{CL})=\{(CL)\}}$. Hence, $(CL)\in\sigma^*(G^N)$ and $(DL)\in\text{ODOM}(\sigma^*,G_{DL})$. Therefore, $(DL)\notin\sigma^*(G_{DL})=\emptyset$, implying that $(DL)\notin\sigma^*(G^N)$. Thus, we conclude that the individual contingent threats situation, (γ^*,Γ^*), associated with the game of Example 7.6.3 admits a **unique OSSB** (hence, a **unique CSSB**) σ^*, which satisfies

$$\boldsymbol{\sigma^*(G^N)=\{(UR),(CL)\}}.$$

Geir Asheim (1989) observed that in the well-known Cournot duopoly model, the unique OSSB (which coincides here with the unique CSSB) for the individual commitments situation yields the monopolist's solution, which, of course, differs from the Cournot–Nash equilibrium. More specifically, consider two firms, 1 and 2, that can produce, **costlessly,** the same commodity c. The demand function is given by $p=120-x_1-x_2$, where x_i, $i=1,2$, is the amount of c firm i produces, and p is the market price. In this case, firm i's profits are px_i. The associated normal form game F^N is, therefore, given by:

$$N=\{1,2\}\ ;\ Z^1=Z^2=[0,120]\ ;\ u^i(x_1,x_2)=(120-x_1-x_2)x_i,\ i=1,2.$$

It is easy to see that the unique Nash equilibrium for this game is $x^*=(x^*_1,x^*_2)$, where $x^*_1=x^*_2=40$. The resulting price is $p^*=40$, and each firm makes profits of 1600. However, since $\text{Max}(120-z)z$ is obtained at $z^*=60$, the maximal joint (monopolist's) profits are $3600>3200$.

We shall now see that the unique OSSB (or CSSB), σ, for the associated individual commitments situation (γ,Γ), satisfies: $\sigma(G^N)=\{(30,30)\}$, yielding, each firm, profits of 1800. That is, the firms split the (joint) monopolist's profits!

Indeed, if i commits to y_i units of c, then j's unique best response is to produce $(120-y_i)/2$, [which maximizes: $z_j(120-y_i-z_j)$]. That is, for all $y\in Z^N$, $\sigma(H^j_y)=\{(y_i,(120-y_i)/2)\}$. It follows that if i commits to y_i, the resulting price is $120-y_i-[(120-y_i)/2)]=(120-y_i)/2$, and his profits are $[(120-y_i)/2)]y_i$. Hence, i's optimal commitment is to produce 60 units of c. Player j will then respond by producing $[(120-60)/2]=30$ units; the resulting price is 30, yielding i the profits of 1800. Thus, by committing to the strategy of producing 60, each firm can assure itself profits of 1800. Therefore, if $z\in\sigma(G^N)$, we must have that for $i=1,2$, $z_i(120-z_i-z_j)\geq 1800$. But the only strategy in Z^N that satisfies these two inequalities is the strategy-tuple (30, 30). Hence, $\sigma(G^N)=\{(30,\ 30)\}$, as we wished to show.

7.7 Coalitional commitments

A modification of the above process is obtained by allowing not only for single individuals to commit themselves to particular strategies, but also for coalitions to make correlated commitments. That is, when the n-tuple of strategies $\zeta\in Z^N$ is proposed to the individuals, a coalition S can declare that it objects to the specified choice of ζ^S and state openly the strategy each of its members will adopt instead. That is, **S has to specify an S-tuple of strategies, $\xi^S\in Z^S$, to which its members are henceforth committed.** The revised proposal then becomes $(\zeta^{N\setminus S},\xi^S)$, from which another coalition (that contains only noncommitted members) can deviate, and so on.

This process is described by the ***coalitional commitments situation*** **(γ,Γ),** where the set of positions is the same as in the individual commitments situation, namely,

$$\Gamma \equiv \{H_\zeta^S \mid S \in 2^N \text{ and } \zeta \in Z^N\},$$

and the inducement correspondence, γ, is given by: For all $H_\zeta^S \in \Gamma$, $\zeta,\xi \in Z^N$, and $T \subset N$,

$$\gamma(T|H_\zeta^S,\xi) \equiv \{H_\rho^{S\setminus T} \mid \rho^{N\setminus S} = \xi^{N\setminus S}\} \quad \text{if } T \subset S,$$
$$\gamma(T|H_\zeta^S,\xi) \equiv \emptyset \qquad \text{otherwise.}$$

Thus, γ captures the fact that at each "round" a group of noncommitted players, T, may decide to commit themselves to follow a particular T-tuple of strategies, $\rho^T \in Z^T$. Analogous to Claim 7.6.1, we have the following.

Claim 7.7.1: *Let F^N be a finite game in normal form and let (γ,Γ) be its associated coalitional commitments situation. Then, there exist a unique OSSB and a unique CSSB for (γ,Γ).*

Using the recursive formulas of Theorems 5.2.1 and 5.4.1, it is possible to explicitly derive these two stable standards of behavior. Thus, for example, the unique OSSB, σ, for the prisoner's dilemma, Example 7.4.4, is given by:

$$\sigma(H_\zeta^\emptyset) = \{\zeta\} \text{ for } \zeta \in Z^N,$$
$$\sigma(H_{DL}^1) = \sigma(H_{UL}^1) = \{(UL)\},$$
$$\sigma(H_{DR}^1) = \sigma(H_{UR}^1) = \{(UR)\},$$
$$\sigma(H_{UL}^2) = \sigma(H_{UR}^2) = \{(UR)\},$$
$$\sigma(H_{DL}^2) = \sigma(H_{DR}^2) = \{(DR)\},$$
$$\sigma(G^N) = \{(DL)\}.$$

That is, $\sigma(G^N)$ consists of the unique Pareto outcome.

Again, Claim 7.7.1 together with Theorem 4.5 offer a characterization of an OSSB for the coalitional commitments situation (γ,Γ) as an abstract stable set for the system $(D,\angle)$, where

$$D \equiv \{(S,\zeta) \mid S \in 2^N \text{ and } \zeta \in Z^N\},$$

and for $\zeta,\xi \in Z^N$, $(S,\zeta) \angle (T,\xi)$ if and only if

$$T \subset S,\ T \neq S \neq \emptyset,\ \zeta^{N\setminus S} = \xi^{N\setminus S}, \text{ and for all } i \in S\setminus T,\ u^i(\xi) > u^i(\zeta).$$

Analogous to Observation 7.5.2, we have the following.

Observation 7.7.2: *Let F^N be a finite game in normal form and let (γ,Γ) be its associated coalitional commitments situation. Then, there exists a unique* *abstract stable set, K, for the abstract system* $(D,\angle)$, *which is given by* $K\equiv\{(S,\xi)|\ \xi\in\sigma(H_\xi^S)\}$, *where* σ *is the unique OSSB for* (γ,Γ).

We now have four different situations that are associated with normal form games where coalitions are allowed to form, namely, the strong Nash, the CPN, the coalitional contingent threats, and the coalitional commitments situations. That the stable standards of behavior for these situations may yield distinct recommendations can be illustrated by the prisoner's dilemma, Example 7.4.4. As we saw, in this example we have: **CPNE** $=\{UR\}$, **SNE** $=\emptyset$, **there exists no OSSB for the coalitional contingent threats situation,** and **the unique OSSB for the coalitional commitments situation satisfies** $\sigma(G^N)=\{DL\}$.

Proofs for Chapter 7

Proof of Theorem 7.1.2: Since (γ,Γ) is a hierarchical situation (e.g., $\Gamma_1\equiv\{G^N\}$ and $\Gamma_2\equiv\Gamma\backslash\{G^N\}$), Theorem 5.2.1 implies that it suffices to show that the SB σ, defined by $\sigma(G^N)=\mathrm{NE}(F^N)$ **and for** $G_\zeta^i\in\Gamma$, $\sigma(G_\zeta^i)=\{(\xi^i,\zeta^{N\backslash\{i\}})|\xi^i\in\mathrm{NE}(F_\zeta^i)\}$, is an OSSB for the Nash situation (γ,Γ).

Since for all $i\in N$, u^i is a continuous function and Z^i is a compact set, it follows that for all $\zeta\in Z^N$, $\mathrm{NE}(F_\zeta^i)=\{\xi^i\in Z^i|\ u^i(\xi^i,\zeta^{N\backslash\{i\}})\geq u^i(\rho^i,\zeta^{N\backslash\{i\}})$ for all $\rho^i\in Z^i\}\neq\emptyset$. Therefore, ζ^i is not a Nash equilibrium in F_ζ^i if and only if there exists a Nash equilibrium, ξ^i, in F_ζ^i such that $u^i(\xi^i,\zeta^{N\backslash\{i\}})>u^i(\zeta)$. Hence, for all $G_\zeta^i\in\Gamma$, $\sigma(G_\zeta^i)=X(G_\zeta^i)\backslash\mathrm{ODOM}(\sigma,G_\zeta^i)$.

By the same argument, ζ is not a Nash equilibrium in the game $F^N=(N,\{Z^i\}_{i\in N},\{u^i\}_{i\in N})$ if and only if there exists a player $i\in N$ such that ζ^i is not a Nash equilibrium in F_ζ^i. That is, $\zeta\notin\sigma(G^N)$ if and only if there exists a player $i\in N$ such that $\zeta\notin\sigma(G_\zeta^i)$. Hence, $\sigma(G^N)=X(G^N)\backslash\mathrm{ODOM}(\sigma,G^N)$. Thus, for all $G\in\Gamma$, $\sigma(G)=X(G)\backslash\mathrm{ODOM}(\sigma,G)$, that is, σ is an OSSB for (γ,Γ).

Q.E.D.

Proof of Theorem 7.2.1: Since γ is a simple inducement correspondence and for all $G\in\Gamma$, $|N(G)|\leq n$, by Proposition 5.1.6 and Theorem 5.2.1, (γ,Γ) admits at most one OSSB. Q.E.D.

Proof of Theorem 7.2.3: By induction on $|S|$. For $|S|=1$, $\zeta\in\sigma(G_\zeta^i)$ if and only if $\zeta^i\in\mathrm{NE}(F_\zeta^i)=\mathrm{CPNE}(F_\zeta^i)$. Hence, the theorem holds. Assume validity for all $|\tilde{S}|<J$, and let $|S|=J$.

i. For all $Q\subset T\subset N$, $\zeta\in\sigma(G_\zeta^T)$ implies $\zeta\in\sigma(G_\zeta^Q)$: Otherwise, by the external stability of σ, $\zeta\notin\sigma(G_\zeta^Q)$ implies that there exist $M\subset Q$ and $\xi\in\sigma(G_\zeta^M)$ with $\xi>_M\zeta$. But then $\zeta\in\mathrm{ODOM}(\sigma,G_\zeta^T)$, contradicting $\zeta\in\sigma(G_\zeta^T)$.

ii. $\zeta^S \in \text{CPNE}(F_\zeta^S)$ implies $\zeta \in \sigma(G_\zeta^S)$: Otherwise, by the external stability of σ, there exist $T \subset S$ and $\xi \in \sigma(G_\zeta^T)$ with $\xi >_T \zeta$. If $|T| < |S|$, then, by the induction hypothesis, $\xi^T \in \text{CPNE}(F_\zeta^T) = \text{CPNE}(F_\xi^T)$. By Claim 7.2.4 below, $\xi >_T \zeta$ contradicts the assumption that $\zeta^S \in \text{CPNE}(F_\zeta^S)$. Hence, $T = S$. By (i) above, $\xi \in \sigma(G_\zeta^Q)$ for all $Q \subset S$. Hence, by the induction hypothesis, ξ^S is self-enforcing for F_ζ^S. But then, $\xi >_S \zeta$ contradicts the assumption that $\zeta^S \in \text{CPNE}(F_\zeta^S)$.

iii. $\zeta \in \sigma(G_\zeta^S)$ implies $\zeta^S \in \text{CPNE}(F_\zeta^S)$: By (i) and the induction hypothesis, ζ^S is self-enforcing for F_ζ^S. Hence, if $\zeta^S \notin \text{CPNE}(F_\zeta^S)$ then there exists another self-enforcing strategy profile ξ^S for F_ζ^S such that $\xi >_S \zeta$. By the internal stability of σ, $\xi \notin \sigma(G_\zeta^S)$. By the external stability of σ, there exist $T \subset S$ and ρ such that $\rho \in \sigma(G_\xi^T)$ and $\rho >_T \xi$. If $T = S$, then $G_\xi^T = G_\zeta^T$ implying $\rho \in \sigma(G_\zeta^S)$, which contradicts $\zeta \in \sigma(G_\zeta^S)$. Thus, $T \subset S$, $T \neq S$. Since ξ is self-enforcing for F_ζ^S, it follows that $\xi^T \in \text{CPNE}(F_\xi^T)$. Hence, by the induction hypothesis, $\xi \in \sigma(G_\xi^T)$, contradicting $\rho \in \sigma(G_\xi^T)$ and $\rho >_T \xi$.

Q.E.D.

Proof of Claim 7.2.4: The proof is by induction on the number of players, n. For $n = 1$, by (i) in Definition 7.2.2, $\text{CPNE}(F^N)$ coincides with the set of all Pareto-optimal strategies. Therefore, if $\zeta \in \text{CPNE}(F^N)$ then there is no $\xi \in \text{CPNE}(F^N)$ with $\xi >_N \zeta$.

Assume the validity of Claim 7.2.4 for all games with fewer than n players. Let $\zeta \in \text{CPNE}(F^N)$. Then, by (iii) in Definition 7.2.2, there is no $\xi \in \text{CPNE}(F^N)$ with $\xi >_N \zeta$. Moreover, by (ii) in Definition 7.2.2, for all $S \subset N$, $S \neq N$, $\zeta^S \in \text{CPNE}(F_\zeta^S)$. Therefore, by the induction hypothesis, there is no $S \subset N$, $S \neq N$, and $\xi^S \in \text{CPNE}(F_\zeta^S)$ with $(\xi^S, \zeta^{N \setminus S}) >_S \zeta$. Q.E.D.

Proof of Claim 7.2.5: The proof is by induction on the number of players, n. For $n = 1$, that is, $N = \{i\}$, (i) in Definition 7.2.2 implies that $\text{CPNE}(F^N)$ coincides with the set of all Pareto-optimal strategies. Therefore, if $\zeta \in Z^N \setminus \text{CPNE}(F^N)$, since Z^i is a compact set and u^i is continuous, there exists $\xi \in \text{CPNE}(F^N)$ with $\xi >_N \zeta$.

Assume the validity of Claim 7.2.5 for all games with fewer than n players, and let $\zeta \in Z^N \setminus \text{CPNE}(F^N)$. Then, ζ violates either (ii) and/or (iii) in Definition 7.2.2.

If (ii) does not hold, then there exists $S \subset N$, $S \neq N$, for which

$$\zeta^S \in Z^S \setminus \text{CPNE}(F_\zeta^S).$$

As the number of players in F_ζ^S does not exceed $n-1$, the induction hypothesis yields that there exist $T \subset S$ and $\xi^T \in \text{CPNE}(F_\zeta^T)$ for which $(\xi^T, \zeta^{N \setminus T}) >_T \zeta$.

Finally, assume that (ii) is satisfied but (iii) in Definition 7.2.2 is violated. Since we assumed that the self-enforcing strategy profiles for F^N is a compact set and $\zeta \in Z^N \setminus \text{CPNE}(F^N)$ satisfies (ii), it follows that there exists a self-enforcing strategy $\xi \in Z^N$ with $\xi >_N \zeta$ such that there is no other self-enforcing strategy ρ with $\rho >_N \xi$. Then, ξ satisfies both (ii) and (iii), implying that $\xi \in \text{CPNE}(F^N)$. Recalling that $\xi >_N \zeta$ concludes the proof. Q.E.D.

Proof of Theorem 7.2.6: Since for all $i \in N$, the cardinality of the set $\{u^i(z) | \; z \in Z^N\}$ does not exceed J, the dominance relation in the abstract system associated with the corresponding CPN situation is strictly acyclic. (Indeed, there is no sequence of length $J+1$ with the property that each element in the sequence dominates it predecessor.) Theorems 4.5 and 4.7 yield, therefore, the validity of this theorem. Q.E.D.

Proof of Theorem 7.2.7: The proof follows immediately from Theorem 4.13. Q.E.D.

Proof of Theorem 7.2.8: By Claim 2.5.6, σ is an OSSB for $(\tilde{\gamma},\tilde{\Gamma})$ if and only if it is also a CSSB for $(\tilde{\gamma},\tilde{\Gamma})$.

Let $\tilde{\sigma}$ be an SB for $(\tilde{\gamma},\tilde{\Gamma})$. Define the SB, σ, for the CPN situation (γ,Γ) as follows. For $G^S_\zeta \in \Gamma$, $\boldsymbol{\sigma}(G^S_\zeta) \equiv \cup \{\tilde{\boldsymbol{\sigma}}(\tilde{H}^S_\xi) | \; \xi \in X(G^S_\zeta)\}$. Then, $\rho \in \text{ODOM}(\sigma, G^S_\zeta)$ if and only if $\rho \in \text{ODOM}(\tilde{\sigma}, \tilde{H}^S_\rho)$. Hence, σ is an OSSB for (γ,Γ) if and only if $\tilde{\sigma}$ is an OSSB for $(\tilde{\gamma},\tilde{\Gamma})$. By Theorem 7.2.3, it follows that if $\tilde{\sigma}$ is an OSSB (hence a CSSB) for $(\tilde{\gamma},\tilde{\Gamma})$, then it is unique, and it is given by:
For all $\tilde{H}^S_\zeta \in \tilde{\Gamma}$,

$$\begin{aligned} \tilde{\sigma}(\tilde{H}^S_\zeta) = X(\tilde{H}^S_\zeta) &= \{\zeta\} && \text{if } \zeta^S \in \text{CPNE}(F^S_\zeta), \\ &= \emptyset && \text{if } \zeta^S \notin \text{CPNE}(F^S_\zeta). \end{aligned}$$

In particular, $\tilde{\sigma}(G^N) = \sigma(G^N) = \text{CPNE}(F^N)$. Q.E.D.

Proof of Theorem 7.2.9: By Theorem 4.5, σ is an OSSB for the CPN situation (γ,Γ) if and only if its graph is a *vN&M* abstract stable set for the abstract system $(D^*, \angle^*)$, where $D^* \equiv \{(G^S_\zeta,\xi) | G^S_\zeta \in \Gamma \text{ and } \xi \in X(G^S_\zeta)\}$, and $(G^S_\zeta,\xi) \angle^* (G^T_\rho,\omega)$ if and only if $T \subset S$, $\xi^{N \setminus T} = \omega^{N \setminus T}$, and $\omega >_T \xi$. Since for all $S \subset N$ and $\zeta \in Z^N$, G^S_ζ can be identified with (S,ζ), and $(G^S_\zeta,\xi) \angle^* (G^T_\rho,\omega)$ if and only if $(S,\xi) \angle (T,\omega)$, it follows that σ is an OSSB for the CPN situation (γ,Γ) if and only if its graph is a *vN&M* abstract stable set for the abstract system $(D,\angle)$. Theorems 7.2.1 and 7.2.3 yield, therefore, Theorem 7.2.9.
Q.E.D.

Proof of Theorem 7.3.2: As γ is hierarchical (e.g., $\Gamma_1 \equiv \{G^N\}$ and $\Gamma_2 \equiv \Gamma \setminus \{G^N\}$), Theorem 5.2.1 implies that it suffices to show that the SB σ, defined by $\boldsymbol{\sigma}(\boldsymbol{G^N}) = \mathbf{SNE}(\boldsymbol{F^N})$ **and, for** $\boldsymbol{G \neq G^N}$, $\boldsymbol{\sigma}(\boldsymbol{G}) = \boldsymbol{X}(\boldsymbol{G})$, is an OSSB for the strong Nash situation (γ,Γ).

Since for all $S \subset N$, $\zeta \in Z^N$, and $G \neq G^N$, $\gamma(S|G,\zeta) = \emptyset$, we have that for $G \neq G^N$, $\text{ODOM}(\sigma,G) = \emptyset$. Hence, for $G \neq G^N$, $\sigma(G) = X(G) \backslash \text{ODOM}(\sigma,G) = X(G)$. Therefore, by the definition of SNE (Definition 7.3.1), ζ is an SNE if and only if $\zeta \notin \text{ODOM}\,(\sigma,G^N)$. Q.E.D.

Proof of Theorem 7.3.3: Note first that $(\tilde{\gamma}^1,\tilde{\Gamma})$ is hierarchical (e.g., let $\tilde{\Gamma}_1 = \{G^N\}$ and $\tilde{\Gamma}_2 = \tilde{\Gamma} \backslash \{G^N\}$). Theorem 5.4.1 implies, therefore, that $(\tilde{\gamma}^1,\tilde{\Gamma})$ admits at least one CSSB. By Claim 2.5.6, σ is an OSSB for $(\tilde{\gamma}^1,\tilde{\Gamma})$ if and only if it is also a CSSB for $(\tilde{\gamma}^1,\tilde{\Gamma})$. Thus, $(\tilde{\gamma}^1,\tilde{\Gamma})$ admits an OSSB. Theorem 5.2.1 yields, therefore, that this is the unique OSSB, hence the unique CSSB for $(\tilde{\gamma}^1,\tilde{\Gamma})$. By Theorem 5.2.1, this CSSB is given by η. Specifically, for all $\tilde{H}^S_\zeta \in \tilde{\Gamma}$,

$$\boldsymbol{\eta}(\tilde{H}^S_\zeta) = \boldsymbol{X}(\tilde{H}^S_\zeta) = \{\zeta\} = \tilde{\boldsymbol{\sigma}}^1(\tilde{H}^S_\zeta),$$

and, by Definition 7.3.1,

$$\boldsymbol{\eta}(\boldsymbol{G^N}) = \mathbf{SNE}(\boldsymbol{F^N}) = \tilde{\boldsymbol{\sigma}}^1(\boldsymbol{G^N}). \qquad \text{Q.E.D.}$$

Proof of Theorem 7.4.1: Let F^N be a game in normal form and let (γ,Γ) be its associated individual contingent threats situation. By Claim 2.5.6, σ is an OSSB for (γ,Γ) if and only if it is also a CSSB for (γ,Γ).

To see the second part of the theorem, assume, in negation, that there exist an OSSB (or a CSSB) for (γ,Γ) and $\zeta \in Z^N$ such that $\zeta \in \text{NE}(F^N) \backslash \sigma(G^N)$. The external stability of σ implies that there exist $i \in N$ and $\xi^i \in Z^i$ such that $u^i(\xi^i,\zeta^{N \backslash \{i\}}) > u^i(\zeta)$, contradicting the fact that $\zeta \in \text{NE}(F^N)$. Q.E.D.

Proof of Observation 7.4.2: By Claim 2.5.6, σ is an OSSB for the situation (γ,Γ) if and only if it is a CSSB for (γ,Γ). By Theorem 4.5, therefore, the SB σ is an OSSB (hence, a CSSB) for (γ,Γ) if and only if its graph is an abstract stable set for the associated abstract system $(D^\circ,\angle^\circ)$, where $D^\circ \equiv \{(G^N,\zeta) |\ \zeta \in Z^N\} \cup \{(G_\zeta,\zeta) |\ \zeta \in Z^N\}$ and $(G,\zeta) \angle^\circ (H,\xi)$ if and only if $H = G_\xi$ and there exists $i \in N$ such that $\zeta^{N \backslash \{i\}} = \xi^{N \backslash \{i\}}$ and $u^i(\xi) > u^i(\zeta)$. Since we can identify the pair (G_ζ,ζ) with the N-tuple of strategies $\zeta \in Z^N$, the definition of the abstract system $(D^*,\angle)$ yields that the SB σ is an OSSB (hence, a CSSB) for (γ,Γ) if and only if $\sigma(G^N) = K$, where K is an abstract stable set for the system $(D^*,\angle)$.

The last part of the theorem follows directly from the definitions of Nash equilibrium, abstract core, and the dominance relation $\angle$. Q.E.D.

Proof of Claim 7.4.3: Assume, in negation, that there exists an OSSB (or a CSSB) for (γ,Γ) such that $\sigma(G^N) = \emptyset$. In view of Claim 2.5.1, it follows that there exists $G_\zeta \in \Gamma$ with $\sigma(G_\zeta) \neq \emptyset$, that is, $\sigma(G_\zeta) = \{\zeta\}$. The (internal) stability of σ implies that $\zeta \notin \text{ODOM}(\sigma, G_\zeta)$, and hence, $\zeta \notin \text{ODOM}(\sigma, G^N)$. By the (external) stability of σ we therefore have that $\zeta \in \sigma(G^N)$, which is a contradiction.

The inducement correspondence γ implies that for all $G_\zeta \in \Gamma$, $\zeta \in$ ODOM (σ, G_ζ) if and only if $\zeta \in \text{ODOM}(\sigma, G^N)$. Therefore, if σ is an OSSB (or a CSSB) for the individual contingent threats situation then for all $G_\zeta \in \Gamma$, $\sigma(G_\zeta) = \sigma(G^N) \cap X(G_\zeta)$, that is, $\sigma(G_\zeta) = \{\zeta\}$ if $\zeta \in \sigma(G^N)$ and $\sigma(G_\zeta) = \emptyset$ if $\zeta \notin \sigma(G^N)$. Q.E.D.

Proof of Theorem 7.4.5: By Observation 7.4.2, we need to show that the abstract system $(D^*, \angle)$ admits an abstract stable set. In fact, we shall prove the stronger result that every system $(D, \angle)$ admits an abstract stable set, where D is a nonempty subset of the set of strategies, that is, $D \subset D^* = Z^N$, and for $\zeta, \xi \in D$, $\zeta \angle \xi \Leftrightarrow \exists\ i \in N$ such that $\zeta^{N \setminus \{i\}} = \xi^{N \setminus \{i\}}$ and $u^i(\xi) > u^i(\zeta)$.

The proof is by induction on the number of elements in D. (Recall that Z^i, $i = 1,2$, is finite.) If $|D| = 1$, then clearly D is an abstract stable set for $(D, \angle)$. Assume the validity of the assertion for all $(\hat{D}, \angle)$ with $|\hat{D}| \leq h-1$ and consider the system $(D, \angle)$ where $|D| = h$. Define the set

$$\boldsymbol{B \equiv \{\zeta \in D \mid u^2(\zeta) \geq u^2(\zeta^1, \xi^2) \text{ for all } (\zeta^1, \xi^2) \in D\}.}$$

That is, $\zeta \in B$ if and only if ζ^2 is player 2's best response, in D, to player 1's choice of ζ^1. B is clearly a vN&M externally stable set for the system $(D, \angle)$. Therefore, if B is also a vN&M internally stable set for the system $(D, \angle)$, we are done. Otherwise, there exist ζ and ξ in B such that $\zeta \angle \xi$. As $\zeta \in B$, it follows that $\zeta^2 = \xi^2$ and $u^1(\xi) > u^1(\zeta)$.

Consider the set $\tilde{D} \equiv D \setminus \{\zeta\}$. (Since $|D| > 1$, $\tilde{D} \neq \emptyset$.) Then, by the induction hypothesis, there exists a vN&M abstract stable set, $\tilde{A}$, for $(\tilde{D}, \angle)$. We shall now verify that $\tilde{A}$ is also a vN&M abstract stable set for $(D, \angle)$. The internal stability of $\tilde{A}$ is guaranteed by the fact that $\tilde{A}$ is a vN&M abstract stable set for $(\tilde{D}, \angle)$. Therefore, it remains to be shown that $\tilde{A}$ is also externally stable for $(D, \angle)$. Since $\tilde{A}$ is externally stable for $(\tilde{D}, \angle)$ we need only to verify that $\zeta \in \Delta(\tilde{A})$.

Now, if $\xi \in \tilde{A}$, then $\zeta \angle \xi$ implies $\zeta \in \Delta(\tilde{A})$. If, on the other hand, $\xi \notin \tilde{A}$, then, since $\tilde{A}$ is externally stable for $(\tilde{D}, \angle)$, there exists $\rho \in \tilde{A}$ with $\xi \angle \rho$. Since $\xi \in B$, it follows that $\rho^2 = \xi^2$ and $u^1(\rho) > u^1(\xi)$. Hence, $\rho^2 = \zeta^2$ and $u^1(\rho) > u^1(\zeta)$, that is, $\zeta \angle \rho$. Therefore, $\zeta \in \Delta(\tilde{A})$. Q.E.D.

Proof of Theorem 7.4.6: By Observation 7.4.2, we need to show that the abstract system $(D^*, \angle)$ admits an abstract stable set. Indeed, every cycle in this system contains an even number of distinct elements of D. Therefore, by Richardson (1946, Theorem 1, p. 578) we have that $(D^*, \angle)$ admits an abstract stable set. Q.E.D.

Proof of Theorem 7.5.1: Let F^N be a game in normal form and let (γ,Γ) be its associated coalitional contingent threats situation. By Claim 2.5.6, σ is an OSSB for (γ,Γ) if and only if it is also a CSSB for (γ,Γ).

To see the second part of the theorem, assume, in negation, that there exist an OSSB (or a CSSB) for (γ,Γ) and $\zeta \in Z^N$ such that $\zeta \in \text{SNE}(F^N) \backslash \sigma(G^N)$. Then, the external stability of σ implies that there exist $S \subset N$ and $\xi^S \in Z^S$ such that for all $i \in S$, $u^i(\xi^S, \zeta^{N \backslash S}) > u^i(\zeta)$, contradicting the fact that $\zeta \in \text{SNE}(F^N)$.

Q.E.D.

Proof of Observation 7.5.2: By Claim 2.5.6, σ is an OSSB for the situation (γ,Γ) if and only if it is a CSSB for (γ,Γ). By Theorem 4.5, therefore, the SB σ is an OSSB (hence, a CSSB) for (γ,Γ) if and only if its graph is an abstract stable set for the associated abstract system $(D^\circ, \angle^\circ)$, where $D^\circ \equiv \{(G^N,\zeta) | \ \zeta \in Z^N\} \cup \{(G_\zeta,\zeta) | \ \zeta \in Z^N\}$ and $(G,\zeta) \angle^\circ (H,\xi)$ if and only if $H = G_\xi$ and there exists $S \subset N$ such that $\zeta^{N \backslash S} = \xi^{N \backslash S}$ and for all $i \in S$, $u^i(\xi) > u^i(\zeta)$. Since we can identify the pair (G_ζ,ζ) with the N-tuple of strategies $\zeta \in Z^N$, the definition of the abstract system $(D^*, \angle^*)$ yields that the SB σ is an OSSB (hence, a CSSB) for (γ,Γ) if and only if $\sigma(G^N) = K$, where K is an abstract stable set for the system $(D^*, \angle^*)$.

The last part of the theorem follows directly from the definitions of strong Nash equilibrium and the dominance relation $\angle^*$. Q.E.D.

Proof of Claim 7.5.3: Assume, in negation, that there exists an OSSB (or a CSSB) for (γ,Γ) such that $\sigma(G^N) = \emptyset$. In view of Claim 2.5.1, it follows that there exists $G_\zeta \in \Gamma$ with $\sigma(G_\zeta) \neq \emptyset$, that is, $\sigma(G_\zeta) = \{\zeta\}$. The (internal) stability of σ implies that $\zeta \notin \text{ODOM}(\sigma, G_\zeta)$, and, hence, $\zeta \notin \text{ODOM}(\sigma, G^N)$. By the (external) stability of σ we therefore have that $\zeta \in \sigma(G^N)$, which is a contradiction.

The inducement correspondence γ implies that for all $G_\zeta \in \Gamma$, $\zeta \in \text{ODOM}(\sigma, G_\zeta)$ if and only if $\zeta \in \text{ODOM}(\sigma, G^N)$. Therefore, if σ is an OSSB (or a CSSB) for the coalitional contingent threats situation then, for all $G_\zeta \in \Gamma$, $\sigma(G_\zeta) = \sigma(G^N) \cap X(G_\zeta)$, that is, $\sigma(G_\zeta) = \{\zeta\}$ if $\zeta \in \sigma(G^N)$ and $\sigma(G_\zeta) = \emptyset$ if $\zeta \notin \sigma(G^N)$.

Q.E.D.

Proof of Claim 7.5.4: Let σ by an OSSB (hence a CSSB) for the coalitional contingent threats situation associated with the 2×2 matrix game F^N. Assume, in negation, that there exists $\zeta \in \text{CPNE} \backslash \sigma(G^N)$. By the external stability of σ, $\zeta \in \text{ODOM}(\sigma, G^N)$. That is, there exist $S \subset N$ and $\xi \in \sigma(G_\xi)$ such that $\xi^{N \backslash S} = \zeta^{N \backslash S}$ and, for all $i \in S$, $u^i(\xi) > u^i(\zeta)$. Since F^N is a two-person game, $\zeta \in \text{CPNE}$ implies that ζ is a Pareto-optimum Nash equilibrium. Hence, $u^i(\xi) > u^i(\zeta)$ for $i = 1,2$, and, in addition, ξ is not a Nash equilibrium. Thus, there exist $i \in N$ and ρ such that $\rho^h = \xi^h$, for $\{h\} = N \backslash \{i\}$, and $u^i(\rho) > u^i(\xi)$. By the stability of σ, therefore, $\rho \in \text{ODOM}(\sigma, G^N)$. That is, there exist $h \in N$ and $\omega \in \sigma(G_\omega)$, hence $\omega \in \sigma(G^N)$, such that $\rho^i = \xi^i$ and $u^h(\omega) > u^h(\rho)$. Since F^N is a 2×2 matrix game, it follows that $\omega = \zeta$, contradicting the assumption that $\zeta \notin \sigma(G^N)$. Q.E.D.

Proof of Claim 7.6.1: Note first that the individual commitments situation (γ, Γ) is strictly hierarchical. The hierarchy of $H^S_\xi \in \Gamma$ can, for example, be based on the cardinality of the coalition S. (That is, H^T_ζ is of a lower hierarchy than H^S_ξ if $T \subset S$, and $T \neq S$.) The validity of the claim is verified by applying Corollary 5.3.3 and Theorem 5.4.1. Q.E.D.

Proof of Observation 7.6.2: By Theorem 4.5, σ is an OSSB for the individual commitments situation if and only if its graph is a vN&M abstract stable set for the associated abstract system $(D^*, \angle^*)$, where $\boldsymbol{D^* \equiv \{(H^S_\xi, \xi) | H^S_\xi \in \Gamma}$ **and** $\boldsymbol{\xi \in X(H^S_\xi)\}}$ and $\boldsymbol{(H^S_\xi, \xi) \angle^* (H^T_\rho, \omega)}$ if and only if there exists $i \in S$ such that $T = S \backslash \{i\}$, $\omega^{N \backslash S} = \xi^{N \backslash S}$, and $u^i(\omega) > u^i(\xi)$. By Theorem 4.5 and Claim 7.6.1, the abstract system $(D^*, \angle^*)$ admits a unique abstract stable set, K^*.

The definition of $X(H^S_\xi)$ implies that $(H^S_\zeta, \xi) \angle^* (H^T_\rho, \omega)$ if and only if $(H^S_\xi, \xi) \angle^* (H^T_\omega, \omega)$. Hence, $(H^S_\zeta, \xi) \in K^*$ if and only if $(H^S_\xi, \xi) \in K^*$. To conclude the proof of the observation, notice that (H^S_ξ, ξ) can be identified with the pair (S, ξ).
Q.E.D.

Proof of Claim 7.7.1: Note first that the coalitional commitments situation (γ, Γ) is strictly hierarchical. The hierarchy of $H^S_\zeta \in \Gamma$ can, for example, be based on the cardinality of the coalition S. (That is, H^T_ζ is of a lower hierarchy than H^S_ξ if $T \subset S$, and $T \neq S$.) The validity of the claim is verified by applying Corollary 5.3.3 and Theorem 5.4.1. Q.E.D.

Proof of Observation 7.7.2: By Theorem 4.5, σ is an OSSB for the coalitional commitments situation if and only if its graph is a vN&M abstract stable set for the associated abstract system $(D^*, \angle^*)$, where $\boldsymbol{D^* \equiv \{(H^S_\zeta, \xi) | H^S_\zeta \in \Gamma}$ **and** $\boldsymbol{\xi \in X(H^S_\xi)\}}$ and $\boldsymbol{(H^S_\xi, \xi) \angle^* (H^T_\rho, \omega)}$ if and only if $T \subset S$, $T \neq S \neq \emptyset$, $\omega^{N \backslash S} = \xi^{N \backslash S}$ and $u^i(\omega) > u^i(\xi)$ for all $i \in S \backslash T$. By Theorem 4.5 and Claim 7.7.1, the associated abstract system $(D^*, \angle^*)$ admits a unique abstract stable set, K^*.

The definition of $X(H^S_\xi)$ implies that $(H^S_\zeta, \xi) \angle^* (H^T_\rho, \omega)$ if and only if $(H^S_\xi, \xi) \angle^* (H^T_\omega, \omega)$. Hence, $(H^S_\zeta, \xi) \in K^*$ if and only if $(H^S_\xi, \xi) \in K^*$. To conclude the proof of the observation, notice that (H^S_ξ, ξ) can be identified with the pair (S, ξ).
Q.E.D.

CHAPTER 8

Extensive form games with perfect information

Of the three game forms, it is the extensive form, or the game tree, that provides the most detailed description of the actions that are available to the players. I shall argue that, as was the case with the other two game forms, this description is not adequate. On the one hand, it fails to specify, for example, the legal institutions, such as whether it is possible for a player to self-commit to his future actions. [It is the answer to this question that lies at the heart of the distinction between Nash and subgame perfect equilibria (see Definitions 8.0.3 and 8.0.4).] And, on the other hand, it involves unnecessarily detailed information:

> The game tree is an extremely useful device for didactic purposes, but one must often pay a high price for its use, in terms of redundancy. The rules of many games permit the same physical "position" to be reached through various different sequences of moves. Yet in a tree each sequence of moves must lead to a different node. The tree convention forces us to remember the history of the position, whether we want to or not (Shubik 1984, p. 48).

Insisting on such a detailed description is not only "wasteful"; it also has serious consequences. Thus, for example, a game in extensive form cannot serve as the framework for analyzing: (i) "human rationality," inherent to which is the empirical observation that individuals often ignore (even relevant) information (see Section 11.3), and, perhaps more importantly, (ii) coalition formation, since it is impossible to provide the complete specifications of the exact way in which individuals can interact.

> In noncooperative equilibrium theory it is assumed that *all* communication takes place within the game. Thus, if discussions are held among players, these must be modeled as part of the game. The difficulty is not with the extensive form but with the description or coding of information and communication. . . . In general there is no easy way to describe complex sets of messages, verbal inflections, and gestures as sets of moves in a game. Yet all these may figure importantly in face-to-face communication during bargaining (Shubik 1984, p. 258).

As we saw in the previous two chapters, the theory of social situations overcomes these shortcomings: The existing legal institutions and the precise negotiation process are clearly stated; the notion of situation is sufficiently flexible, allowing for the (perceptual) simplification of the social environment; and coalition formation is naturally accommodated (indeed, the inducement correspondence specifies the opportunities that are available not only to single individuals but also to groups of individuals).

The representation of an extensive form game (with perfect information and without chance moves) as a "tree situation" (see the next section) has the following additional merits:

i. It simplifies the analysis considerably. In particular, it employs the notion of a ***path,*** rather than the much more complicated, and somewhat artificial, concept of ***strategy.***
ii. Points out the close relationship between the CSSB and the most important game-theoretic notion for games in extensive form – the subgame perfect equilibrium. This observation suggests a new characterization of subgame perfect equilibrium (Theorem 8.2.6), in which the beliefs of a player concerning the reaction of other players to his deviation are very different from those implicit in the classical definition of this notion (Definition 8.0.4). In addition to its conceptual contents, this characterization yields new results in classical game theory (see, e.g., Theorem 8.2.7).
iii. Produces new and interesting solution concepts. In particular, the unique OSSB for a finite tree situation refines subgame perfection. This refinement is quite attractive; several authors promoted it (in the particular models they studied) by resorting to appealing, but ad hoc, assumptions (see Examples 8.3.3, 8.3.4, 8.3.5, and 8.3.7). Other new solution concepts are obtained by allowing players to form coalitions (see Example 8.4.3 and Remark 8.4.4).

The theory of extensive form games employs some basic concepts from graph theory. In addition to the terms introduced in Definition 5.1.3, we need the following definition.

A ***rooted tree*** is a digraph with a unique source, called its ***root,*** which has the property that there exists a unique walk (path) from the root to each other vertex. Alternatively, a rooted tree is an acyclic digraph which has exactly one vertex of indegree 0 and all of its other vertices of indegree 1.

Definition 8.0.1: An n-person extensive form game with perfect information *(and without chance moves) is represented by a rooted tree, T, called the* ***game tree,*** *that has the following structure:*

E.1. The set of nodes, $\mathbf{V(T)}$, is partitioned into $n+1$ sets, $\mathbf{V_0(T), V_1(T), V_2(T), \ldots, V_n(T)}$. The length of the unique path which connects the *root of T with a vertex $v \in V_i(T)$, $i=1,2,\ldots,n$, is finite. The set* $\mathbf{V_0(T)}$ *contains the* ***terminal nodes,*** *that is, those nodes whose outdegree is 0.*

E.2. *Each terminal node, $v \in V_0(T)$, is assigned a* ***payoff vector*** *in $\mathbb{R}^N$.*

The interpretation of this structure is as follows. For each $i \in N$, $V_i(T)$ is the set of decision nodes of player i. Once $v \in V_i(T)$ is reached, player i has to choose one of the nodes adjacent from v. If a terminal node $v \in V_0(T)$ is reached, then no more choices by the individuals can be made, and player i receives a utility level equal to the ith coordinate of the payoff vector assigned to v.

Let T be a game tree. Denote by $\boldsymbol{v^*(T)}$ the root of T, and by $\boldsymbol{\Pi(T)}$ the set of all paths in the tree T that originate in the root $v^*(T)$ and end in some terminal node in $V_0(T)$. [Since each vertex is fully characterized by the unique path that connects it with the root of the tree, **the set $V_0(T)$ can be identified with the set $\Pi(T)$.**] By (E.2), each path $x \in \Pi(T)$ is assigned a vector, $\boldsymbol{\mu(x)}$, in $\mathbb{R}^N$. The scalar $\mu^i(x)$ is the utility level player i receives if the path x in $\Pi(T)$ is followed. This notation is particularly useful for infinite game trees, where the set of terminal nodes $V_0(T)$ is not defined, but we can assign to each path x (finite or infinite) in $\Pi(T)$ the payoff vector $\mu(x)$ in $\mathbb{R}^N$. Since each vertex $v \in V(T)$ is reachable from $v^*(T)$ by a unique path, we shall extend the domain of the function μ to include all paths in all subtrees, $\tilde{T}$, of T. Thus, for $x \in \Pi(\tilde{T})$, $\mu(x) \equiv \mu(v^*(T),\ldots,v^*(\tilde{T})=x_1,x_2,x_3,\ldots)$.

For a vertex $v \in V(T)$, denote by $\boldsymbol{(T|v)}$ the (sub)tree whose root is v. That is, $\Pi(T|v)$ is the set of all paths that originate at v and end in some terminal vertex in $V_0(T)$. [Thus, for example, $T=(T|v^*(T))$.] It is easily verified that if T is a game tree, that is, T satisfies (E.1) and (E.2), then for any $v \in V(T)$, $(T|v)$ is also a game tree.

When a game tree T is represented by a diagram, the symbol $\boxed{i}$ is attached to every vertex v which belongs to $V_i(T)$. For example, Figure 8.0.1 represents the game tree T, where

$$N=\{1,2,3\},\ V(T)=\{v_1,v_2,\ldots,v_{13}\},$$
$$V_1(T)=\{v_1,v_8,v_{11}\},\ V_2(T)=\{v_2,v_7\},\ V_3(T)=\{v_4\},$$
$$V_0(T)=\{v_3,v_5,v_6,v_9,v_{10},v_{12},v_{13}\}.$$

The two most important game-theoretic solution concepts for a game tree[1] T are the Nash and subgame perfect equilibria. Both notions make use of the notion of a strategy in a game tree.

Definition 8.0.2: *Let T be a game tree. A (pure)* ***strategy (for player i)*** *is a function f^i that associates with each node $v \in V_i(T)$ a node w that is adjacent, in T, from v.*

[1] Throughout this chapter the term extensive form game or game tree corresponds to games with perfect information and without chance moves.

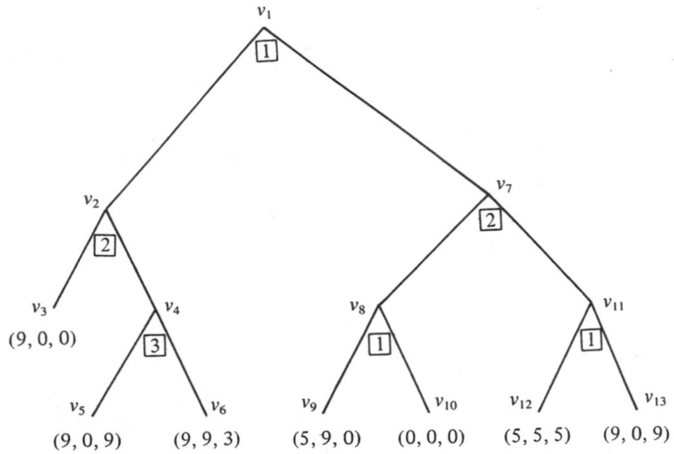

Figure 8.0.1

That is, a strategy f^i specifies the choice, or move, player i will make in any contingency that might arise. Thus, for $i \in N$ and $v \in V_i(T)$, $f^i(v)$ is a node w adjacent from v, which i will choose (if he follows f^i) if and when v is reached. The notion of strategy is not only complex but also demanding. Individuals have to decide and specify (in advance) what actions they will take in all possible contingencies, including in those that player i knows for sure will never be reached if he adopts f^i. For example, let the strategy f^1 for player 1 in the game tree represented in Figure 8.0.1 satisfy $f^1(v^*(T)) = f^1(v_1) = v_2$. Observe that once v_2 is reached, player 1 will never be asked to make another decision. The strategy f^1 must, nevertheless, specify also the choices player 1 will make in all the vertices that belong to $V_1(T)$. In particular, the domain of f^1 must include the vertices v_8 and v_{11}, even though they are not reachable from v_2. It is important to note that the notion of subgame perfect equilibrium (Definition 8.0.4) is based on this very feature of a strategy, that is, on the choices a strategy specifies for unreachable vertices. As we shall shortly see, these difficulties are avoided when the theory of social situation is applied to game trees; outcomes in "the tree situation" are paths rather than strategies.

Every ***strategy profile,*** that is, an n-tuple of strategies, $f = (f^1, f^2, \ldots, f^n)$, naturally defines (inductively) a unique path, $\pi(f)$, in $\Pi(T)$: The first vertex in $\pi(f)$ is $v^*(T)$, and the vertex that follows, in $\pi(f)$, a vertex v that belongs to $\pi(f)$ is the vertex w, where $w \equiv f^i(v)$ and i is the (unique) player for whom $v \in V_i(T)$. Therefore, the utility level that player i derives from an n-tuple of strategies, f, is given by

$$h^i(f) \equiv \mu^i(\pi(f)).$$

That is, $h^i(f)$ is the ith coordinate of the payoff vector assigned to the path $\pi(f)$.

Definition 8.0.3: *Let T be a game tree. A* ***Nash Equilibrium for T*** *is an n-tuple of strategies* $f=(f^1,f^2,\ldots,f^n)$ *such that for all* $i \in N$, $h^i(f) \geq h^i(g)$ *for all g, with* $g^j = f^j$ *for all* $j \neq i$, *and* g^i *is a strategy for i. The set of Nash equilibria for T is denoted by* ***NE(T)***.

The notion of NE(T) rests on behavioral assumptions and beliefs which are similar to those for the notion of a Nash equilibrium (Definition 7.1.1) in games in normal form. That is, no single individual finds it beneficial to unilaterally deviate, believing that all other players will stick to their strategies. A refinement of the notion of NE(T) is provided by the following definition.

Definition 8.0.4: *Let T be a game tree. The strategy profile* $f=(f^1,f^2,\ldots,f^n)$ *constitutes a* ***(subgame) Perfect Equilibrium for T,*** *if it has the property that for every* $v \in V(T)$, *the restriction of f to the (sub)tree* $(T|v)$ *belongs to* $NE(T|v)$. *The set of subgame perfect equilibria for T is denoted by* ***PE(T)***.

That is, an n-tuple of strategies is a subgame perfect equilibrium for T if it is the case that no matter at what vertex $v \in V(T)$ the players happen to find themselves, no player will find it beneficial to unilaterally deviate from his strategy [restricted to the subgame $(T|v)$], believing that all other players will continue to follow their (restricted) strategies. [Observe that these beliefs are held at any vertex $v \in V(T)$, even if reaching it requires many players to repeatedly deviate from the strategy profile f.] In particular, every perfect equilibrium for the game tree T is a Nash equilibrium for T.

8.1 The tree situation

Let $\tilde{T}$ be a (sub)tree. [$\tilde{T}$ might represent either the original extensive form game or one of its subgames $(T|v)$, $v \in V(T)$.] Associate with $\tilde{T}$ the position $\boldsymbol{G(\tilde{T})}$, defined as follows. The set of players in $G(\tilde{T})$ is the set of players, N, in the original extensive form game. Thus,

$$N(G(\tilde{T})) \equiv N = \{1,2,\ldots,n\}.$$

The set of outcomes, $X(G(\tilde{T}))$, in position $G(\tilde{T})$ is the set of all paths in the tree $\tilde{T}$ that originate in the root $v^*(\tilde{T})$ and end in some terminal node in $V_0(T)$, that is,

$$X(G(\tilde{T})) \equiv \Pi(\tilde{T}).$$

For player $i \in N$, the utility function, $u^i(G(\tilde{T}))$, is given by: For $x \in X(G(\tilde{T}))$, $u^i(G(\tilde{T}))(x)$ is the ith coordinate of the payoff vector assigned to the path x; that is, for all $i \in N$ and $x \in \Pi(\tilde{T})$,

$$u^i(G(\tilde{T}))(x) \equiv \mu^i(x).$$

Observe that for a terminal node $v \in V_0(T)$, $G(T|v) = (N, \{v\}, \{\mu^i(v)\}_{i \in N})$. The ***tree situation*** (γ, Γ) associated with the game tree T is defined as follows. The set Γ contains all the positions that correspond to subtrees in the original game tree T. That is,

$$\Gamma = \{G(T|v) |\ v \in V(T)\}.$$

Since every vertex $v \in V(T)$ uniquely defines the subtree $(T|v)$, we may simplify the notation and write $G(v)$ for $G(T|v)$. Thus,

$$\Gamma = \{G(v) |\ v \in V(T)\} = \{G(\tilde{T}) | \tilde{T} = (T|v),\ v \in V(T)\}.$$

Let us now turn to the definition of the inducement correspondence γ. The rules of the (extensive form) game are such that player i is called upon to make a decision in vertex v, $v \in V(T)$, only if v belongs to the set of vertices assigned to player i by the partition of the set of nodes of the game tree, that is, if and only if $v \in V_i(T)$. In this case, player i can induce all the positions associated with the subtrees that result from the decision he chooses to make, namely, all positions of the form $G(w)$, where the node w is adjacent from v.

Let $G(\tilde{T}) \in \Gamma$ and let $x \in X(G(\tilde{T}))$. As just discussed, if x is followed then player i is called upon to make a choice in each of the vertices that lie along the path x, and, in addition, belong to $V_i(\tilde{T})$. Therefore, when x is proposed in $G(\tilde{T})$, player i can induce all positions $G(w)$ where the node w is adjacent from a node v, which both belongs to $V_i(\tilde{T})$ and lies along the path x. With a slight abuse of notation, the last two conditions imposed on v will be written as $v \in \{x\} \cap V_i(\tilde{T})$. [Note that since $x \in \Pi(\tilde{T})$ we have that $\{x\} \cap V_i(\tilde{T}) = \{x\} \cap V_i(T)$.]

Assuming that coalitions are not allowed to form (which is the fundamental feature of a "noncooperative game"), the inducement correspondence γ, for all $i \in N$, $G(\tilde{T}) \in \Gamma$, and $x \in X(G(\tilde{T}))$, is given by

$$\gamma(\{i\} | G(\tilde{T}), x) = \{G(w) |\ \exists\ v \in \{x\} \cap V_i(T) \text{ such that } w \text{ is adjacent from } v\},$$
$$\gamma(S | G(\tilde{T}), x) = \emptyset \quad \text{otherwise.}$$

Recall from Definition 5.1.3 that a game tree in which the lengths of all paths do not exceed a finite integer, J, is called a ***bounded game tree,*** and the ***length of a bounded game tree*** is the maximal length of its paths. Notice also that there are no restrictions on the cardinality of the set of vertices, $V(T)$, of a bounded game tree. That is, a bounded game tree might contain an infinite number of vertices. A game tree where $V(T)$ contains only a finite number of vertices is called a ***finite game tree.*** Clearly, every finite game tree is bounded. For bounded game trees we have the following result.

Claim 8.1.1: *Let T be a bounded game tree and let* (γ,Γ) *be its associated tree situation. Then, there exist a unique OSSB and a unique CSSB for* (γ,Γ).

The nature of these two SBs and their relationship to classical solution concepts will be discussed in the next sections. Claim 8.1.3 points out another notable and useful feature of tree situations: The "truncation" of a "stable path" is itself a "stable path" in the "truncated" subtree. This property holds for every tree situation, including those associated with unbounded game trees.

Definition 8.1.2: *Let T be a game tree,* $x\in\Pi(T)$, *and* $w\in\{x\}$. *The* ***truncation of x from w*** *is the path obtained by restricting x to the game tree* $(T|w)$.

Thus, for example, if $x=(x_1,x_2,x_3,\ldots,x_j,\ldots)$, and $w=x_m$ for some m, then the truncation of x from w is the path $y\in\Pi(T|w)$, $y=(y_1,y_2,\ldots,y_j,\ldots)$, where $y_j\equiv x_{j+m-1}$, $j=1,2,\ldots$.

Claim 8.1.3: *Let T be a game tree and let* (γ,Γ) *be its associated tree situation. Let* σ *be an OSSB, or a CSSB, for* (γ,Γ). *For any subtree* $\tilde{T}$, *and every* $x\in\sigma(G(\tilde{T}))$, if $w\in\{x\}$ *then the truncation of x from w belongs to* $\sigma(G(w))$.

Claim 8.1.3 can be interpreted to say that if the players agree to follow the path x at the beginning of the game, then even if they could revoke their decision later on, they would not choose to do so. For finite game trees we have the following strong result.

Theorem 8.1.4: *Let T be a game tree with* $|V(T)|<\infty$, *and let* (γ,Γ) *be its associated tree situation. Then, there exist a unique OSSB,* σ^o, *and a unique CSSB,* σ^c, *for* (γ,Γ). *Furthermore, both of these SBs are nonempty-valued, and for all* $G\in\Gamma$, $\sigma^o(G)\subset\sigma^c(G)$.

As asserted at the beginning of this section, the notions of OSSB and CSSB for tree situations are intimately related to the notion of perfect equilibrium. Since the set of outcomes in a position $G(\tilde{T})$ is the set of paths $\Pi(\tilde{T})$, rather than strategies, it is useful to consider the set of paths in $\Pi(\tilde{T})$ that result from an n-tuple of strategies that is a subgame perfect equilibrium in the game tree $\tilde{T}$. This set will be called the ***set of perfect equilibrium paths,*** denoted **PEP($\tilde{T}$).** That is,

$$\mathbf{PEP}(\tilde{T})=\{\pi(f)|\ f\in\mathbf{PE}(\tilde{T})\}.$$

8.2 CSSB for the tree situation

The concept of CSSB is closely related to the notion of PEP: In all game trees that possess perfect equilibria, PEP is a CSSB. Moreover, in bounded game trees PEP is the unique CSSB. These two remarkable results provide a new characterization for, and shed new light on, the notion of subgame perfect equilibrium.

Theorem 8.2.1: *Let T be a game tree and let (γ,Γ) be its associated tree situation. Assume that PEP(T)$\neq\emptyset$. Define the SB, σ, for (γ,Γ) by: For every subtree $\tilde{T}$ of T, $\sigma(G(\tilde{T}))\equiv$PEP($\tilde{T}$). Then, σ is a CSSB for (γ,Γ).*

The condition in Theorem 8.2.1 that PEP(T) be nonempty is indispensable. Indeed, there are unbounded game trees for which PEP($\tilde{T}$)$=\emptyset$ for all subtrees $\tilde{T}$. But, by Claim 2.5.1, the SB which assigns to every position the empty set cannot be a CSSB.

Example 8.2.4 is another demonstration of the necessity, even in bounded game trees, to impose the condition that PEP(T)$\neq\emptyset$ for Theorem 8.2.1 to hold.

One implication of Theorem 8.2.1 is that for a large class of bounded game trees, the PEP correspondence is the only CSSB for the associated tree situation.

Theorem 8.2.2: *Let T be a bounded game tree and let (γ,Γ) be its associated tree situation. Assume that the unique CSSB, σ, for (γ,Γ) is nonempty-valued. Then, for all $G(\tilde{T})\in\Gamma$, $\sigma(G(\tilde{T}))=PEP(\tilde{T})$. (Hence, for such game trees, $PEP(\tilde{T})\neq\emptyset$ for all subtrees $\tilde{T}$* of *T*.)

Theorems 8.1.4 and 8.2.2 immediately imply that in finite game trees the PEP correspondence is the only CSSB for the associated tree situation and yield the well-known result that in finite game trees the PEP correspondence is nonempty-valued.

Corollary 8.2.3: *Let T be a game tree with $|V(T)|<\infty$, and let (γ,Γ) be its associated tree situation. Then, there exists a unique CSSB, σ, for (γ,Γ), which is given by: For all $G(\tilde{T})\in\Gamma$, $\sigma(G(\tilde{T}))=PEP(\tilde{T})$. Moreover, for any subtree $\tilde{T}$, $\sigma(G(\tilde{T}))$ is nonempty.*

The following example shows that the requirement that the CSSB be nonempty-valued is indispensable for Theorem 8.2.2 to hold.

Example 8.2.4: Consider the game where player 1 can choose between Left and Right. If he chooses Left, his payoff is 5. If he chooses Right, he then

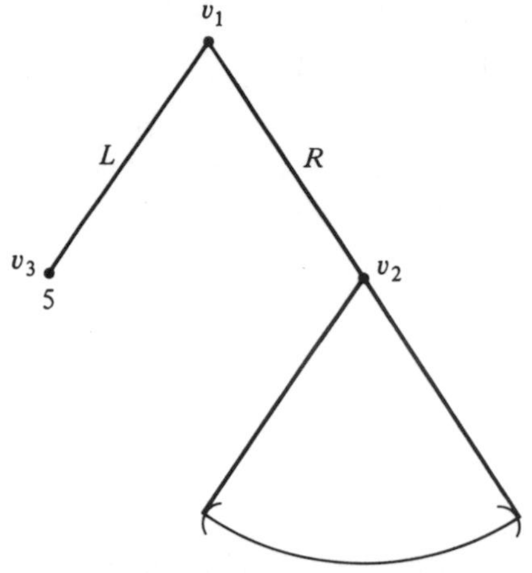

Figure 8.2.4a

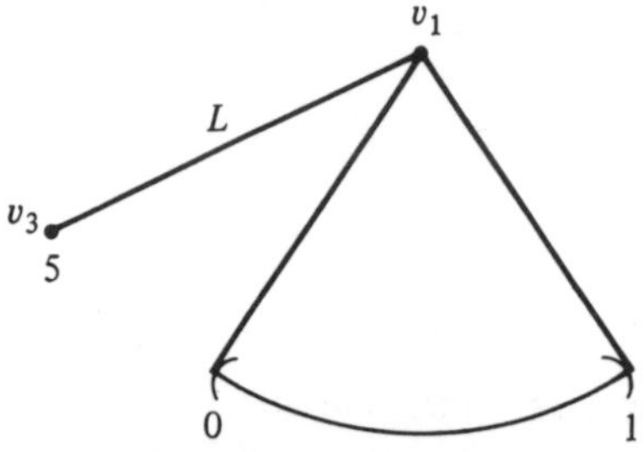

Figure 8.2.4b

has to quote a number t in the open interval (0,1) and his payoff is t. (The bounded game tree T that represents this game is depicted in Figure 8.2.4a). It is easy to see that the associated tree situation (γ,Γ) admits a unique CSSB, σ, which is given by:

$$\sigma(G(v))=\{v\}, \text{ if } v\in V_0(T);\ \sigma(G(v_2))=\emptyset; \text{ and } \sigma(G(T))=\{(v_1,v_3)\}.$$

The recommendations of this SB are quite appealing. It is most reasonable to recommend, at the beginning of this game, that the player choose Left. Indeed, $\sigma(G(T))=\{(v_1,v_3)\}$, and, no "best" recommendation can be given regarding the number that should be quoted once v_2 is reached. Indeed, $\sigma(G(v_2))=\emptyset$.

In contrast, this game tree admits no perfect equilibrium. Example 8.2.4 also points out the following difficulty with the notion of perfect equilibrium: A social environment can be represented as two, "essentially the same," game trees, but, nevertheless, their PEPs differ drastically. Indeed, Figure 8.2.4b is a slight variant of Figure 8.2.4a: Instead of choosing first between Left and Right, and then, if Right is chosen, to decide on the number t, the player can, at the beginning of the game, decide whether to say Left, or else, to (directly) quote a number $t\in(0,1)$. This latter game tree does have a perfect equilibrium, namely the choice Left, whereas the game tree in Figure 8.2.4a admits, as we saw, no perfect equilibrium.

The following example, due to Benyamin Shitovitz (private communication), shows that the converse of Theorem 8.2.1 does not hold. That is, there exists an infinite tree situation whose CSSB is totally unrelated to PEP.

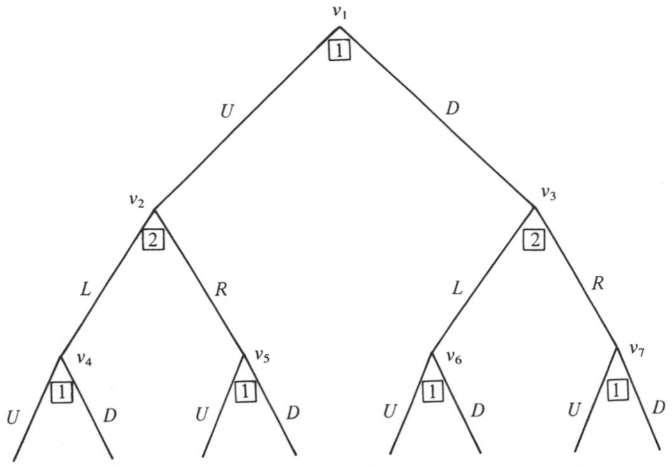

Figure 8.2.5

Example 8.2.5: There are two players, 1 and 2, who each can choose, in his turn, one of two actions. Player 1 can choose either Up or Down, and player 2 can choose either Left or Right. Turns are alternating, with player 1 being the one to start. Let T be the game tree that represents this two-person extensive form game. (See Figure 8.2.5.) By identifying a vertex $v \in V(T)$ with the sequence of actions that leads to it, the set of all outcomes in $G(T)$ can be written as

$$\Pi(T) = \{x = (x_1, x_2, \ldots) \mid x_t \in \{U, D\} \text{ if } t \text{ is odd and } x_t \in \{L, R\} \text{ if } t \text{ is even}\}.$$

Given an infinite sequence of choices, $x \in \Pi(T)$, the payoffs, $\mu(x)$, are as follows. If x contains each of the choices $U, D, L,$ and R infinitely many times, then player 1 receives 5 dollars (or utils) and player 2 receives 0 dollars, that is, in that case, $\mu(x) = (5,0)$. Any other sequence of choices, that is, any sequence in which either U and/or D and/or L and/or R is chosen only a finite number of times, yields 0 dollars to player 1 and 5 dollars to player 2, that is, in that case, $\mu(x) = (0,5)$. That is,[1]

$$\mu(x) = (5,0) \Leftrightarrow \text{for all } j \in \{U, D, L, R\},\ \#\{t \mid x_t = j\} = \infty,$$
$$\mu(x) = (0,5) \Leftrightarrow \exists\, j \in \{U, D, L, R\} \text{ such that } \#\{t \mid x_t = j\} < \infty.$$

It is straightforward to see that for any subtree $\tilde{T}$, if the path x belongs to PEP($\tilde{T}$) then the resulting payoff, $\mu(x)$, is (0,5). Indeed, player 2 can adopt, for example, the (weakly dominating) strategy "always choose Left," thereby guaranteeing himself the payoff 5, and no other path in $\Pi(T)$ yields him a

[1] For a set A, $\#A$ denotes the cardinality of A. Thus, $\#A = |A|$.

higher payoff. Thus, for every subtree $\tilde{T}$ of the game tree T of this example, we have

$$\mathbf{PEP}(\tilde{T})=\{x\in\Pi(\tilde{T})|\ \mu(x)=(0,5)\}.$$

By Theorem 8.2.1, therefore, the SB σ^1, defined by

$$\sigma^1(G(\tilde{T}))\equiv \mathbf{PEP}(\tilde{T})=\{x\in\Pi(\tilde{T})|\ \mu(x)=(0,5)\},$$

is a CSSB for (γ,Γ).

I shall now show that in addition to σ^1, there exists another CSSB, σ^2, for (γ,Γ). And, quite remarkably, for every subtree $\tilde{T}$, the solution assigned by σ^2 to $G(\tilde{T})$ is disjoint from PEP($\tilde{T}$). This SB is defined as follows: For all $G(\tilde{T})\in\Gamma$,

$$\sigma^2(G(\tilde{T}))=\{x\in\Pi(\tilde{T})|\ \mu(x)=(5,0)\}.$$

To see that σ^2 is indeed a CSSB for (γ,Γ), observe that in view of the inducement correspondence of the tree situation, and since $\sigma^2(G)\neq\emptyset$ for all $G\in\Gamma$, we can write CDOM as

CDOM$(\sigma^2,G)=\{x\in X(G)|\ \exists\ i\in N$ and $H\in\gamma(\{i\}|G,x)$ such that for all $y\in\sigma^2(H)$, $\mu^i(x)<\mu^i(y)\}=\{x\in X(G)|\ \mu^1(x)<5\}$.

It is, therefore, evident that for all $G\in\Gamma$, $\sigma^2(G)=X(G)\backslash\text{CDOM}(\sigma^2,G)$, that is, the SB σ^2 is a CSSB for (γ,Γ). Furthermore,

$$\mathbf{PEP}(\tilde{T})\cap\sigma^2(G(\tilde{T}))=\emptyset \quad \textbf{for every subtree } \tilde{T}.$$

As we saw in the two previous chapters, some of the results obtained through the application of the theory of social situations can be stated and proved within the paradigm of classical game theory. That such is also the case with extensive form games is verified by the following theorem, which provides a complete and new characterization of PEP.

Theorem 8.2.6: *Let T be a game tree and let $x^*\in\Pi(T)$. Then, $x^*\in PEP(T)$ if and only if x^* satisfies the following condition:*

C. *for every $i\in N$ and every vertex w adjacent from $v\in V_i(T)\cap\{x^*\}$, there exists $y\in PEP(T|w)$ such that $\mu^i(y)\leq\mu^i(x^*)$.*

The importance of Theorem 8.2.6, whose proof is quite straightforward, lies in its interpretation. There are fundamental and significant differences between the original definition of PEP and its equivalent formulation as provided in Theorem 8.2.6. First, and perhaps most important, the deviating individual expects a ***correlated retaliation;*** the other players will unite and choose a path, from the set of subgame perfect equilibrium paths in the resulting subgame, which will make the deviating player (weakly) worse off than he was under the proposed path. Second, the characterization of PEP in Theorem 8.2.6 replaces the notion of a **strategy** by the much simpler notion of a ***path.*** Consequently, a player can deviate **at most once** from a proposed path and generate a new subtree. But in this subtree, the player does accept the paths recommended by its PEP. In contrast, when players are free to choose their strategies, there can be multiple vertices in which deviations occur. [It is this subtle but significant difference that accounts for the fact that the SB σ^2 is a CSSB for the tree situation in Example 8.2.5, but none of the paths contained in the solution assigned by σ^2 to a subtree $\tilde{T}$ belongs to PEP($\tilde{T}$).]

We shall now see that Theorem 8.2.6 can be instrumental also in establishing new results of interest for a class of extensive form games, called ***generalized sequential bargaining games.*** Assume that a "cake of size 1" is to be divided among n players, provided they reach an agreement on how to divide it. If the n players cannot reach an agreement, then each player receives nothing. Specifically, denote the set of **possible agreements** by Δ, that is, $\boldsymbol{\Delta \equiv \{a \in \mathbb{R}^n_+ |\ \Sigma_{i=1}^n a_i \leq 1\}}$. Events in the bargaining process are confined to times in the set $\{1,2,\ldots,t,\ldots\}$. When it is player i's turn to make an offer, he has to choose an element in Δ, which represents the way he proposes to divide the cake. Turns are alternated, with player i proposing at times $t=i$, $i+n$, $i+2n$, $i+3n,\ldots$. After a proposal $z \in \Delta$ has been made at time t, the players vote sequentially in favor of or against the proposal. If all vote in favor of the proposal (say "yes," denoted by Y), the game ends at time t with player i receiving z^i units of the cake, yielding him the utility level $\boldsymbol{u^i(z^i,t)}$. Otherwise, the game proceeds to time $t+1$ when a new proposal is made.

The only assumptions on the utility functions $u^i(z^i,t)$ that I impose are that for every player $i \in N$, every offer $z \in \Delta$, and any period t,

A.1. $u^i(z^i,1)=z^i$, and
A.2. $(u^1(z^1,t),u^2(z^2,t),\ldots,u^n(z^n,t)) \in \Delta$.

The first assumption states that in the first period the utility function of every player is linear with the amount of cake he receives at that period. Condition (A.2) states that the utility level a player attains from any division at any period is always nonnegative, and, moreover, the sum of the utility levels attained never exceeds 1. Conditions (A.1) and (A.2) together imply that any payoff (vector of utility levels) that can be attained by the players at period t can also be attained in the first period. Observe, however, that (A.1) and (A.2) do not imply (the commonly employed assumption) that $u^i(z^i,t)$ is monotone decreasing in t.

A special class of utility functions that satisfy the two conditions is the set of functions of the form $u^i(z^i,t)=(\delta^i)^{t-1}z^i$, with δ^i, $\delta^i\in[0,1]$, being the "future discount factor" of player i. (See Rubinstein 1982). Note that δ^i can assume the value 1, that is, players need not discount the future at all.

Theorem 8.2.6 together with the particular structure of the game tree, T, that represents a generalized sequential bargaining game allows for a partial characterization of the payoffs supported by a subgame perfect equilibrium in T (see Greenberg 1988b). Denote this latter set by PEU(T), that is,

$$\mathbf{PEU}(T)\equiv\{a\in\mathbb{R}^n|\ \text{there exists } x\in\mathbf{PEP}(T) \text{ such that } \mu(x)=a\}.$$

Theorem 8.2.7: *Let T be a generalized sequential bargaining game that satisfies (A.1) and (A.2). Then PEU(T) is a convex set in* $\mathbb{R}^n$.

8.3 OSSB for the tree situation

An important result of this section is that in many game trees, including all finite game trees, the OSSB for the associated tree situation leads to an attractive refinement of the notion of perfect equilibrium paths. This unexpected result is quite remarkable because the motivation behind the notion of OSSB is totally unrelated to that which underlies Nash, and, hence, subgame perfect equilibrium.[1]

Let T be a game tree. The payoff function μ is said to be ***continuous*** if and only if for every $\epsilon>0$ there exists an integer κ such that if x and y are two paths in $X(G(T))$ whose first κ vertices coincide, then for all $i\in N$, $|\mu^i(x)-\mu^i(y)|<\epsilon$. Intuitively, continuity requires that the difference between the utility levels a player receives from two paths that coincide "long enough" is "negligible." We shall say that the game tree T is a ***continuous game tree*** if its payoff function μ is continuous. It is evident that all bounded game trees are continuous games.

Theorem 8.3.1: *Let T be a continuous game tree, and let* (γ,Γ) *be its associated tree situation. Let* σ *be an OSSB for* (γ,Γ) *such that* $\sigma(G(\tilde{T}))\neq\emptyset$ *for all* $G(\tilde{T})\in\Gamma$. *Then, for every* $G(\tilde{T})\in\Gamma$, $\sigma(G(\tilde{T}))\subset PEP(\tilde{T})$.

The requirement that the payoffs be continuous is essential for Theorem 8.3.1 to hold. Indeed, Claim 2.5.5 implies that both σ^1 and σ^2 in Example 8.2.5 are OSSBs for (γ,Γ). Yet, we saw that for every $G(\tilde{T})\in\Gamma$, $\sigma^2(G(\tilde{T}))\cap \mathrm{PEP}(\tilde{T})=\emptyset$.

[1] After the completion of the manuscript, Shitovitz and I noticed that the same is true for CSSB; it, too, refines subgame perfection. In particular, the analog of Theorem 8.3.1 holds also for CSSB (see Greenberg and Shitovitz 1990).

Theorems 8.1.4 and 8.3.1 imply that the unique OSSB for the tree situation associated with a finite game tree yields a nonempty refinement of PEP.

Corollary 8.3.2: *Let T be a finite game tree, and let* (γ,Γ) *be its associated tree situation. Then, there exists a unique OSSB,* σ*, for* (γ,Γ)*. Moreover, for every* $G(\tilde{T})\in\Gamma$, $\sigma(G(\tilde{T}))\neq\emptyset$ and $\sigma(G(\tilde{T}))\subset PEP(\tilde{T})$.

The following example demonstrates that the inclusion in Corollary 8.3.2 (and hence in Theorem 8.3.1) can be strict. That is, there exists a finite game tree T such that the unique OSSB, σ, for the associated tree situation assigns to the position $G(T)$ a **nonempty strict subset** of PEP(T).

Example 8.3.3: Let (γ,Γ) be the tree situation associated with the game tree depicted in Figure 2.1.2. Then, $\mathbf{\Gamma=\{G^1,G^2,...,G^7\}}$, corresponding to the seven subtrees $T^1,....,T^7$, where

$$V(T^1)\equiv\{v_1,v_2,\ldots,v_7\},\ V(T^2)\equiv\{v_2,v_4,v_5\},\ V(T^3)\equiv\{v_3,v_6,v_7\},$$
$$\text{and for } h=4,5,6,7,\ V(T^h)\equiv\{v_h\}.$$

The inducement correspondence γ is given by:

$$\gamma(\{1\}|G^1,x)=\{G^2,G^3\},$$
$$\gamma(\{2\}|G^1,(v_1,v_2,v_4))=\gamma(\{2\}|G^1,(v_1,v_2,v_5))=\{G^4,G^5\},$$
$$\gamma(\{2\}|G^1,(v_1,v_3,v_6))=\gamma(\{2\}|G^1,(v_1,v_3,v_7))=\{G^6,G^7\},$$
$$\gamma(\{2\}|G^2,x)=\{G^4,G^5\},\ \gamma(\{2\}|G^3,x)=\{G^6,G^7\},$$

and

$$\gamma(S|G,x)=\emptyset \quad \text{otherwise.}$$

(Observe that this tree situation is essentially the same as, but notationally different from, the situation we associated in Chapter 2 with Example 2.1.2.) Theorem 5.2.1 allows the explicit construction of the unique OSSB, σ, for the tree situation (γ,Γ) which is associated with a bounded game tree. Since (γ,Γ) is strictly hierarchical, $\alpha(G)=\emptyset$ for all $G\in\Gamma$, and, therefore, σ is given by: $\sigma(G)=\beta(G)$ for all $G\in\Gamma$. It is easy to see that

$$\text{PEP}(T)=\{(v_1,v_2,v_4),\ (v_1,v_2,v_5),\ (v_1,v_3,v_6)\},$$

yielding the utility levels

$$\text{PEU}(T)=\{(100,0),(0,0),(0,100)\}.$$

That is, each of the three possible payoff configurations is supported by some PE. In contrast, the unique OSSB σ for (γ,Γ) satisfies

$$\sigma(G(T))=\{(v_1,v_2,v_4)\};$$

that is, player 1 proposes that he raises the child and player 2 consents, leading to the unique payoff (100,0).[1]

The refinement of PEP obtained by the OSSB for the tree situation of Example 8.3.3 is rather appealing. The following three examples show that the refinement the OSSB yields (both in bounded and unbounded game trees) coincides with the one promoted (in the particular cases and without general theoretical foundations) by other scholars.

Example 8.3.4: McKelvey and Ordeshook (private communication) consider the problem of **"retrospective voting,"** in which candidates cannot commit themselves before the election to adopting particular policies. The following description exposes the basic problem. There is a single voter, player 1, who can vote for either candidate 2 or candidate 3. The candidate that player 1 elects becomes the incumbent, and must then choose a policy from the set $\{a,b\}$. After the incumbent chooses a policy, the voter must vote again for the candidate who will be the incumbent in the next period. The voter's preferences are a function only of the policy selected, and he receives a unit of utility every time a is chosen and 0 utility every time b is chosen. The candidates get utility only from being elected, obtaining one unit of utility whenever they are elected. This game proceeds a finite number of periods. (Figure 8.3.4 depicts the game tree if it is repeated twice.)

There are many subgame perfect equilibria in this game, because of the following feature of this model. The decision made by the voter affects the utility of the candidate, but not the utility of the voter (except indirectly, insofar as the candidate that is elected by the voter may later adopt a policy more or less favorable to the voter). Similarly, when the candidate adopts a policy, it affects the utility of the voter, but not the utility of the candidate (except insofar as it might affect future decisions by the voter about whom to vote for). It is for this reason that, as is easily verified, PEP(T) [or the solution assigned to $G(T)$ by the unique CSSB for the associated tree situation] coincides with $\Pi(T)$. That is, **every path in the game tree is supported by a subgame perfect equilibrium.**[2]

Clearly, the "plausible" equilibrium is where the voter "rewards" the candidate who chooses the policy a, and "punishes" the candidate who gives him the policy b, thereby inducing the candidate to select the preferred policy,

[1] It is interesting to note that the refinement obtained by the OSSB refines other refinements of PEP. Thus, both Selten's (1975) "trembling hand" and Kohlberg and Mertens' (1986) "stability" yield, for Example 8.3.3, the set of the two paths $\{(v_1,v_2,v_4),(v_1,v_2,v_5)\}$, which strictly includes $\sigma(G(T))$.

[2] It is interesting to note that in this game neither Selten's (1975) "trembling hand" nor Kohlberg and Mertens' (1986) "stability" refines subgame perfection.

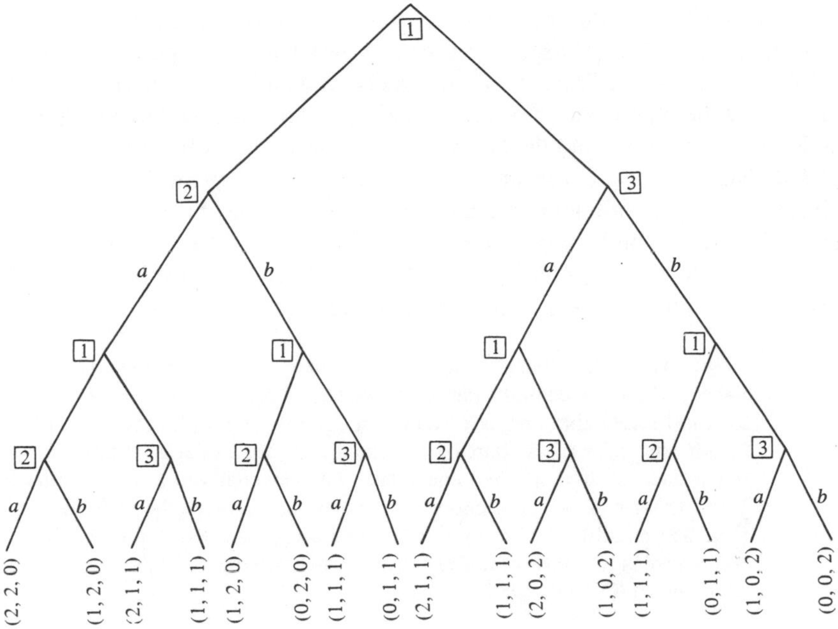

Figure 8.3.4

in anticipation of being reelected. These equilibria result in paths for which the voter always gets maximum utility, and the initial incumbent always gets reelected. Quite remarkably, these are precisely the paths assigned by the unique OSSB, σ, for the associated tree situation. More specifically, σ is given by: For positions $G(v) \in \Gamma \cap V_1(T)$ (that correspond to elections), $\sigma(G(v)) = \{(2,a,2,a,\ldots,2,a),(3,a,3,a,\ldots,3,a)\}$,[1] that is, $\sigma(G(v))$ consists of the two paths that yield the voter the maximum utility and in which the initial incumbent is always reelected. For positions $G(v) \in \Gamma \cap V_i(T)$ (that correspond to candidate i, $i \in \{2,3\}$, being elected), $\sigma(G(v)) = \{(a,i,a,i,a,\ldots,i,a),(b,i,a,i,a,\ldots,i,a)\}$, that is, $\sigma(G(v))$ consists of the two paths which, with perhaps the exception of the current period, yield the voter the maximum utility, and, again, the initial incumbent is always reelected. Winer (1989) shows that this characterization holds also for the infinite case. In particular, the tree situation associated with the (unbounded) game tree admits a unique OSSB.

The following is another example where the unique OSSB yields the promoted refinement of subgame perfect equilibrium.

[1] It is, at times, convenient to identify a path with the actions the players take along it.

Example 8.3.5: Consider the **dollar auction game with a budget constraint** (Shubik 1971; O'Neil 1986), where two players bid for an object which is worth s dollars, $\boldsymbol{s>1}$. Players bid alternately, and all bids are in integers. At each round the player who bids can either "give up," denoted by Θ, or else he has to (strictly) overbid the last offer. Each player has a budget constraint of b dollars, $\boldsymbol{b>s}$, which means that no player can bid more than b for the object. The important feature of this game is that the object is awarded to the higher bidder, but **both players pay** (to the auctioneer) their final bids.

The multiplicity of equilibria was O'Neil's main concern and he suggested resolving this problem by drawing on "risk-aversion."

> However, too many possible strategies would result from finding all sequential equilibria, so we find a particular sequential equilibrium that we think is the most reasonable one. We state a simple rule about players' choice behavior and regard it as part of the concept of sequential rationality for a dollar auction: If more than one branch has maximal value, it is assumed that a rational player will choose the move that involves the smallest bid, including possibly the bid of zero (that is, dropping out). A player will be risk-averse in the sense of not venturing money without some positive reason for doing so (O'Neil, 1986, p. 36).

Quite remarkably, as Proposition 8.3.6 asserts, the tree situation associated with the dollar auction game admits a unique OSSB which yields O'Neil's choice of "the most reasonable" perfect equilibrium!

In view of the particular structure of the dollar auction game, it is convenient to identify a vertex $v \in V(T)$ with the (unique) history of bids that leads from $v^*(T)$ to v. As we shall see, the last two bids play an important role. Let r and t be two integers such that $b \geq t > r \geq 0$. Denote by $\boldsymbol{\Gamma(r,t)}$ the set of positions $G(v) \in \Gamma$ where the last two bids [on the path of bids from $v^*(T)$ to v] were r and t (and, hence, the current bidder is the player who bid r). Let $\boldsymbol{\Gamma(0,0)}$ consist of the original position, and let $\boldsymbol{\Gamma(0,t)}$ consist of the position where player 1 bid t and it is player 2's turn to respond. Recall that Θ denotes the decline of a player to continue the bidding, in which case the object is awarded to the other player.

Proposition 8.3.6: *There exists a unique OSSB for the tree situation associated with the dollar auction game. This OSSB, σ, is given by: For a position corresponding to a terminal node, that is, for $G \in \Gamma(r,t)$ with $t \in \{b,\Theta\}$, σ assigns the payoffs attached to that node. For $G \in \Gamma(r,t)$, with $\boldsymbol{0 \leq t < b}$,*

$$
\begin{aligned}
\sigma(G) &\equiv \{(\varphi(t),\Theta)\} && \text{if } \varphi(t) < s+r, \\
&\equiv \{\Theta,(\varphi(t),\Theta)\} && \text{if } \varphi(t) = s+r, \\
&\equiv \{\Theta\} && \text{if } \varphi(t) > s+r,
\end{aligned}
$$

where[1] *for all* $t \leq b-1$,

$$\varphi(t) = t+1+[(b-t-1)mod(s-1)].$$

In particular, at the beginning of the game, player 1 has to bid $\varphi(0)=1+(b-1)\text{mod}(s-1)$ dollars, which is exactly the solution promoted by O'Neil (1986).

The third (sketch of an) example shows that the refinement offered by the OSSB is of interest also in unbounded game trees.

Example 8.3.7: Asheim (1987, 1988a) considered an intergenerational model where each generation inherits capital stocks from the previous generation and has to decide on its consumption and on the capital stocks it will leave for the next generation. The (subjective) utility function of a generation is additively separable in its consumption and the utility of the next generation. The overall (ethical) welfare function of a generation is equal to the lowest (subjective) utility level of the remaining generations.

This economy can be represented by an infinite game tree where the payoff to each generation is its welfare level. Since zero consumption by all generations is subgame perfect (and can, therefore, serve as a "punishment" for the deviating player), we have that for every subtree $\tilde{T}$, PEP($\tilde{T}$) = $\Pi(\tilde{T})$. Thus, the notion of subgame perfection has no predictive power in this model; it excludes no path in T. In contrast, Asheim shows that there exists a unique OSSB for the corresponding tree situation. This OSSB assigns the unique time-consistent optimal path to any position that corresponds to a subgame with strictly positive capital stocks. Thus, this OSSB implies that the present generation chooses the best path among those which later generations will carry out. It is precisely this refinement of PEP which, because of its optimality properties, is promoted in Asheim (1987, 1988a).

It might be interesting to note that by Claim 2.5.5, this unique OSSB is also a CSSB for the tree situation (but, by Theorem 8.2.1, it is not the unique CSSB).

As we saw in the previous chapters, Theorem 4.5 enables us to define an OSSB for the tree situation (associated with an arbitrary game tree) as an abstract stable set. Since each position $G(\tilde{T}) \in \Gamma$ is fully characterized by the set of paths $\Pi(\tilde{T})$, the abstract system associated with (γ,Γ) can be simplified to the abstract system $(D,\angle)$, defined as follows. The elements of D are all truncated paths. That is,

$$D \equiv \cup\{\Pi(\tilde{T}) \mid \tilde{T} \text{ is a subtree of the original game tree } T\}.$$

[1] Recall that $s>1$, and that for two positive integers p and q, $(p)\text{mod}(q)=m$, where m is the unique integer which satisfies $p=kq+m$, $0 \leq m < q$, for some integer k.

The dominance relation captures the inducement correspondence γ. Specifically, for $x,y \in D$,

$$x \angle y \Leftrightarrow \exists\, i \in N \text{ and } J \geq 1, \text{ such that } y_1 \text{ is adjacent from } x_J,\ x_J \in V_i(T), \text{ and } \mu^i(y) > \mu^i(x).$$

Observation 8.3.8: *The SB σ is an OSSB for the tree situation (γ,Γ) if and only if for all subtrees $\tilde{T}$ of T, $\sigma(G(\tilde{T})) = K \cap \Pi(\tilde{T})$, where K is an abstract stable set for the above abstract system $(D,\angle)$.*

Observation 8.3.8 offers a new interpretation to the negotiation process which leads to the OSSB. Assume that the path $x \in \Pi(T)$ is proposed. Player i can then deviate from x [once the vertex $x_J \in V_i(T) \cap \{x\}$ is reached] and bring the game to an adjacent node (y_1). Now, according to the above dominance relation $\angle$, once y_1 is reached player i proposes to all the players to follow a particular path y in the subtree $(T|y_1)$.

I close this section by establishing the existence of a unique ϵ-OSSB for generalized sequential bargaining games. The only restriction imposed is that the utility level a player derives from infinite paths (that is, from never reaching an agreement) is 0. [Recall that for all $i \in N$, $z \in \Delta$, and t, $u^i(z^i,t) \geq 0$.] That is, the following assumption holds.

B. For every player i and every agreement $z \in \Delta$, $u^i(z^i,t) \rightarrow 0$ as $t \rightarrow \infty$.

For this class of generalized sequential bargaining games we have the following result.

Theorem 8.3.9: *Let T be a generalized bargaining game that satisfies (B), and let (γ,Γ) be its associated tree situation. Then, for every $\epsilon > 0$, there exists a unique ϵ-OSSB for (γ,Γ).*

Observe that in the important special case where the utility functions are of the form $u^i(z^i,t) = (\delta^i)^{t-1} z^i$, with $\delta^i \in [0,1)$, all three assumptions, (A.1), (A.2), and (B), are satisfied. Let σ^ϵ, $\epsilon > 0$, denote the unique ϵ-OSSB for the tree situation associated with such a sequential bargaining game. Asheim (1989) proved that these σ^ϵs are nested, as a function of ϵ, and in the limit as $\epsilon \rightarrow 0$, $\sigma^\epsilon(G(T))$ contains only the stationary division $[(1-\delta)/(1-\delta^n), \delta(1-\delta)/(1-\delta^n), \ldots, \delta^{n-1}(1-\delta)/(1-\delta^n)]$. (See also Section 11.3.)

8.4 The coalitional tree situation

As repeatedly emphasized, the representation of a social environment as an extensive form game prohibits a group of individuals from coordinating their actions unless there are extremely rigid and explicit rules concerning exactly how such a group can form. Clearly, this is not the case with the theory of social situations. This observation will now be used to define the "coalitional tree situation," which yields a new solution concept that differs from both the Nash and the subgame perfect equilibria.

Let T be a game tree and let $S \subset N$. Denote $\mathbf{V_S(T)} \equiv \cup_{i \in S} V_i(T)$; that is, $V_S(T)$ consists of all the vertices in $V(T)$ which belong to $V_i(T)$, for some $i \in S$. Thus, for example, $V(T) = V_0(T) \cup V_N(T)$.

Definition 8.4.1: *Let T be a game tree, let* $v,w \in V(T)$, *and let* $S \subset N$. *Then* **v is S-adjacent to w,** *and* **w is S-adjacent from v,** *if there exists a sequence of vertices,* $(v_1,v_2,\ldots,v_H)$, *such that* $v_1 = v$, $v_H = w$, $\{v_1,v_2,\ldots,v_{H-1}\} \subset V_S(T)$, *and for all h,* $h = 1,2,\ldots,H-1$, v_h *is adjacent to* v_{h+1}.

That is, v is S-adjacent to w if w is reachable, in T, from v, and all the vertices that connect v and w, with the possible exception of w, belong to the decision set of vertices of some $i \in S$. The ***coalitional tree situation,*** (γ,Γ), is defined as follows. The collection of positions Γ coincides with that of the tree situation, that is, it consists of all positions that correspond to some subtree $\tilde{T}$. Thus,

$$\Gamma \equiv \{G(v) \mid v \in V(T)\} = \{G(\tilde{T}) \mid \tilde{T} \text{ is a subtree of } T\}.$$

The inducement correspondence allows every coalition, and not just single players, to deviate from a proposed path x. More specifically, when a vertex $v \in \{x\}$ is reached, members of S can induce any position $G(w)$ provided that v is S-adjacent to w. They do so by committing to follow the path $(v_1,v_2,\ldots,v_H)$ specified in Definition 8.4.1. It follows that, if the path $x \in \Pi(T)$ is proposed, members of S can induce all positions $G(w)$, where w is S-adjacent from a vertex v for some v that lies along x, that is, for $v \in \{x\} \cap V_S(T)$. The inducement correspondence in the coalitional tree situation is, therefore,

$$\gamma(S|G(\tilde{T}),x) = \{G(w) \mid \exists\ v \in \{x\} \cap V_S(T) \text{ such that } w \text{ is } S\text{-adjacent from } v\}.$$

Observe that the coalitional tree situation describes a social environment where the formation of coalition S implies that its members commit never to break away from it, and upon its formation its members decide on the course of action they agree to follow. [See (C.1) and (C.2) at the beginning of Chapter 6.]

Analogous to Claim 8.1.1, we have the following result.

Claim 8.4.2: *Let T be a bounded game tree and let* (γ,Γ) *be its associated coalitional tree situation. Then* (γ,Γ) *admits a unique OSSB and a unique CSSB.*

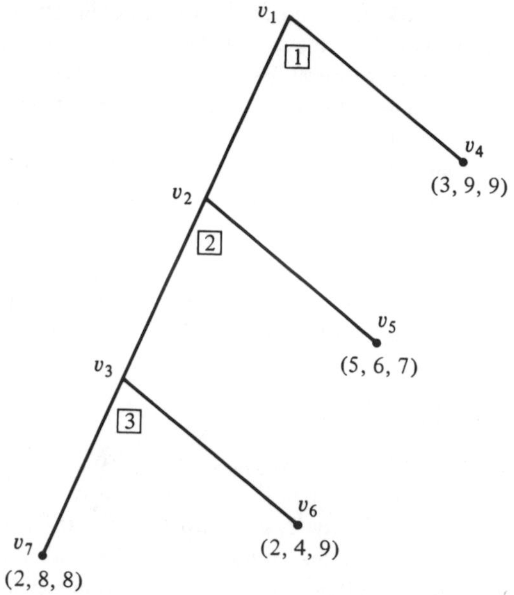

Figure 8.4.3

The following example illustrates two interesting distinctions between the tree situation and the coalitional tree situation. First, the analog of Theorem 8.1.4 need not hold: There exist finite game trees, T, such that the solution assigned to $G(T)$ by the unique OSSB (which happens to coincide with the unique CSSB) for the associated coalitional tree situation is the empty set. Second, it is possible, even in finite game trees, T, that the solution assigned to $G(T)$ by the unique OSSB, σ, for the associated coalitional tree situation is nonempty and yet no path in that solution is a perfect equilibrium path. That is, $\sigma(G(T)) \neq \emptyset$, but $\sigma(G(T)) \cap \mathrm{PEP}(T) = \emptyset$. This is reminiscent of the last society considered in the voting-by-veto model of Example 3.6, where the set of nonvetoed alternatives that results when coalitions are allowed to form is disjoint from the choice set when only single individuals are allowed to object to a proposed alternative.

Example 8.4.3: Consider the finite game tree depicted in Figure 8.4.3. It is easy to verify that the unique OSSB coincides with the unique CSSB for the associated coalitional tree situation. Denote this SB by σ. Then, σ is given by:

$$\boldsymbol{\sigma(G(T)) = \{(v_1, v_4)\},\ \sigma(G(v_2)) = \emptyset,\ \sigma(G(v_3)) = \{(v_3, v_6)\},}$$
$$\textbf{and, for } \boldsymbol{k = 4,5,6,7,\ \sigma(G(v_k)) = \{v_k\}.}$$

And, it is easily verified that:

$$\mathbf{PEP}(T)=\{(v_1,v_2,v_5)\}.$$

In particular, $\sigma(G(v_2))=\emptyset$, $\sigma(G(T))\neq\emptyset$, and $\sigma(G(T))\cap \mathrm{PEP}(T)=\emptyset$. [The reason that $(v_2,v_5)\notin\sigma(G(v_2))$ is that the coalition $\{2,3\}$ can induce, from $G(v_2)$, the position $G(v_7)$, where each of the two players gets a higher payoff than he gets in $\mu(v_2,v_5)$.]

Remark 8.4.4: Since the theory of social situations unifies the analysis of all three types of games (see Section 1.4 point VII), it is possible to transform the game tree to a game in normal form and investigate the solution concepts defined in the preceding chapter, in particular, those derived from the four open negotiation situations of Sections 7.4–7.7.

Proofs for Chapter 8

Proof of Claim 8.1.1: Note first that (γ,Γ) is strictly hierarchical. Indeed, let K be the length of the tree T. Define, inductively, the sets $\Gamma_1,\Gamma_2,\ldots,\Gamma_K$ as follows:

$$\Gamma_1\equiv\{G(T)\}, \text{ and } \Gamma_{k+1}\equiv\{G(\tilde{T}|v)|G(\tilde{T})\in\Gamma_k \text{ and } v \text{ is adjacent from } v^*(\tilde{T})\}.$$

That is, Γ_k consists of all the positions that correspond to subtrees whose roots are reachable by a path of length $k-1$ from the root $v^*(T)$ of the original game tree T. It is easily verified that, since T is bounded, this partition of Γ satisfies condition (H.1) of Definition 5.11. Moreover, no position can be induced from itself, by any coalition, no matter what outcome is being proposed. Thus, (γ,Γ) is strictly hierarchical. The validity of the claim follows, therefore, from Corollary 5.3.3 and Theorem 5.4.1. Q.E.D.

Proof of Claim 8.1.3: Let σ be an SB for the tree situation (γ,Γ) that is associated with the game tree T. Let $\tilde{T}=(T|v)$ be a subtree, let $x\in\sigma(G(\tilde{T}))$, and let y be the truncation of x from w. Then, by the definition of the inducement correspondence γ, $y\in\mathrm{ODOM}(\sigma,G(w))$ implies that $x\in\mathrm{ODOM}(\sigma,G(\tilde{T}))$, and $y\in\mathrm{CDOM}(\sigma,G(w))$ implies that $x\in\mathrm{CDOM}(\sigma,G(\tilde{T}))$. Therefore, if σ is an OSSB (respectively, CSSB) for (γ,Γ), then $x\in\sigma(G(\tilde{T}))$ implies $y\in\sigma(G(w))$.
Q.E.D.

Proof of Theorem 8.1.4: By Claim 8.1.1 and Theorem 5.4.4 it suffices to show that the unique OSSB is nonempty valued. The proof is by induction on the length of T. Let (γ,Γ) be the tree situation associated with the finite game tree T, and let σ be its unique OSSB. Clearly, for every subtree of length 0, that is, for every subtree, $\tilde{T}$, consisting of a single (terminal) node, v, we have $\sigma(G(\tilde{T}))=\{v\}\neq\emptyset$. The induction hypothesis is that for every subtree of length less than m, the solution assigned by σ to the corresponding position is nonempty.

Let $\tilde{T}$ be a finite subtree of length m, with $v^*(\tilde{T})\in V_i(\tilde{T})$ for some $i\in N$. Let $\boldsymbol{A(\tilde{T})}$ denote the set of vertices that are adjacent from $v^*(\tilde{T})$. By the induction hypothesis, if $w\in A(\tilde{T})$, then $\sigma(G(w))$ is nonempty. Moreover, $|V(T)|<\infty$ implies that $|A(\tilde{T})|<\infty$, and for all $w\in A(\tilde{T})$, $|\sigma(G(w))|<\infty$. Therefore, there exists $z^*\in \text{ArgMax}\{\mu^i(z)|z\in\sigma(G(w)), w\in A(\tilde{T})\}$. By construction, $(v^*(\tilde{T}),z^*)\notin$ ODOM$(\sigma,G(\tilde{T}))$. The (external) stability implies, therefore, that $(v^*(\tilde{T}),z^*)\in \sigma(G(\tilde{T}))$. Hence, $\sigma(G(\tilde{T}))\neq\emptyset$. Q.E.D.

Proof of Theorem 8.2.1: We make use of Theorem 8.2.6 (which is a restatement of this theorem using the terminology of classical game theory). Let T be a game tree, (γ,Γ) be its associated tree situation, and σ the PEP mapping as defined in the theorem. By Theorem 8.2.6, $x^*\in\sigma(G(\tilde{T}))$ if and only if for all $i\in N$, $G(\hat{T})\in\gamma(\{i\}|G(\tilde{T}),x^*)$ implies that there exists $y\in\sigma(G(\hat{T}))$ such that $\mu^i(y)\leq\mu^i(x^*)$. To conclude that σ is a CSSB for (γ,Γ) it suffices to show that σ is nonempty valued. It is for this reason that we assumed that PEP$(T)\neq\emptyset$, since then, for all subtrees $\tilde{T}$, $\sigma(G(\tilde{T}))$ is also nonempty. [Indeed, if $f\in$PE(T) then the restriction of f to a subtree $\tilde{T}$ belongs to PE$(\tilde{T})$.]

Q.E.D.

Proof of Theorem 8.2.2: Let T be a bounded game tree, and let (γ,Γ) be its associated tree situation. In view of Claim 8.1.1 and Theorem 8.2.1, it suffices to show that for all subtrees $\tilde{T}$ of T, PEP$(\tilde{T})\neq\emptyset$. Alternatively, since we assumed that $\sigma(G(\tilde{T}))\neq\emptyset$ for all $G(T)\in\Gamma$, it suffices to show that for all subtrees $\tilde{T}$ of T, PEP$(\tilde{T})\supset\sigma(G(\tilde{T}))$.

The proof of this last statement is by induction on the length of T. Clearly, if T is of length 0, that is, $V(T)=\{v\}$, the assertion holds. Assume the validity of the induction hypothesis for all game trees of length $m-1$, and let T be a bounded game tree of length m.

Denote by $A(T)$ the set of vertices adjacent from $v^*(T)$. Without loss of generality, $v^*(T)\in V_1(T)$. Consider $x^*=(x^*_1,x^*_2,x^*_3,\ldots)\in\sigma(G(T))$ (such x^* exists since we assumed that $\sigma(G(\tilde{T}))\neq\emptyset$ for all $G(\tilde{T})\in\Gamma$). Since σ is assumed to be nonempty-valued, the internal conservative stability of σ implies that for all $w\in A(T)$ there exists a path $x_w\in\sigma(G(w))$ such that $\mu^1(x^*)\geq\mu^1(x_w)$. By the induction hypothesis, $x_w\in$PEP$(T|w)$. That is, there exists an n-tuple of strategies $f_w\in$PE$(T|w)$ such that $\pi(f_w)=x_w$. By Claim 8.1.3, and the induction hypothesis, the truncation of x^* from x^*_2 is in $\sigma(G|x^*_2)$, and is supported by an n-tuple of strategies $f_2\in$PE$(T|x^*_2)$.

For the game tree T, define the n-tuple of strategies f as follows: $\mathbf{f^1(v^*(T))=x^*_2}$, **the restriction of f to $(T|x^*_2)$ is f_2, and the restriction of f to $(T|w)$ for**

$w \in A(T) \setminus \{x^*_2\}$ **is** f_w. Then, clearly, $\pi(f) = x^*$. Moreover, the fact that the restriction of f to any proper subtree is a perfect equilibrium in that subtree together with the choice of the strategy profiles f_w (that support the paths x_w) yield that $f \in \mathrm{PE}(T)$. Hence, $x^* \in \mathrm{PEP}(T)$, as we wished to show.

Proof of Corollary 8.2.3: The proof follows from Theorems 8.1.4 and 8.2.2. Q.E.D.

Proof of Theorem 8.2.6:

i. Assume that $x^* \in \mathrm{PEP}(T)$. Then, there exists a subgame perfect equilibrium, f^*, that supports x^* [that is, $f^* \in \mathrm{PE}(T)$ and $\pi(f^*) = x^*$]. By the definition of perfect equilibrium, for every subtree $\tilde{T}$, the restriction, $f^*(\tilde{T})$, of f^* to $\tilde{T}$ belongs to $\mathrm{PE}(\tilde{T})$. Therefore, the path $y \equiv \pi(f^*(\tilde{T}))$ belongs to $\mathrm{PEP}(\tilde{T})$. Moreover, since f^* is a PE in T, f^* is an NE in T, and hence y satisfies condition (C).

ii. Assume that $x^* \in \Pi(T)$ satisfies condition (C). For every $i \in N$ and each position $G(\tilde{T})$ that i can induce from $G(T)$ when x^* is proposed, let $f(\tilde{T})$ be an n-tuple of strategies in $\mathrm{PE}(\tilde{T})$ that supports the path $y \in \mathrm{PEP}(\tilde{T})$ such that $\mu^i(y) \leq \mu^i(x^*)$. Define the n-tuple of strategies, f, in T as follows: Along x^* follow x^*. Otherwise, for every position $G(\tilde{T})$ that belongs to $\gamma(\{i\}|G(T), x^*)$, the restriction of f to $\tilde{T}$ coincides with $f(\tilde{T})$.

It is easy to see that for every vertex $v \in V(T) \setminus \{x^*\}$ there exists a (unique) player, $k \in N$, that can induce the position $G(\tilde{T})$ from $G(T)$ when x^* is proposed such that $v \in V(\tilde{T})$. Therefore, f is, indeed, an n-tuple of strategies for T. And, clearly, $\pi(f) = x^*$. Therefore, to conclude the proof of the theorem it suffices to show that $f \in \mathrm{PE}(T)$.

Assume, in negation, that $f \notin \mathrm{PE}(T)$, that is, there exists a subtree $\tilde{T}$ for which the restriction of f to $\tilde{T}$ is not a Nash equilibrium. Since the restriction of a perfect equilibrium is a perfect equilibrium in the restricted game tree, the construction of f yields that the restriction of f to any subtree whose root does not lie on x^* is a PE in that subgame. Therefore, since the restriction of f to $\tilde{T}$ is not a Nash equilibrium in $\tilde{T}$ it follows that $v^*(\tilde{T}) \in \{x^*\}$ and that the only player who finds it beneficial to deviate from the restriction of f to $\tilde{T}$ is player k, where $v^*(\tilde{T}) \in V_k(T)$. Since the restriction to any strict subtree of $\tilde{T}$ is a PE in that subgame, player k will find it beneficial to deviate from the restriction of f to $\tilde{T}$ only once. Thus, player k benefits from inducing a position $G(w)$, where w is adjacent from $v^*(\tilde{T})$. That is, $\mu^k(y^*) > \mu^k(x^*)$, where $y^* = \pi(f(T|w))$. But by the choice of $f(T|w)$, $\mu^k(y^*) \leq \mu^k(x^*)$, which is a contradiction. Hence, $f \in \mathrm{PE}(T)$.

Q.E.D.

Proof of Theorem 8.2.7: Let $a,b \in \text{PEU}(T)$, and let $c \equiv \lambda a + (1-\lambda)b$ for some $\lambda \in [0,1]$. We need to show that $c \in \text{PEU}(T)$.

By Lemma 2 below, the paths $x \equiv (a,Y,Y,\ldots,Y)$ and $y \equiv (b,Y,Y,\ldots,Y)$ belong to PEP(T). We shall show that the path $z \equiv (c,Y,Y,\ldots,Y) \in \text{PEP}(T)$. By Theorem 8.2.6 it suffices to show that if i can induce $G(\tilde{T})$ from $G(T)$ when z is proposed, then there exists a payoff $d \in \text{PEU}(\tilde{T})$ such that $d_i \leq \mu^i(z)$.

Let $i \in N$. Without loss of generality, assume that $a_i \leq b_i$, implying that $a_i \leq c_i$, that is, $\mu^i(x) \leq \mu^i(z)$. By (A.2), $c \in \Delta$. Hence, by Lemma 1 below, if $G(\tilde{T}) \in \gamma(\{i\}|G(T),z)$ and $v^*(\tilde{T}) \notin \{z\}$, then there exists $G(\hat{T}) \in \gamma(\{i\}|G(T),x)$, with $\text{PEU}(\hat{T}) = \text{PEU}(\tilde{T})$. Since $x \in \text{PEP}(T)$, by Theorem 8.2.6, we have that there exists a payoff $d \in \text{PEU}(\hat{T}) = \text{PEU}(\tilde{T})$, $d_i \leq \mu^i(x)$. As $\mu^i(x) \leq \mu^i(z)$, we conclude that there exists $d \in \text{PEU}(\tilde{T})$, with $d_i \leq \mu^i(z)$, as we wished to show.

Q.E.D.

Lemma 1: *Let T be a generalized bargaining game, $x \in \Pi(T)$, and $a \in \Delta$. Denote $y \equiv (a,Y,Y,\ldots,Y)$. Then, for every $i \in N$, $G(\tilde{T}) \in \gamma(\{i\}|G(T),y)$ with $v^*(\tilde{T}) \notin \{y\}$ implies there exists a position $G(\hat{T})$ that i can induce from G(T) when x is proposed such that $PEU(\hat{T}) = PEU(\tilde{T})$.*

Proof of Lemma 1: Since $a \in \Delta$, $y \equiv (a,Y,Y,\ldots,Y) \in \Pi(T)$. The particular structure of the generalized bargaining game is such that all subtrees whose roots are reached after t periods have the same PEU. The validity of the claim follows, therefore, from the fact that the length of every path in $\Pi(T)$, in particular, of x, is at least that of y. Q.E.D.

Lemma 2: *Let T be a generalized bargaining game that satisfies (A.1) and (A.2), $x \in PEP(T)$, and $\mu(x) \equiv a \in \mathbb{R}^n$. Then, the path $y \equiv (a,Y,Y,\ldots,Y)$ belongs to PEP(T).*

Proof of Lemma 2: By Theorem 8.2.6 we need to show that for any position $G(\tilde{T}) \in \gamma(\{i\}|G(T),y)$ there exists a payoff $b \in \text{PEU}(\tilde{T})$ such that $b_i \leq \mu^i(y)$.

By (A.1) and (A.2), $a \in \Delta$. By Lemma 1, therefore, if $G(\tilde{T}) \in \gamma(\{i\}|G(T),y)$ with $v^*(\tilde{T}) \notin \{y\}$, then there exists $G(\hat{T}) \in \gamma(\{i\}|G(T),x)$ with $\text{PEU}(\hat{T}) = \text{PEU}(\tilde{T})$. Applying Theorem 8.2.6 again, we have that since $x \in \text{PEP}(T)$ there exists a payoff $b \in \text{PEU}(\hat{T})$ such that $b_i \leq \mu^i(x)$. Thus, by (A.1), there exists a payoff $b \in \text{PEU}(\tilde{T})$ such that $b_i \leq \mu^i(y) = \mu^i(x)$. Q.E.D.

Proof of Theorem 8.3.1: Let $x^* \in \sigma(G(T))$. We need to show that there exists a PE, f^*, that supports the path x^*. We shall construct such an n-tuple of strategies. To this end, we shall first choose, inductively, a sequence of disjoint paths, which partitions the (possibly infinite) set of vertices of T, in the sense that each vertex $v \in V(T)$ belongs to one and only one of these paths.

Define, as in the proof of Claim 8.1.1, the sets $\Gamma_1, \Gamma_2, \ldots, \Gamma_k, \ldots$ by

$$\Gamma_1 \equiv \{G(T)\}$$

and

$$\Gamma_{k+1} \equiv \{G(\tilde{T}|v) \mid G(\tilde{T}) \in \Gamma_k \text{ and } v \text{ is adjacent from } v^*(\tilde{T})\}.$$

That is, Γ_k consists of all the positions that correspond to subtrees whose roots are reachable by a path of length $k-1$ from the root, $v^*(T)$, of the original game tree, T. Denote

$$\begin{aligned} &\boldsymbol{\nabla_1 \equiv \{G(T)\}}, \\ &\boldsymbol{x(G(T)) \equiv x^*}, \\ &\boldsymbol{\Lambda_1 \equiv \{v \in V(T) \mid v \in \{x(G(T))\}\}}. \end{aligned}$$

That is, Λ_1 is the set of all vertices of T that lie along the given path x^*. Recall that $x(G(T)) \in \sigma(G(T))$. Assume now that the sets Λ_j and ∇_j were defined for all j, $j=1,2,\ldots,J$, and that for each $G \in \cup_{j=1}^{J} \nabla_j$, the path $\boldsymbol{x(G) \in \sigma(G)}$ is also defined. Let

$$\boldsymbol{\nabla_{J+1} \equiv \{G(v) \in \Gamma_{J+1} \mid v \notin \Lambda_J\}}.$$

Thus, ∇_{J+1} contains all positions that are associated with subtrees, $\tilde{T}$, such that the length of the (unique) path that connects its root, $v^*(\tilde{T})$, with $v^*(T)$ is of length J, and, moreover, $v^*(\tilde{T})$ does not belong to any of the paths $x(G)$, $G \in \cup_{j=1}^{J} \nabla_j$. For each $G \in \nabla_{J+1}$, choose a path

$$\boldsymbol{x(G) \in \sigma(G)}.$$

Recall that by our assumption, $\sigma(G) \neq \emptyset$ for all $G \in \Gamma$, and hence $x(G)$ exists. Define

$$\boldsymbol{\Lambda_{J+1} \equiv \{v \in V(T) \mid v \in \{x(G)\}, \quad G \in \bigcup_{j=1}^{J+1} \nabla_j\}}.$$

Thus, a vertex $v \in V(T)$ belongs to Λ_{J+1} if it belongs to one of the paths $x(G)$, $G \in \cup_{j=1}^{J+1} \nabla_j$. Continuing in this manner we get the collection of paths,

$$\boldsymbol{\Pi \equiv \{x(G) \mid G \in \nabla_j \quad \text{for some } j, \quad j=1,2,\ldots\}}.$$

Clearly, each vertex $v \in V(T)$ belongs to one and only one path in $\boldsymbol{\Pi}$.

Using the set Π we shall now define the n-tuple of strategies f^* that supports the path $x^* \in \sigma(G(T))$ and which will be shown to belong to PE(T).

For $i \in N$ define the strategy for player i, f^{*i}, as follows: For $v \in V_i(T)$, $\boldsymbol{f^{*i}(v) \equiv w}$, where w is the vertex that is adjacent from v along the unique path in $\boldsymbol{\Pi}$ that passes through v. For every node $v \in V(T)$, denote by $z^*(v)$ the path defined by restricting the strategy profile f^* to the subtree $(T|v)$. Since $x^* \in \Pi$, we have that $x^* = z^*(v^*(T))$, that is, $\boldsymbol{f^*}$ **supports** $\boldsymbol{x^*}$.

Next, observe that for any $v \in V(T)$, $z^*(v) \in \sigma(G(v))$. Indeed, if $G(v) \in \nabla_j$ for some j, then, by the definition of f^*, $z^*(v) = x(G(v))$, and by construction, $x(G(v)) \in \sigma(G(v))$. Thus, for this case, $z^*(v)$ belongs to $\sigma(G(v))$. If, on the other hand, for all j, $G(v) \notin \nabla_j$, then $v \in \{x(G(w))\}$ for some vertex $w \in V(T)$ that precedes v. By construction, $x(G(w)) \in \sigma(G(w))$, and hence, by Claim 8.1.3, its truncation from v, that is, $z^*(v)$, belongs to $\sigma(G(v))$.

Assume, in negation, that f^* is not a PE in T. That is, there exists a subtree $\tilde{T}$ such that the restriction of f^* to $\tilde{T}$ is not a Nash equilibrium in $\tilde{T}$. Thus, there exist $i \in N$ and a strategy for player i, g^i, such that the path $y^* = (y^*_1, y^*_2, \ldots)$ resulting from player i choosing the strategy g^i, when the other $n-1$ players all follow f^*, yields player i a higher payoff. That is, $\boldsymbol{y^* = \pi(g^i, f^{*N \setminus \{i\}})}$ and $\boldsymbol{\mu^i(y^*) > \mu^i(z^*(y^*_1))}$. To conclude the proof of the theorem it suffices to show that for every y^*_j which is not a terminal node we have that $\mu^i(z^*(y^*_j)) \geq \mu^i(z^*(y^*_{j+1}))$, since then, the continuity of μ^i implies that $\mu^i(z^*(y^*_1)) \geq \mu^i(y^*)$. This is a contradiction. Hence, f^* is a perfect equilibrium.

Let $y^*_j \notin [V_i(T) \cup V_0(T)]$. Since every player $k \in N \setminus \{i\}$ follows the strategy f^{*k}, we have that $z^*(y^*_j) = (y^*_j, z^*(y^*_{j+1}))$, implying $\mu^i(z^*(y^*_j)) = \mu^i(z^*(y^*_{j+1}))$. Assume, next, that $y^*_j \in V_i(T)$. Since $z^*(y^*_j) \in \sigma(G(y^*_j))$ and $z^*(y^*_{j+1}) \in \sigma(G(y^*_{j+1}))$, the fact that $G(y^*_{j+1}) \in \gamma(\{i\} | G(y^*_j), z^*(y^*_j))$ together with the optimistic (internal) stability of σ imply that $\mu^i(z^*(y^*_j)) \geq \mu^i(z^*(y^*_{j+1}))$. Thus, for all j, $j = 1, 2, \ldots$, $\mu^i(z^*(y^*_j)) \geq \mu^i(z^*(y^*_{j+1}))$. Q.E.D.

Proof of Corollary 8.3.2: This proof follows immediately from Theorems 8.1.4 and 8.3.1 (or, alternatively, Corollary 8.2.3). Q.E.D.

Proof of Proposition 8.3.6: Since the game tree that represents the dollar auction game is finite, Theorem 8.1.4 yields that the associated tree situation admits a unique OSSB. It is left to be verified that this OSSB is given by the SB σ described in the theorem.

By definition, for all t, $0 \leq t < b$, $\varphi(t) = t + 1 + [(b - t - 1) - k(s - 1)] = b - k(s - 1)$, where k is the unique integer such that $\varphi(t)$ satisfies:

1. $\varphi(t) < t + s$ and $\varphi(t) > t$.

Therefore, for all t, $0 \leq t < b$,

2. $\varphi(\varphi(t)) \geq t + s$.
3. $\varphi(q) = \varphi(t)$ for all q, $t < q < \varphi(t)$.

To conclude the proof of the theorem, we use induction on the hierarchy of the position. For $G \in \Gamma_K$, that is, for a position corresponding to a terminal node, σ coincides with $\beta(G)$ of Theorem 5.2.1. Assume validity for all positions in Γ^{k+1}, and let $G \in \Gamma_k$, $G \in \Gamma(r,t)$. Call i the player who has to bid. By (2) and the definition of σ, $\{\Theta\} \in \sigma(H)$ for $H \in \Gamma(t,\varphi(t))$. Therefore, player i will never bid more than $\varphi(t)$. By (3), he will never bid less than $\varphi(t)$. So, the question reduces to whether to bid at all. But the only case in which he will choose not to bid is when bidding $\varphi(t)$ benefits him by no more than s dollars. Indeed, $\sigma(G) = \{\Theta\}$ if $(\varphi(t) - r) < s$, and $\Theta \in \sigma(G)$ if $(\varphi(t) - r) = s$. Q.E.D.

Proof of Observation 8.3.8: The proof follows immediately from Theorem 4.5 and the definition of the tree situation. Q.E.D.

Proof of Theorem 8.3.9: Condition (B) implies that the dominance relation $\angle^\epsilon$ in the abstract system $(D, \angle^\epsilon)$ that corresponds to (γ, Γ) is strictly acyclic. Theorems 4.11 and 4.7 yield that (γ, Γ) admits a unique ϵ-OSSB for every $\epsilon > 0$. Q.E.D.

Proof of Claim 8.4.2: See Proof of Claim 8.1.1. Q.E.D.

CHAPTER 9

Infinitely repeated games

In this chapter, which is closely related to Greenberg (1989b), the theory of social situations is applied to infinitely repeated games. Representing a repeated game as a situation simplifies the analysis: It employs the notion of path, rather than the much more complex concept of strategy. In addition, the CSSB for the repeated game Nash situation fully characterizes the set of perfect equilibrium paths. This result is remarkable since the motivation behind the notion of CSSB is totally different from the one which underlies the notion of subgame perfection. Furthermore, the application of the theory of social situations to repeated games enables the analysis of coalition formation, that is, when players may correlate their actions.

A novel aspect introduced in this chapter is that, depending on the particular application that is under consideration, we may wish to impose some (natural) restrictions on the standard of behavior. In this case, in view of the inherent feature of an infinitely repeated game, namely, that after any "history of actions" the game continues to be repeated infinitely many times, we shall require that the SB be "nondiscriminating" (Definition 9.2.1).

The repeated game is obtained by repeating a normal form game, called "the one shot game," infinitely many times, and evaluating the payoffs in terms of their present values. It is assumed that at each period t, $t=2,3,4,\ldots$, each player knows the previous actions of all players.

Let $(N,\{Z^i\}_{i\in N},\{u^i\}_{i\in N})$ denote the ***one shot*** (normal form) ***game***. Let X denote the set of all sequences of all possible actions by the players, that is,

$$X \equiv \{x=(x_1,x_2,x_3,\ldots) \mid x_t \in Z^N \text{ for } t=1,2,3,\ldots\}.$$

Each player $i\in N$ has a utility function U^i, $U^i: X \to \mathbb{R}$, which represents the discounted value of the stream of payoffs in the one shot game. Specifically, player i's discount factor is δ^i, $\delta^i \in (0,1)$, and his overall utility level from $x\in X$ is

$$U^i(x) \equiv \sum_{t=1}^{\infty} (\delta^i)^t u^i(x_t).$$

9.1 The repeated game Nash situation

It is the inherent characteristic of a repeated game that it will continue in the next period to be a repeated game after the present payoffs are paid. Therefore, an individual i can choose at any period τ any action (strategy in the one shot game) $\zeta^i_\tau \in Z^i$, thereby generating a new repeated game which is identical to the original one, except that it starts at period $\tau+1$ (after i's choice of ζ^i_τ was detected) and the utility functions are those derived from the original utility functions by incorporating the payoffs up to, and including, period τ. This description is captured by the ***repeated game Nash situation,*** (γ,Γ), which is defined as follows.

Observe that in any "subgame," that is, a repeated game that starts at some period, $\tau+1$, reached after the finite sequence of actions $(x_1,x_2,\ldots,x_\tau)$, $x_t \in Z^N$, $t=1,2,\ldots,\tau$, the utility function of player i, defined over X, is of the form $\boldsymbol{a+bU^i}$, where a is the total amount of the discounted utility received up to period τ and b is obtained from the discount factor. Specifically,

$$a = \sum_{t=1}^{\tau} (\delta^i)^t u^i(x_t) \quad \text{and} \quad b = (\delta^i)^\tau.$$

Moreover, the nature of a repeated game is such that the set of players remains N after every history, and the set of all potentially possible outcomes by the n players remains X.

It therefore seems natural to let the collection Γ of positions in the repeated game Nash situation be the set

$$\Gamma \equiv \{G \mid N(G) \equiv N;\ X(G) \equiv X;\ u^i(G) \equiv a + bU^i,\ 0 < b \leq 1,\ i \in N\}.$$

That is, the set of players in all positions in Γ is the original set of players, N; the set of outcomes is the set of all sequences of actions that they can take; and the utility level a player derives from following, in position $G \in \Gamma$, the sequence $x \in X$, is a positive linear transformation of his discounted value of the stream of payoffs from the path x.

I now turn to the definition of the inducement correspondence γ. Suppose that it is proposed to the players to follow, in position G, the sequence of actions $x \in X$. Player i can decide to deviate from x at some period τ, that is, to choose an action $\zeta^i_\tau \in Z^i$ which might differ from x^i_τ – the one that was proposed for him to take at period τ. In this case, player i induces the repeated game that starts at period $\tau+1$, after the players have received the τ payoffs resulting from their actions up to and including period τ. The following notation is, therefore, useful for the definition of γ. For a positive integer τ, $G \in \Gamma$, $x \in X$, $i \in N$, and $\zeta^i_\tau \in Z^i$, denote by $\boldsymbol{H = (G|x;\zeta^i_\tau)}$ the position reached if x is followed from G for the first $\tau-1$ periods, and at period τ player i chooses $\zeta^i_\tau \in Z^i$ while all other players follow x_τ. Formally, $H = (G|x;\zeta^i_\tau)$ is given by

$$N(H) = N,\ X(H) = X,\ u^k(H)(y) \equiv u^k(G)(x_1,x_2,\ldots,x_{\tau-1},\zeta_\tau,y),$$

where $\zeta_\tau \in Z^N$, **with** $\zeta^j_\tau = x^j_\tau$ **for all** $j \neq i$.

That is, $u^k(H)(y)$ is the utility level player $k \in N$ derives from following in position $G \in \Gamma$ the sequence of actions: In the first $\tau-1$ periods the players take the actions $(x_1,x_2,\ldots,x_{\tau-1})$, $x_t \in Z^N$, $t=1,2,\ldots,\tau-1$, at period τ they choose the actions $\zeta_\tau \in Z^N$, and thereafter they follow the sequence $y \in X$.

Following Nash, assume that coalitions are not allowed to form. Then, in view of the above discussion, it is natural to associate the following inducement correspondence with the repeated game. For every $G \in \Gamma$, $i \in N$, and $x \in X$,

$$\boldsymbol{\gamma(\{i\}|G,x) = \{(G|x;\zeta^i_\tau) | \tau \in \{1,2,\ldots,\} \text{ and } \zeta^i_\tau \in Z^i\},}$$
$$\boldsymbol{\gamma(S|G,x) = \emptyset \quad \text{if } |S| > 1.}$$

I close this section with a technical remark that will prove useful. Recall that, by Definition 7.0.1, for all $i \in N$, Z^i is a nonempty compact metric space and $u^i: Z^N \rightarrow \mathbb{R}$ is a continuous function. Therefore, by endowing X with the product topology, we have, by Tychonoff's Theorem, that X is a compact metric space. Moreover, for all $i \in N$, $U^i: X \rightarrow \mathbb{R}$ is continuous, implying that for all $G \in \Gamma$, $u^i(G)$ is a continuous function over $X(G)$.

9.2 Nondiscrimination

Notice that all positions in Γ have identical sets of players and identical sets of outcomes, and, moreover, the preferences (though not the utility functions) of every player over the set X are also independent of the particular position. Therefore, and in view of the inducement correspondence, it seems reasonable to require that an SB assign the same solution to all positions in Γ. Such an SB will be called nondiscriminating (among positions).

Definition 9.2.1. *Let (γ,Γ) be the repeated game Nash situation. A standard of behavior, σ, is **nondiscriminating** if for all $G,H \in \Gamma$, $\sigma(H) = \sigma(G)$.*

Let G^0 be the position associated with the original repeated game, that is, for all $i \in N$, $u^i(G^0) \equiv U^i$ [and, of course, $N(G^0) = N$ and $X(G^0) = X$]. A useful advantage of a nondiscriminating SB σ is that it is sufficient to investigate the solution $\sigma(G^0)$.

Because of Theorem 9.3.4, we shall devote most of this chapter to the analysis of nondiscriminating CSSBs for the repeated game Nash situation (γ,Γ). Observe that if σ is a nondiscriminating CSSB for (γ,Γ) then, by Claim 2.5.1, $\sigma(G) \neq \emptyset$ for all $G \in \Gamma$. Therefore, by the definition of γ, in this case we can write CDOM as

$$\boldsymbol{\text{CDOM}(\sigma,G) = \{x \in X | \exists\ i \in N,\ \tau \geq 1, \text{ and } \zeta_\tau \in Z^N \text{ with } \zeta^k_\tau = x^k_\tau \text{ for all } k \in N,\ k \neq i, \text{ such that } U^i(x_\tau,x_{\tau+1},\ldots) < U^i(\zeta_\tau,y) \text{ for all } y \in \sigma(G)\}.}$$

Claim 9.2.2: *Let σ be a nondiscriminating conservative internally stable SB for the repeated game Nash situation (γ,Γ). Let $\tilde{\sigma}(G)$ be the closure of $\sigma(G)$.*

Then, the SB $\tilde{\sigma}$ is also a nondiscriminating conservative internally stable SB for (γ,Γ). If, in addition, $\sigma(G^0)$ is not empty, then $\tilde{\sigma}$ satisfies:

Condition 9.2.3: *For all $i\in N$, the set Arg Min$\{U^i(x)|x\in\tilde{\sigma}(G^0)\}$ is nonempty.*

That is, an SB σ satisfies Condition 9.2.3 if and only if for each $i\in N$ and every $G\in\Gamma$, there is a worst path for player i, in $\sigma(G^0)$, among all paths in that set.

Let σ^c be a nondiscriminating CSSB for the repeated game Nash situation (γ,Γ) which satisfies Condition 9.2.3. Since for all $G\in\Gamma$ and all $i\in N$, $u^i(G)$ is a positive linear transformation of U^i, we have that for all $G\in\Gamma$ and for all $i\in N$, Arg Min$\{U^i(x)|x\in\sigma^c(G^0)\}=$ Arg Min$\{u^i(G)(x)|x\in\sigma^c(G)\}$. That is, the set of worst paths for player i is independent of the particular position $G\in\Gamma$. Let $z(i|\sigma^c)$ be one such worst path, that is, for a nondiscriminating SB σ^c that satisfies Condition 9.2.3,

$$z(i|\sigma^c) \in \text{Arg Min}\{U^i(x)|x\in\sigma^c(G^0)\}.$$

As the next proposition asserts, these paths, $z(i|\sigma^c)$, $i\in N$, essentially characterize CDOM(σ^c,G^0), and, hence, characterize the SB σ^c if it is a CSSB. First, we need the following notation. Let $x,y\in X$, τ be a positive integer, $i\in N$, and $\zeta^i_\tau\in Z^i$. Denote the path

$$(x;\zeta^i_\tau;y)\equiv(x_1,x_2,\ldots,x_{\tau-1},\zeta_\tau,y_1,y_2,\ldots),$$

where $\zeta^k_\tau=x^k_\tau$ **for all** $k\in N$, $k\neq i$. That is, the path $(x;\zeta^i_\tau;y)$ describes the following sequence of actions: In the first $\tau-1$ periods, all players take the actions $(x_1,x_2,\ldots,x_{\tau-1})$, $x_t\in Z^N$, $t=1,2,\ldots,\tau-1$, at time $t=\tau$ each player k other than i chooses the action x^k_τ and player i chooses the action $\zeta^i_\tau\in Z^i$, and from period $\tau+1$ on, all players follow the sequence $y\in X$.

Proposition 9.2.4: *Let σ^c be a nondiscriminating SB for the repeated game Nash situation (γ,Γ) which satisfies Condition 9.2.3, and let $x\in X$. Then,*

$$x\notin CDOM(\sigma^c,G^0)$$

if, and only if, for all $i\in N$, all τ, $\tau=1,2,\ldots$, and all $\zeta^i_\tau\in Z^i$,

$$** \quad U^i(x)\geq U^i(x;\zeta^i_\tau;z(i|\sigma^c)).$$

9.3 PEP is the maximal nondiscriminating CSSB

In this section we shall relate the nondiscriminating CSSBs for the repeated game Nash situation to game-theoretic equilibrium notions. First, recall the following definitions.

A ***strategy*** of player $i \in N$ in the repeated game is a sequence of functions $\boldsymbol{f^i(t)}$, $t=1,2,\ldots$. The function for period t determines player i's action at t a a function of the actions of all players in all previous periods. Formally, for all $i \in N$, $f^i(1) \in Z^i$, and for $t=2,3,\ldots$, $f^i(t)$: $Z^{N(t-1)} \rightarrow Z^i$, where $Z^{N(t-1)}$ denotes the Cartesian product of Z^N, $(t-1)$ times. Let Ω denote the set of all n-tuples of strategies, $f=(f^1,\ldots,f^n)$. Every $f \in \Omega$ generates a path $\boldsymbol{\pi(f)} \in X$, where $\pi(f)_1=f(1)$ and $\pi(f)_t=f(t)(\pi(f)_1,\ldots,\pi(f)_{t-1})$. That is, $\pi(f)$ is the sequence of actions that will actually occur if players follow the strategy profile $f \in \Omega$. With a slight abuse of notation, define for $i \in N$ and $f \in \Omega$, $\boldsymbol{U^i(f) \equiv U^i(\pi(f))}$.

As was the case with normal and extensive form games, the n-tuple of strategies $f \in \Omega$ is a ***Nash Equilibrium (NE)*** (for the repeated game) if for all $i \in N$, $U^i(\pi(f)) \geq U^i(\pi(g))$ for all $g \in \Omega$ with $g^k=f^k$, for all $k \in N$, $k \neq i$.

For any positive integer J, a ***J*-history,** denoted $\boldsymbol{H(J)}$, is an ordered list of J actions (of the n players), that is, $H(J)=(x_1,\ldots,x_J) \in Z^{NJ}$. For $f \in \Omega$ and a J-history $H(J)=(x_1,\ldots,x_J)$, denote by $f|_{H(J)}$ the n-tuple of strategies $g \in \Omega$, where for all $i \in N$ and all t, $t=1,2,3,\ldots$,

$$\boldsymbol{g^i(t)(y_1,\ldots,y_{t-1})=f^i(t+J)(x_1,\ldots,x_J,y_1,\ldots,y_{t-1})}.$$

Analogous to extensive form games, the n-tuple of strategies $f \in \Omega$ is a (subgame) ***Perfect Equilibrium (PE)*** if f is an NE, and for all J, $J=1,2,\ldots$, and all histories $H(J) \in Z^{NJ}$, $f|_{H(J)}$ is an NE.

Denote the sets of ***Nash equilibrium paths*** and ***perfect equilibrium paths*** by NEP and PEP, respectively, that is,

$$\textbf{NEP}=\{\boldsymbol{\pi(f)} \mid \boldsymbol{f} \textbf{ is an NE}\}\ ;\ \textbf{PEP}=\{\boldsymbol{\pi(f)} \mid \boldsymbol{f} \textbf{ is a PE}\}.$$

Let the SB, which assigns to each position G in Γ the NEP (respectively, PEP) in the repeated game with which G is associated, be denoted by $\boldsymbol{\sigma}^N$ (respectively, $\boldsymbol{\sigma^P}$).

Claim 9.3.1: *Both σ^N and σ^P are nondiscriminating SBs for the repeated game Nash situation (γ,Γ).*

Claim 9.3.2: *If the set of perfect equilibria is not empty, then the nondiscriminating SB σ^P satisfies Condition 9.2.3.*

Henceforth, I shall assume that the set of perfect equilibria is nonempty. Observe that a sufficient condition for this assumption to hold is that the one shot game has a Nash equilibrium $z^* \in Z^N$, since then the n-tuple of (stationary) strategies $f \in \Omega$ is a perfect equilibrium in the repeated game, where for all $i \in N$, and any J-history $H(J)$, $f^i(J+1)(H(J)) \equiv z^{*i}$.

The following characterization (using our notation) of PEP in repeated games with discounting, which is due to Abreu (1988), turns out to be very useful for establishing that the SB σ^P is the unique maximal nondiscriminating CSSB for (γ,Γ).

Theorem 9.3.3: *The path $x^0 \in X$ belongs to PEP if and only if there exist n paths, $x^i \in X$, $i \in N$, such that for all $i \in N$, all k, $k=0,1,2,\ldots,n$, all τ, $\tau=1,2,\ldots$, and all $\zeta^i_\tau \in Z^i$,*

$$U^i(x^k;\zeta^i_\tau;x^i) \leq U^i(x^k).$$

The following is the main result of this section.

Theorem 9.3.4: *σ^P is the unique maximal (with respect to set inclusion) nondiscriminating CSSB for the repeated game Nash situation (γ,Γ). That is, σ^P is a nondiscriminating CSSB, and if σ is a nondiscriminating CSSB for (γ,Γ), then for all $G \in \Gamma$, $\sigma(G) \subset \sigma^P(G)$.*

The following example establishes that the notion of nondiscriminating CSSB for the repeated game Nash situation might serve as a refinement of the notion of perfect equilibrium. That is, there might exist a nondiscriminating CSSB σ for (γ,Γ) that satisfies: $\sigma(G^0) \subset \sigma^P(G^0)$ but $\sigma(G^0) \neq \sigma^P(G^0)$.

Example 9.3.5: The one shot game is given by the payoff matrix

	L	*R*
U	(1,1)	(20,20)
D	(0,0)	(1,1)

That is, player 1's set of actions in the one shot game is $Z^1 \equiv \{U,D\}$ and player 2's is $Z^2 \equiv \{L,R\}$. Let $f^* \in \Omega$ denote the nondiscriminating (stationary) strategy defined by

$$f^*(t) \equiv (U,R) \text{ for all } t=1,2,\ldots .$$

That is, regardless of the history, player 1 always chooses U and player 2 always chooses R. Define the nondiscriminating SB σ^* where, for all $G \in \Gamma$,

$$\sigma^*(G) = \{\pi(f^*)\} = \{((U,R),\ldots,(U,R),\ldots)\}.$$

Observe, first, that σ^* is a nondiscriminating CSSB for (γ,Γ). Indeed, $\sigma^*(G)$ is the best path in X, for both players, and, hence, $\sigma^*(G) \subset X(G) \backslash \text{CDOM}(\sigma^*,G)$. To realize that the reverse inclusion also holds note that (U,R) is the unique Nash equilibrium, as well as the unique Pareto-optimum, in the one shot game. Since $z(i|\sigma^*) = \pi(f^*)$, $i=1,2$, it follows that every path $x \in X$ which differs from $\pi(f^*)$ violates condition (**) in Proposition 9.2.4. Therefore, by Proposition 9.2.4, $x \in \mathrm{CDOM}(\sigma^*, G^0)$.

We shall now verify that $\sigma^P(G^0)$ includes paths other than $\pi(f^*)$. Notice that in the one shot game the individually rational (that is, MinMax) payoff for each player is 1. As the well-known Folk Theorem states (see, e.g., Fudenberg and Maskin 1986), for sufficiently large discount factors, δ^i, $0<\delta^i<1$, there exists a path $y \in \mathrm{PEP}$ such that $U^i(y)<2(\delta^i/(1-\delta^i))$, $i=1,2$. Since $U^i(\pi(f^*))=20(\delta^i/(1-\delta^i))$, $i=1,2$, it follows that $y \in \mathrm{PEP} \backslash \sigma^*(G^0)$.

Thus, the nondiscriminating CSSB σ^* for (γ,Γ) assigns to G^0 a strict subset of PEP.

Remark 9.3.6: Note that every path which results from always playing a Nash equilibrium in the one shot game belongs to every nondiscriminating CSSB for the repeated game Nash situation (γ,Γ) that is closed valued (in the product topology). That is, let σ be a nondiscriminating CSSB for (γ,Γ) such that $\sigma(G^0)$ is a closed set, and let $\boldsymbol{\zeta \in Z^N}$ be a Nash equilibrium in the one shot game. Then, $\boldsymbol{x \in} \sigma(G^0)$, where $\boldsymbol{x_t \equiv \zeta}$ **for all** $\boldsymbol{t=1,2,\ldots}$. Indeed, by nondiscrimination, $\sigma(G^0) \neq \emptyset$. Let $y \in \sigma(G^0)$, hence, by stability, $y \notin \mathrm{CDOM}(\sigma, G^0)$. Since ζ is a Nash equilibrium in the one shot game, the definitions of CDOM and γ imply that the path $(\zeta,y) \notin \mathrm{CDOM}(\sigma,G^0)$. As σ is a CSSB, $(\zeta,y) \in \sigma(G^0)$. Therefore, by applying to (ζ,y), instead of y, the above argument, we have that $(\zeta,\zeta,y) \in \sigma(G^0)$. Continuing in this manner yields that for any finite number J, $(\zeta \otimes J, y) \in \sigma(G^0)$, where $\zeta \otimes J$ denotes the J-history $\mathrm{H}(J)=(\zeta,\zeta,\ldots,\zeta)$. Since $\sigma(G^0)$ is closed, we conclude that $x \in \sigma(G^0)$.

9.4 The coalitional repeated game situation

As repeatedly emphasized, an important feature of the theory of social situations is that it naturally accommodates coalition formation. I close this chapter by suggesting an extension of the notion of PEP, which allows players to coordinate their actions. Specifically, players in coalition S, $S \subset N$, can decide to deviate from x at period τ and choose the correlated actions $\zeta^S_\tau \in Z^S$. In this case, S induces the repeated game that starts at period $\tau+1$, after the players have received the τ payoffs resulting from their actions up to and including period τ. Formally, the ***coalitional repeated game situation*** $\boldsymbol{(\gamma^C,\Gamma)}$ is defined as follows.

The collection of positions in (γ^C,Γ) is the same as that in the repeated game Nash situation, namely,

$$\boldsymbol{\Gamma \equiv \{G \mid N(G) \equiv N\,;\, X(G) \equiv X;\, u^i(G) \equiv a+bU^i,\, 0<b\leq 1,\, i \in N\}.}$$

For any positive integer τ, $G \in \Gamma$, $x \in X$, $S \subset N$, and $\zeta^S_\tau \in Z^S$, denote by $\boldsymbol{H=(G \mid x;\, \zeta^S_\tau)}$ the position $H \in \Gamma$, where

$$N(H)=N\ ;\ X(H)=X\ ;\ u^k(H)(y)\equiv u^k(G)(x_1,x_2,\ldots,x_{\tau-1},\zeta_\tau,y),$$

for $\zeta_\tau \in Z^N$, with $\zeta^j_\tau = x^j_\tau$ **for all** $j \in N \backslash S$. The inducement correspondence γ^C is given by: For every $G \in \Gamma$, $x \in X$, and $S \subset N$,

$$\gamma^C(S|G,x)=\{(G|x;\zeta^S_\tau)|\ \tau\in\{1,2,\ldots\} \text{ and } \zeta^S_\tau \in Z^S\}.$$

The analogy between the coalitional repeated game and the Nash situations suggests that it is reasonable to require that the solutions to all positions in Γ be identical, that is, that the SB for (γ^C,Γ) be nondiscriminating. Theorem 9.3.4 advances the following new solution concept.

Definition 9.4.1: A **coalitional PEP (CPEP)** *is a maximal nondiscriminating CSSB for the situation* (γ^C,Γ).

The following observation shows that CPEP refines the notion of PEP. (This is to be contrasted with the tree situation; see Example 8.4.3.)

Observation 9.4.2: *Let σ be a CPEP for the coalitional repeated game situation (γ^C,Γ). Then, for every $G \in \Gamma$, $\sigma(G) \subset \sigma^P(G)$.*

As is the case with several of the other solution concepts proposed in this book, no general results have as yet been established for the notion of CPEP. It might, however, be interesting to note that the coalitional repeated game situation corresponding to Example 9.3.5 admits a unique nondiscriminating CSSB (hence, a unique CPEP). This CSSB is given by σ^*, which consists of the unique Pareto-optimal path in X.

Indeed, arguments similar to those given in Example 9.3.5 establish that σ^* is a nondiscriminating CSSB for (γ^C,Γ). To see that σ^* is the only nondiscriminating CSSB for (γ^C,Γ), let $\hat{\sigma}$ be a nondiscriminating CSSB for (γ^C,Γ) and let $\hat{\sigma}^c$ be its closure. By the proof of Claim 9.2.2, $\hat{\sigma}^c$ is a nondiscriminating conservative internally stable SB for (γ^C,Γ), and $z(i|\hat{\sigma}^c)$ is well defined for $i=1,2$. Since each strategy profile in the one shot game yields both players the same payoff, every path X also yields the same payoff to both individuals. Therefore, we can choose an identical worst path in $\sigma^c(G^0)$ for both players. Thus, let

$$y \equiv z(1|\hat{\sigma}^c) = z(2|\hat{\sigma}^c).$$

Since $\sigma^*(G^0)$ consists of the best path in X for both players, to conclude that $\sigma^c(G^0)=\sigma^*(G^0)$ it suffices to show that $\{y\}=\sigma^*(G^0)$. Otherwise, $U^i(y) < U^i(\sigma^*(G^0)) = 20\delta^i/(1-\delta^i)$. Let τ be the first period for which $y_\tau \neq (U,R)$. Denote: $\zeta_\tau \equiv (U,R)$; $\tilde{y} \equiv (y_\tau, y_{\tau+1}, \ldots)$; $\tilde{z} \equiv (\zeta_\tau, y_1, y_2, \ldots)$. Thus, $\tilde{z} = ((U,R), y_1, y_2, \ldots, y_{\tau-1}, \tilde{y}) = ((U,R), \ldots, (U,R), \tilde{y})$, and therefore, we have, for $i=1,2$,

$$U^i(\tilde{z})=20\sum_{t=1}^{\tau}(\delta^i)^t+(\delta^i)^\tau U^i(\tilde{y})=20\delta^i[1-(\delta^i)^\tau]/(1-\delta^i)+(\delta^i)^\tau U^i(\tilde{y}).$$

Since $y_\tau\neq(U,R)$, $U^i(\tilde{y})<20\delta^i/(1-\delta^i)$. Therefore, $20\delta^i[1-(\delta^i)^\tau]/(1-\delta^i)>[1-(\delta^i)^\tau]U^i(\tilde{y})$. Thus, $U^i(\tilde{z})>U^i(\tilde{y})$, implying that $U^i(y)<U^i(y;\zeta_\tau;y)$. By the proof of Proposition 9.2.4, the last inequality yields that $y\in\text{CDOM}(\hat{\sigma}^c,G^0)$. But then $y\in\hat{\sigma}^c(G^0)$ contradicts the conservative internal stability of $\hat{\sigma}^c$.

Although this chapter is devoted to the analysis of CSSB, it is certainly interesting to study also the (nondiscriminating and discriminating) OSSBs for the two repeated game situations. Preliminary results due to Shitovitz (private communication) suggest that each of these two situations admits at most one nondiscriminating OSSB. Moreover, Shitovitz showed that if σ is the nondiscriminating OSSB for the repeated game Nash situation then $x\in\sigma(G)$ implies that for all $\tau\geq 1$, x_τ is a Nash equilibrium in the one shot game. Similarly, if σ is the nondiscriminating OSSB for the coalitional repeated game situation then $x\in\sigma(G)$ implies that for all $\tau\geq 1$, x_τ is a strong Nash equilibrium in the one shot game.

Proofs for Chapter 9

Proof of Claim 9.2.2: By definition, for $G\in\Gamma$, $\tilde{\sigma}(G)$ is the closure (in X) of $\sigma(G)$. The nondiscrimination of σ implies, therefore, that $\tilde{\sigma}$ is also a nondiscriminating SB for (γ,Γ), that is, for all $G\in\Gamma$, $\tilde{\sigma}(G)=\tilde{\sigma}(G^0)$.

To see that $\tilde{\sigma}$ is conservative internally stable, let $x\in\tilde{\sigma}(G^0)$ and assume, in negation that $x\in\text{CDOM}(\tilde{\sigma},G^0)$. Then, there exist $i\in N$ and $\zeta_\tau\in Z^N$ with $\zeta_\tau^k=x_\tau^k$ for all $k\in N$, $k\neq i$, such that $U^i(x_\tau,x_{\tau+1},\ldots)<U^i(\zeta_\tau,y)$ for all $y\in\tilde{\sigma}(G^0)$.

By definition, $x\in\tilde{\sigma}(G^0)$ implies that there exists a sequence $\{x^r\}$, $r=1,2,\ldots$, such that $x^r\in\sigma(G^0)$, and $x^r\to x$. The internal conservative stability of σ implies that $x^r\notin\text{CDOM}(\sigma,G^0)$, $r=1,2,\ldots$. In particular, for every $r=1,2,\ldots$, there exists $y^r\in\sigma(G^0)$ such that $U^i(x_\tau^r,x_{\tau+1}^r,\ldots)\geq U^i(\zeta_\tau^r,y^r)$, where $\zeta_\tau^r\in Z^N$ is given by: For $k\in N$, $k\neq i$, $(\zeta_\tau^r)^k=(x_\tau^r)^k$, and $(\zeta_\tau^r)^i=\zeta_\tau^i$.

Since σ is an SB for Γ, $\sigma(G^0)\subset X$. The compactness of X implies that $\tilde{\sigma}(G^0)$ is a compact subset of X. Therefore, without loss of generality, $y^r\to y^*\in\tilde{\sigma}(G^0)$. By the continuity of U^i, it follows that $U^i(x_\tau,x_{\tau+1},\ldots)\geq U^i(\zeta_\tau,y^*)$, contradicting $U^i(x_\tau,x_{\tau+1},\ldots)<U^i(\zeta_\tau,y)$ for all $y\in\tilde{\sigma}(G^0)$. Hence, $\tilde{\sigma}$ is conservatively internally stable.

Finally, assume that $\sigma(G^0)$ is nonempty. Then, $\tilde{\sigma}(G^0)$ is also nonempty. Recall that $\tilde{\sigma}(G^0)$ is a compact subset of X. Therefore, the continuity of $u^i(G^0)=U^i$ yields that $\tilde{\sigma}$ satisfies Condition 9.2.3. Q.E.D.

Proof of Proposition 9.2.4: By definition, $x \in \mathrm{CDOM}(\sigma^c, G^0)$ if and only if there exist $i \in N$ and $H \in \gamma(\{i\}|G^0, x)$ such that $\sigma^c(H) \neq \emptyset$ and for all $y \in \sigma^c(H)$, $u^i(H)(y) > u^i(G)(x)$. Since σ^c satisfies Condition 9.2.3, $z(i|\sigma^c)$ is well defined. Since $z(i|\sigma^c)$ is a worst outcome for player i in the solution to any position in Γ, $x \in \mathrm{CDOM}(\sigma^c, G)$ if and only if $u^i(H)(z(i|\sigma^c)) > u^i(G)(x)$. Thus, $x \notin \mathrm{CDOM}(\sigma^c, G)$ if and only if there is no $i \in N$ and $H \in \gamma(\{i\}|G, x)$ for which the last strict inequality is true. By the definition of γ, $x \notin \mathrm{CDOM}(\sigma^c, G)$ if and only if (**) holds. Q.E.D.

Proof of Claim 9.3.1: All positions in Γ are of the form $G = (N, X, \{a + bU^i\}_{i \in N})$, with $b > 0$. Therefore, for all $G, H \in \Gamma$, $x, y \in X$, and $i \in N$, we have $u^i(G)(x) > u^i(G)(y)$ if and only if $u^i(H)(x) > u^i(H)(y)$. Hence, for every $i \in N$ and any two n-tuples of strategies $f, g \in \Omega$, $U^i(G)(\pi(f)) > u^i(G)(\pi(g))$ if and only if $u^i(H)(\pi(f)) > u^i(H)(\pi(g))$. It follows from the definitions of Nash and perfect equilibrium that $f \in \Omega$ is an NE (PE) in the game with which $G \in \Gamma$ is associated if and only if it is an NE (PE) in the game with which $H \in \Gamma$ is associated. Thus, for all $G, H \in \Gamma$, $\sigma^N(G) = \sigma^N(H)$, and $\sigma^P(G) = \sigma^P(H)$.
Q.E.D.

Proof of Claim 9.3.2: Follows from the fact that PEP(T) is a nonempty and compact set (see, e.g., Abreu 1988). Q.E.D.

Proof of Theorem 9.3.3: See Abreu, (1988, Propositions 1 and 5).
Q.E.D.

Proof of Theorem 9.3.4: The following two lemmas establish the theorem.

Lemma 1: *σ^P is a nondiscriminating CSSB for* (γ, Γ).

Proof of Lemma 1: By Claim 9.3.2, $z(i|\sigma^P)$ is well defined for all $i \in N$. By definition, $U^i(z(i|\sigma^P)) \leq U^i(x)$ for all $x \in \mathrm{PEP}$. Since $z(i|\sigma^P) \in \mathrm{PEP}$, Theorem 9.3.3 yields that the path $x^0 \in X$ belongs to PEP if and only if for all $i \in N$, all τ, $\tau = 1, 2, \ldots$, and all $\zeta^i_\tau \in Z^i$,

$$*** \quad U^i(x^0) \geq U^i(x^0; \zeta^i_\tau; z(i|\sigma^P)).$$

To see that σ^P is conservative internally stable, assume, in negation, that there exist $G \in \Gamma$ and $x \in X(G)$ such that $x \in \sigma^P(G)$ and, at the same time, $x \in \mathrm{CDOM}(\sigma^P, G)$. By Claim 9.3.2, σ^P satisfies Condition 9.2.3. Hence, Proposition 9.2.4 implies that Condition (**) is violated. But then, $x \in \sigma^P(G)$ contradicts (***).

By Claim 9.3.1, therefore, it is left to be shown that σ^P is also externally stable. Indeed, by Proposition 9.2.4, Claim 9.3.2, and (***), we have that $x \notin \text{CDOM}(\sigma^P, G)$ implies $x \in \sigma^P(G)$. Q.E.D.

Lemma 2: *Let σ be a nondiscriminating conservative internally stable SB for (γ,Γ). Then, $\sigma(G^0) \subset PEP$.*

Proof of Lemma 2: Let $\tilde{\sigma}$ be the closure of σ. By Claim 9.2.2, $\tilde{\sigma}$ is a nondiscriminating conservative internally stable SB for (γ,Γ). Since $\sigma(G^0) \subset \tilde{\sigma}(G^0)$, it suffices to show that $\tilde{\sigma}(G^0) \subset \text{PEP}$.

If $\tilde{\sigma}(G^0) = \emptyset$ we are done. Otherwise, since $\tilde{\sigma}$ is conservative internally stable, $x \in \tilde{\sigma}(G)$ implies $x \notin \text{CDOM}(\tilde{\sigma}, G)$. Therefore, by Proposition 9.2.4, condition (**) is satisfied for all $x \in \tilde{\sigma}(G^0)$. Let $x^0 \in \tilde{\sigma}(G^0)$. Then condition (**) holds for x^0 as well as for $x^i \equiv z(i|\tilde{\sigma})$, $i \in N$. That is, for all $i \in N$, all k, $k = 0,1,2,\ldots,n$, all τ, $\tau = 1,2,\ldots$, and all $\zeta^i_\tau \in Z^i$, $U^i(x^k;\zeta^i_\tau;x^i) \leq U^i(x^k)$. By Theorem 9.3.3, $x^0 \in \text{PEP}$. Q.E.D.

Proof of Observation 9.4.2: The proof of Lemma 2 establishes that if σ is a nondiscriminating conservative internally stable SB for the repeated game Nash situation (γ,Γ), then $\sigma(G) \subset \sigma^P(G)$ for all $G \in \Gamma$. And, it is easy to see that if σ is a nondiscriminating CSSB for the coalitional repeated game situation (γ^C,Γ), then it is also a nondiscriminating conservative internally stable SB for (γ,Γ). Q.E.D.

CHAPTER 10

Implementation by means of situations

In this chapter the theory of social situations is applied to the problem of implementing a social choice rule. As was the case in the previous chapters, here, too, this application yields a new result within the implementation area itself – the characterization of social choice rules that satisfy the strong positive association condition (Definition 10.1.1) – and, in addition, sheds new light on this condition by pointing out its strategic (rather than normative) aspect.

Moreover, the methodology developed in this chapter is likely to prove useful in the important task of incorporating, into the theory of social situations, social environments where individuals have incomplete and/or imperfect information (in particular, about the preferences of the other players they are facing). (See also Section 11.9.)

Definition 10.0.1: *A* ***society*** *is a triple* $(N,A,\{u^i\}_{i\in N})$, *where N is the* ***set of individuals,*** *A is the set of* ***feasible social alternatives,*** *and for* $i\in N$, u^i *denotes individual i's* ***utility function*** *over A,* $u^i:A\to\mathbb{R}$.

The problem of implementation concerns circumstances in which "the social planner" does not know the society he is facing. His knowledge is limited only to the class of "potential societies." That is, although he does know the sets N and A, he has only partial information concerning the preferences of the individuals. Specifically, the social planner knows, for each $i\in N$, the set of utility functions, U^i, to which "the true" preferences of individual i belong.

Definition 10.0.2: *The* ***set of potential societies*** *is a triple* (N,A,U^N), *where N and A are as in Definition 10.0.1, and for* $i\in N$, U^i *denotes* ***individual i's set of admissible utility functions,*** *that is, for all* $i\in N$, *if* $u^i\in U^i$, *then* $u^i:A\to\mathbb{R}$. U^N *denotes the Cartesian product of* U^i *over* $i\in N$, *and an element* $u^N\in U^N$ *is called a* ***utility profile.***

As both sets N and A are the same in all potential societies, a society can be characterized by the utility profile $u^N\in U^N$. The correspondence that assigns to each society $u^N\in U^N$ its "socially desirable outcomes," $f(u^N)\subset A$, is called a social choice rule.

Definition 10.0.3: *A* ***social choice rule (SCR)*** *for the set of potential societies* (N,A,U^N), *is a nonempty-valued correspondence* f, $f: U^N \rightarrow 2^A$ *such that for each* $a \in A$ *there exists* $u^N \in U^N$ *with* $a \in f(u^N)$.

Observe that, in principle, the social choice rule is allowed to depend on the particular form of the utility profiles $u^N \in U^N$ that represent the (ordinal) preference orderings. This flexibility will not, however, be exploited in this chapter. The requirement that the range of an SCR coincides with the set A is not essential, and is imposed only to simplify the exposition.

Let (N,A,U^N) be the set of potential societies, and let f be an SCR for (N,A,U^N). The task of the social planner is to implement the SCR f. That is, he has to design a "mechanism" that "generates outcomes" which have the properties that are desirable according to the given SCR. It is assumed that each individual knows the precise form of the mechanism that the planner is using. The difficulties arise because, in view of the information structure, this mechanism cannot depend on the explicit form of the ("true") utility profile u^N. (See Dasgupta, Hammond, and Maskin 1979).

Within the framework of the theory of social situations, a "mechanism" is a situation. The planner must, therefore, specify a situation, (γ,Γ), with the property that the inducement correspondence γ is independent of u^N. It is because of this condition that we need to introduce the notions of *position-form* and *situation-form,* which are the analogs of positions and situations except that they do not include utility functions.

Definition 10.0.4: *A* ***position-form*** *is a pair* $D=(N(D),X(D))$, *where* $N(D)$ *is the set of players and* $X(D)$ *is the set of feasible outcomes in* D.

Definition 10.0.5: *A* ***situation-form*** *is a pair* (δ,Δ), *where* Δ *is a collection of position-forms and* δ *is a mapping that assigns to each* $D \in \Delta$, $S \subset N(D)$, *and* $x \in X(D)$, *a subset,* $\delta(S|D,x)$, *of* Δ. *Moreover, if* $C \in \delta(S|D,x)$ *then* $S \subset N(C)$.

The notion of situation-form formalizes the requirement that the inducement correspondence γ is independent of u^N. Thus, the task of the planner is to specify a situation-form (δ,Δ) such that for all $u^N \in U^N$, the "resulting (stable) outcomes" for the society u^N yield the social desiderata, $f(u^N)$. Therefore, Δ must contain a position-form with which we shall be able to identify the particular society (N,A,u^N).

Definition 10.0.6: *Let* (N,A,U^N) *be the set of potential societies. The* ***situation-form for*** (N,A,U^N) *is a situation-form* (δ,Δ), *where* Δ *contains a "distinguished position-form"* $\mathbf{D^N}$, *whose set of players is the set of individuals* N, *that is,* $\mathbf{N(D^N)=N}$, *and*

1. *For all* $D \in \Delta$, $N(D) \subset N$ *and* $X(D) \subset X(D^N)$.
2. $C \in \delta(S|D,x)$ *implies* $N(C) \subset N(D)$ *and* $X(C) \subset X(D)$.

That is, if (δ,Δ) is a situation-form for (N,A,U^N), then for every position-form D in Δ, the set of players, $N(D)$, is a subset of the set N, and the set of outcomes, $X(D)$, is a subset of the set of outcomes, $X(D^N)$, in the distinguished position-form D^N. Moreover, if the position-form C can be induced from the position-form D, then both the set of players and the set of outcomes in C are contained in the corresponding sets in D. Loosely speaking, inducements can only "delete" players and/or alternatives. Denote $\boldsymbol{X(\Delta) \equiv X(D^N)}$.

In order to relate outcomes in position-forms to alternatives in the set A (which is also the domain of the SCR f), we need the following concept of a procedure (or mechanism).

Definition 10.0.7: *A* ***procedure for*** $\boldsymbol{(N,A,U^N)}$ *is a triple* (δ,Δ,μ), *where* (δ,Δ) *is a situation-form for* (N,A,U^N), *and* $\mu : X(\Delta) \rightarrow A$, *that is,* μ *assigns to every outcome* $x \in X(\Delta)$ *an alternative* $\mu(x) \in A$.

Let (δ,Δ,μ) be a procedure for (N,A,U^N). Then, since for all $D \in \Delta$, $X(D) \subset X(\Delta)$, it follows that $X(D)$ belongs to the domain of μ. Thus, every outcome $x \in X(D)$, for $D \in \Delta$, is mapped, by the function μ, to an alternative in A. Therefore, a position-form $D \in \Delta$ together with a utility profile $u^N \in U^N$ generate the position $\boldsymbol{G(D,u^N)}$, defined by

$$\boldsymbol{G(D,u^N) \equiv (N(D),X(D),\{u^i \circ \mu\}_{i \in N(D)})},$$

where, for all $x \in X(D)$,

$$\boldsymbol{(u^i \circ \mu)(x) \equiv u^i(\mu(x))}.$$

That is, the sets of players and outcomes in position $G = G(D,u^N)$ coincide with the corresponding sets in the position-form D, and the utility player $i \in N(G)$ derives from an outcome $x \in X(G)$ equals the utility level $u^i(a)$ which i derives from alternative $a \in A$, where $a = \mu(x)$. The reason for this choice of preferences is quite clear. If the procedure (δ,Δ,μ) is employed, then the outcome $x \in X(\Delta)$ leads to alternative $\mu(x)$. Therefore, the value of an outcome x for player i is the level of utility he derives from alternative $\mu(x)$, that is, $u^i(\mu(x))$, which we denote by $u^i \circ \mu(x)$. Thus, we naturally have the following definition.

Definition 10.0.8: *Let* (δ,Δ,μ) *be a procedure for* (N,A,U^N). *The* ***situation*** $\boldsymbol{(\gamma,\Gamma)}$ ***associated with*** $\boldsymbol{(N,A,U^N,\delta,\Delta,\mu)}$ *is given by*

$$\boldsymbol{\Gamma \equiv \{G(D,u^N) | D \in \Delta \text{ and } u^N \in U^N\}},$$

and for all $S \subset N(D)$ *and* $x \in X(D)$,

$$\gamma(S|G(D,u^N),x) = \{G(C,u^N)|\, C \in \delta(S|D,x)\}.$$

It is clear that we can have $D \in \Delta$ and two distinct societies with which we associate the same position, that is, $u^N, w^N \in U^N$, $u^N \neq w^N$, and yet $G(D,u^N) = G(D,w^N)$. The following two claims establish that this fact is inconsequential, since the preferences of the players in $N(D)$ over outcomes in $X(\Delta) \backslash X(D)$ play no role.

Claim 10.0.9: *Let* (γ,Γ) *be the situation that is associated with* $(N,A,U^N,\delta,\Delta,\mu)$. *If* $H \in \gamma(S|G,x)$ *then* $u^i(H)(z) = u^i(G)(z)$ *for all* $i \in N(H)$ *and all* $z \in X(H)$.

Claim 10.0.10: *Let* (δ,Δ,μ) *be a procedure for the society* (N,A,U^N). *Assume that for some* $D \in \Delta$ *and* $u^N, w^N \in U^N$, $G(D,u^N) = G(D,w^N)$. *Then, for all* $S \subset N(D)$ *and* $x \in X(D)$, $\gamma(S|G(D,u^N),x) = \gamma(S|G(D,w^N),x)$.

The "distinguished" position-form $D^N \in \Delta$ together with a particular society $u^N \in U^N$ give rise to the position $G(u^N)$, where,

$$G(u^N) \equiv G(D^N,u^N) \equiv (N,X(\Delta),\{u^i \circ \mu\}_{i \in N}).$$

Since $D^N \in \Delta$, we have that for all $u^N \in U^N$, $G(u^N) \in \Gamma$. It is this position that we identify with the society u^N.

Definition 10.0.11 formalizes the task of the social planner who has to implement the SCR f by means of situations; that is, he has to specify a situation (γ,Γ) that has the following four properties:

i. The inducement correspondence γ is independent of u^N.
ii. There exists a unique OSSB, which coincides with the unique CSSB, σ, for (γ,Γ).
iii. Every potential society, $u^N \in U^N$, is associated with a particular position in Γ, denoted $G(u^N)$.
iv. For all $u^N \in U^N$, $\sigma(G(u^N))$ yields the socially optimal alternatives, as specified by $f(u^N)$.

Definition 10.0.11: *A social choice rule* f *for the set of potential societies* (N,A,U^N) *is said to be (fully)* ***implementable*** *(by means of situations) if there exists a procedure* (δ,Δ,μ) *for* (N,A,U^N) *such that the situation* (γ,Γ) *associated with* $(N,A,U^N,\delta,\Delta,\mu)$ *has a unique OSSB which coincides with the unique CSSB,* σ, *with the property that:*

$$f(u^N) = \mu(\sigma(G(u^N))) \quad \textit{for all } u^N \in U^N,$$

where, for $Y \subset X(\Delta)$, $\mu(Y) \equiv \{\mu(x)|\, x \in Y\}$. *In this case, we shall say that* f ***is implementable by the situation*** (γ,Γ) *associated with* $(N,A,U^N,\delta,\Delta,\mu)$.

Definition 10.0.11 is the formal generalization of the definition of implementation; there has to be a one-to-one correspondence between the set of equilibria and the set of welfare-optimal social alternatives (see, for example, Dasgupta et al. 1979). The usual definition of (full) implementation is obtained by substituting, in Definition 10.0.11, ''game form'' or ''mechanism'' for procedure and ''equilibria'' for stable (optimistic or conservative) SB.

10.1 Strong positive association

One of the most important conditions imposed on an SCR is that it satisfy the *strong positive association* (or ''monotonicity'') property.

Definition 10.1.1: *Let f be a social choice rule for the set of potential societies* (N,A,U^N). *Then, f satisfies* ***strong positive association (SPA)*** *if and only if for all* $u^N \in U^N$, *if* $a \in f(u^N)$ *then* $a \in f(w^N)$ *whenever* $w^N \in U^N$ *satisfies: For all* $i \in N$ *and all* $b \in A$, $u^i(a) \geq u^i(b)$ *implies* $w^i(a) \geq w^i(b)$.

The main result of this section is that a necessary and sufficient condition for a situation (γ,Γ) to implement an SCR f which satisfies SPA is that no coalitions are allowed to form. That is, only a single individual can induce a position, in which case he is the only member of it. Moreover, no position can be induced from a position whose set of players is a singleton.

Theorem 10.1.2: *Let f be a social choice rule for* (N,A,U^N). *Then, f satisfies SPA if and only if f is implementable by a situation* (γ,Γ) *that is associated with* $(N,A,U^N,\delta,\Delta,\mu)$, *where* (γ,Γ) *satisfies the following condition:*

C.1. ***For all*** $G \in \Gamma$, ***if*** $H \in \gamma(S|G,x)$ ***then*** $N(G)=N$ ***and*** $N(H)=S=\{i\}$ ***for some*** $i \in N$.

Condition (C.1) implies that no position can be induced from an induced position, and that the set of players of an induced position contains a single individual. In particular, therefore, we have:

Claim 10.1.3: *Let* (γ,Γ) *be a situation that satisfies (C.1). Then,* (γ,Γ) *admits a unique OSSB,* σ^o, *and a unique CSSB,* σ^c. *Moreover, for all* $G \in \Gamma$ *with* $N(G) \neq N$, $\sigma^o(G)=\sigma^c(G)=X(G)$.

In addition to characterizing SCRs that satisfy SPA, the proof of Theorem 10.1.2 has led to the following straightforward observation (Greenberg 1988a) which provides an explanation for the fact that SPA has played a central role in the theory of implementation. (I know of no other intuitive reason suggested to account for this fact.)

Observation 10.1.4: *Let f be a social choice rule for the set of potential societies (N,A,U^N). Then, f satisfies SPA if and only if it satisfies the following condition:*

* **For all u^N, $w^N \epsilon U^N$, if $a \in f(u^N) \setminus f(w^N)$, then $\exists$ $i \in N$ and $b \in A$ such that $u^i(a) \geq u^i(b)$ and $w^i(b) > w^i(a)$.**

Observation 10.1.4 points out the strategic aspect implicit in condition (*), and hence in SPA. Indeed, assume that the planner believes (guesses, or is told by the players) that the preference profile is u^N, and that on this basis the planner chooses some alternative $a^* \in f(u^N)$. Assume further that the true preference profile is w^N (which might, of course, differ from u^N). Suppose that an individual i tells the planner that the true profile is not u^N, and that the planner ought to choose alternative b, which differs from a^*. Why should the planner accept i's suggestion? After all, a^* might well be socially optimal but not i's best alternative, that is, it is possible that $a^* \in f(u^N)$ but $u^i(b) > u^i(a^*)$. But, if under u^i – the preferences the planner believes i to have – i does not benefit from replacing b by a^*, then the planner is assured that u^N could not have been the true profile. That is, if i objects to a^* by proposing an alternative $b \in A$, where $u^i(a^*) \geq u^i(b)$, then i's true preferences cannot be represented by u^i, and hence his objection is "credible."

By Observation 10.1.4, if the outcome the planner proposes does not belong to the social welfare-optimal alternatives for the true preference profile, that is, if $a^* \notin f(w^N)$, then a^* could be credibly objected to. Note that even if no individual can credibly object to a^*, the planner cannot be sure that u^N is indeed the true preference profile. All he can be certain of is that a^* is socially optimal for the true preference profile, whatever it may be.

Theorem 10.1.2 generalizes the well-known result that SPA is a necessary (though not sufficient) condition for Nash implementation (see, e.g., Dasgupta et al. 1979).

Definition 10.1.5: *Let (N,A,U^N) be a society. A* **Nash procedure** *(for that society) is a procedure (δ,Δ,μ) for (N,A,U^N), where*

$$X(\Delta) = Z^N \textit{ for some } Z^N \equiv \prod_{i \in N} Z^i,$$

$$\Delta \equiv \{D^N\} \cup \{D^i(\zeta) \mid i \in N \text{ and } \zeta \in Z^N\}, \text{ where } D^i(\zeta) \equiv (\{i\},\{\zeta\}),$$

$$\delta(\{i\} \mid D^N, \zeta) = \{D^i(\eta^i, \zeta^{N \setminus \{i\}}) \mid \eta^i \in Z^i\}, \text{ and } \delta(S \mid D, x) \equiv \emptyset \quad \text{otherwise.}$$

Let (γ,Γ) be the situation associated with $(N,A,U^N,\delta,\Delta,\mu)$, where (δ,Δ,μ) is a Nash procedure. Using Claim 2.5.6, it is easily verified that there exists a unique OSSB that coincides with the unique CSSB for (γ,Γ), and which assigns to the position $G(D^N,u^N)\in\Gamma$ the set of Nash equilibria for the game $(N,\{Z^i\}_{i\in N},\{u^i\circ\mu\}_{i\in N})$. Since (γ,Γ) clearly satisfies condition (C.1), Theorem 10.1.2 implies that SPA is indeed a necessary condition for Nash implementation.

Notice that the procedure constructed in the proof of Theorem 10.1.2 is not a Nash procedure [indeed, $X(\Delta)$ is not a Cartesian product of Z^i over $i\in N$] and, moreover, it cannot be replaced by a Nash procedure because SPA is not a sufficient condition for Nash implementation.

Proofs for Chapter 10

Proof of Claim 10.0.9: By definition, $G\in\Gamma$ if and only if $G=G(D,u^N)$ for some $D\in\Delta$ and $u^N\in U^N$. Moreover, $H\in\gamma(S|G,x)$ implies $H=G(C,u^N)$ for some $C\in\delta(S|D,x)$. Hence, for all $i\in N(G)$, $u^i(G)$ is the restriction of $u^i\circ\mu$ to $X(G)$, and for all $i\in N(H)$, $u^i(H)$ is the restriction of $u^i\circ\mu$ to $X(H)$. By condition (2) of Definition 10.0.6, $N(H)=N(C)\subset N(D)=N(G)$ and $X(H)=X(C)\subset X(D)=X(G)$. Q.E.D.

Proof of Claim 10.0.10: By the definition of γ, $H\in\gamma(S|G(D,u^N),x)$ if and only if $H=G(C,u^N)$ for some $C\in\delta(S|D,x)$. By Claim 10.0.9, $u^i(H)(z)=u^i(G(D,u^N))(z)$ for all $i\in N(H)$ and all $z\in X(H)$. Since $G(D,u^N)=G(D,w^N)$, $u^i(H)(z)=u^i(G(D,w^N))(z)$ for all $i\in N(H)$ and all $z\in X(H)$. Therefore, $H=G(C,u^N)=G(C,w^N)$, implying $H\in\gamma(S|G(D,w^N),x)$. Q.E.D.

Proof of Theorem 10.1.2: Lemmas 1 and 2, which follow the proof of Observation 10.1.4, establish the validity of this theorem. Q.E.D.

Proof of Claim 10.1.3: Let (γ,Γ) be a situation that satisfies (C.1). Define

$$\Gamma_1\equiv\{G\in\Gamma|N(G)=N\} \text{ and } \Gamma_2\equiv\Gamma\setminus\Gamma_1.$$

Then, by (C.1), (γ,Γ) is strictly hierarchical. Therefore, by Theorem 5.2.1, Corollary 5.3.3, and Theorem 5.4.1, (γ,Γ) admits a unique OSSB, σ^o, and a unique CSSB, σ^c, and for $G\in\Gamma_2$, $\sigma^o(G)=\sigma^c(G)=\eta(G)=X(G)$.

Q.E.D.

Proof of Observation 10.1.4:

i. SPA implies (*): Assume, in negation, that SPA holds but condition (*) does not hold. Then, there exist u^N and w^N in U^N, and $a\in f(u^N)\setminus f(w^N)$, such that for all $i\in N$ and $b\in A$, $u^i(a)\geq u^i(b)$ implies $w^i(a)\geq w^i(b)$. But for such u^N and w^N, SPA implies that $a\in f(w^N)$. This is a contradiction.

ii. Condition (*) implies SPA: Assume, in negation, that (*) holds but SPA does not hold. Then, there exist u^N, $w^N \in U^N$, and $a \in f(u^N) \setminus f(w^N)$, such that for all $i \in N$ and $b \in A$, $u^i(a) \geq u^i(b)$ implies $w^i(a) \geq w^i(b)$. But this contradicts (*). Q.E.D.

Lemma 1: *Let f be a social choice rule for the set of potential societies* (N,A,U^N) *which is implementable by a situation* (γ,Γ) *that is associated with* $(N,A,U^N,\delta,\Delta,\mu)$, *where* (γ,Γ) *satisfies (C.1). Then, f satisfies SPA.*

Proof of Lemma 1: Let u^N and w^N in U^N be such that $a^* \in f(u^N)$ and for all $i \in N$ and all $b \in A$, $u^i(a^*) \geq u^i(b)$ implies $w^i(a^*) \geq w^i(b)$. We need to show that $a^* \in f(w^N)$.

Since f is implementable by (γ,Γ), $f(u^N) = \mu(\sigma(G(u^N)))$, where σ is the unique OSSB which coincides with the unique CSSB for (γ,Γ). Since $a^* \in f(u^N)$, it follows that there exists $x^* \in \sigma(G(u^N))$ with $\mu(x^*) = a^*$. To conclude that $a^* \in f(w^N)$, we need to show that $x^* \in \sigma(G(w^N))$.

Assume, in negation, that $x^* \notin \sigma(G(w^N))$. Since σ is stable, $x^* \in \text{ODOM}(\sigma, G(w^N))$. By (C.1) and Claim 10.1.3, there exist $H \in \gamma(\{i\}|G(w^N),x^*)$ and $y^* \in \sigma(H) = X(H)$ with $u^i(H)(y^*) > u^i(G(w^N))(x^*)$. Since (γ,Γ) is associated with $(N,A,U^N,\delta,\Delta,\mu)$, there exists $\tilde{H} \in \gamma(\{i\}|G(u^N),x^*)$ with $N(\tilde{H}) = N(H) = \{i\}$ and $X(\tilde{H}) = X(H)$. By Claim 10.1.3, $\sigma(\tilde{H}) = X(\tilde{H})$, and, hence, $y^* \in \sigma(\tilde{H})$. Using the supposition that for all $i \in N$ and all $b \in A$, $u^i(a^*) \geq u^i(b)$ implies $w^i(a^*) \geq w^i(b)$, we have, by Claim 10.0.9, that $u^i(H)(y^*) > u^i(G(w^N))(x^*)$ implies $u^i(\tilde{H})(y^*) > u^i(G(u^N))(x^*)$. But then, $x^* \in \text{ODOM}(\sigma, G(u^N))$, contradicting $x^* \in \sigma(G(u^N))$. Q.E.D.

Lemma 2: *Let f be a social choice rule for the set of potential societies* (N,A,U^N). *If f satisfies SPA then f is implementable by a situation* (γ,Γ) *that is associated with* $(N,A,U^N,\delta,\Delta,\mu)$, *where* (γ,Γ) *satisfies (C.1).*

Proof of Lemma 2: The proof is by construction. Let f be a social choice rule for the society (N,A,U^N). Define the procedure (δ,Δ,μ) as follows:

$$\begin{aligned}
&\mathbf{X(\Delta) \equiv X \equiv \{(u^N,a) \mid u^N \in U^N \text{ and } a \in f(u^N)\}},\\
&\mathbf{\mu(x) = \mu((u^N,a)) \equiv a},\\
&\mathbf{\Delta \equiv \{D^N\} \cup \{D^i(x) \mid i \in N \text{ and } x \in X\}},
\end{aligned}$$

where

$$\begin{aligned}
&\mathbf{D^N \equiv (N,X) \text{ and } D^i(x) \equiv (\{i\},\{x\})},\\
&\mathbf{\delta(\{i\}|D^N,(w^N,a)) = \{D^i(x) \mid x = (u^N,b) \in X \text{ and } w^i(a) \geq w^i(b)\}},\\
&\mathbf{\delta(S|D,x) \equiv \emptyset \quad \text{otherwise}.}
\end{aligned}$$

It is easily verified that the conditions in Definition 10.0.6 are satisfied, that is, (δ,Δ,μ) is a procedure for (N,A,U^N). Let (γ,Γ) be the situation associated with $(N,A,U^N,\delta,\Delta,\mu)$. Clearly, (γ,Γ) satisfies (C.1). By Claims 2.5.6 and 10.1.3, (γ,Γ) admits a unique OSSB which coincides with the unique CSSB, σ, which satisfies: For all $G\in\Gamma$ with $N(G)=\{i\}$, $\sigma(G)=X(G)$. To conclude the proof of Lemma 2 it remains to be verified that for all $u^N\in U^N$, $f(u^N)=\mu(\sigma(G(u^N)))$.

i. **For all $G(u^N)\in\Gamma$, $f(u^N)\subset\mu(\sigma(G(u^N)))$:** Indeed, for all $u^N\in U^N$ and all $a\in f(u^N)$, $(u^N,a)\notin\{(w^N,a)\in X \mid \exists\, i\in N$ and $b\in A$ such that $w^i(a)\geq w^i(b)$ and $u^i(b)>u^i(a)\}$. Therefore, by Claim 10.0.9, $(u^N,a)\notin$ ODOM$(\sigma,G(u^N))$, that is, $(u^N,a)\in\sigma(G(u^N))$.

ii. **For all $G(u^N)\in\Gamma$, $\mu(\sigma(G(u^N)))\subset f(u^N)$:** Assume, in negation, that $(w^N,b)\in\sigma(G(u^N))$, but $\mu(w^N,b)=b\notin f(u^N)$. Since f satisfies SPA, Observation 10.1.4 yields that f satisfies condition (*). Therefore, $b\in f(w^N)\setminus f(u^N)$ implies, using Definition 10.0.3, that $(w^N,b)\in$ ODOM$(\sigma,G(u^N))$, contradicting the assumption that $(w^N,b)\in\sigma(G(u^N))$. Q.E.D.

CHAPTER 11

Closing remarks

Now that the reader is familiar with the theory of social situations and some of its applications, he is invited to go over Section 1.4 once again and convince himself of the validity of the assertions made there concerning some of the merits of the proposed approach and its potential. Making this point is, as emphasized there, the main purpose of this book.

This last chapter includes some general comments and offers several directions for further research. As stated above, I did not attempt to reach the most general statements of the theorems; my purpose was to whet the appetite of the reader and to suggest that the approach is worth pursuing. I have little doubt that many, and perhaps the more interesting, results and applications are yet to be discovered.

11.1 Equilibria versus recommendations

The theory of social situations is concerned with ***recommendations,*** as opposed to ***predictions.*** It is sometimes argued that equilibrium in classical game theory describes how players (who are "uneducated" and do not consult with "experts") will actually behave. The following example, inspired by Aumann and Maschler (1972), illustrates that the (perhaps most prominent) game-theoretic notion of **Nash equilibrium is in fact prescriptive rather than descriptive.** The example makes another interesting point: A "rational recommendation" to (all the) players might conflict with the "rationality of the players" (see point VII in Section 1.4).

Consider the following two-person normal form game where the payoff matrix is

	L	M	R
U	(4,0)	(0,0)	(0,3)
C	(2,6)	(2,0)	(2,3)
D	(0,0)	(2,3)	(0,3)

As the reader can easily verify, the only (pure strategies) Nash equilibrium is the pair (D,M), yielding the payoff (2,3). But each of the two players can guarantee himself his equilibrium payoff if, instead of following the proposed equilibrium, player 1 chooses C and player 2 chooses R. Moreover, **C (weakly) dominates D and R (weakly) dominates M.** Thus, it seems that no rational player will follow the equilibrium strategies (D,M) unless he is **absolutely convinced** that the other player will also follow it. The slightest doubt a player has, he is better off adopting a different strategy which guarantees him the equilibrium payoff, **no matter what the other player does.** But, recommending such a course of action to both players results in the **recommendation** itself not being acceptable: The pair (C,R) is not a Nash equilibrium.

11.2 Design of institutions

The ease with which some of the better known game-theoretic solution concepts emerge from the theory of social situations might suggest that the associated situations were constructed in order to attain these results. Chronologically this is not true. I first represented "interesting" social environments as situations and only then studied the solutions resulting from the stability requirement. I therefore believe (as Example 3.6 shows) that casting a particular social environment as a situation and then studying the stability implications will, most likely, prove to be very fruitful.

But starting at the other end, that is, with the solution concept, and then working backwards to discover the situation that leads to the desired solution (as we did in Chapter 10) is equally important and innovative. Indeed, players in "the real world" are seldom faced with a precise "game" or situation. Often, the ingenious task is to design the institution or negotiation process in such a way that the final (stable) outcome will be the favorable one.

11.3 Human rationality

The theory of social situations allows for **bounded rationality on both the perception and the computation abilities of the players.** This is to be contrasted with the current trend of identifying bounded rationality only with the players' ability to calculate, ignoring individuals' tendency to simplify the discernment of the environment they are in.

The sequential bargaining game (see Section 8.2) where all players have the same discount factor [that is, for all $i \in N$, $u^i(z^i,t) = \delta^{(t-1)} z^i$, $\delta \in (0,1)$], illustrates this point. As the quote from Shubik (1984, p. 48) at the beginning of Chapter 8 states, the representation of this example as a game in extensive form (or its associated tree situation) forces us, whether we want to or not, to remember the entire history of offers and rejections. But, the theory of social situations allows players to represent this game by the following (less sophisticated and perhaps oversimplified, but more realistic) situation, (γ^*,Γ^*). For period τ, $\tau=1,2,\ldots$, define the position G_τ

$$G_\tau \equiv (N,\Delta,\{u^i(G_\tau)\}_{i\in N}),$$

where $\Delta \equiv \{x\in R^N_+ \mid \Sigma^n_{i=1} x^i \leq 1\}$, and for $x\in\Delta$,

$$u^i(G_\tau)(x) \equiv \delta^{\tau-1}x^i.$$

That is, at every period τ, the set of players is N and the player who is making the offer can suggest an element from Δ, which is evaluated by the players according to the discount factor δ. Observe that the position G_τ is independent of the history of offers and rejections that lead to it. Recall that at period τ, $\tau=1,2,\ldots$, it is player $\boldsymbol{i(\tau)=1+[(\tau-1)\mathrm{mod}(n)]}$ who is making the offer, and he is free to choose any distribution from the set Δ. Player $i(\tau)$'s offer can then be rejected by any of the other players $h\in N\setminus\{i(\tau)\}$, in which case it is player $i(\tau+1)$ who will be making the offer in the next period. Assuming that coalitions are not allowed to form, we can (perhaps, naively) associate the situation (γ^*,Γ^*) with this sequential bargaining game, where

$$\Gamma^* \equiv \{G_\tau \mid \tau=1,2,\ldots\},$$

and for all $S\subset N$, $G_\tau\in\Gamma$, and $x\in\Delta$,

$$\begin{aligned}
&\gamma^*(\{i\}|G_\tau,x)=\{G_\tau\} && \text{if } i=i(\tau),\\
&\gamma^*(\{i\}|G_\tau,x)=\{G_{\tau+1}\} && \text{if } i\neq i(\tau),\\
&\gamma^*(S|G_\tau,x)=\emptyset && \text{if } |S|>1.
\end{aligned}$$

That is, the set of positions Γ^* contains all possible positions, G_τ, that originate at some period τ. The player who proposes at τ is free to choose any offer from Δ, and can, therefore, "reconsider" the offer proposed to him. Thus, $i(\tau)$ can induce G_τ from itself. Every other player can reject the proposal made by $i(\tau)$ by saying "No," in which case player $i(\tau+1)$ will make the offer in the next period. Thus, every $i\neq i(\tau)$ can induce the position $G_{\tau+1}$.

On the perceptual level, the situation (γ^*,Γ^*) greatly simplifies that of the tree situation. And, it seems likely that most people (who are not "game theorists") would not perceive the sequential bargaining game as a tree situation (γ,Γ), but rather in a manner closer to (γ^*,Γ^*).

We now turn to simplifying the computation of the solution. Observe that all positions in $G\in\Gamma^*$ have identical sets of players (namely, N) and identical sets of outcomes (namely, Δ), and, moreover, the preferences (though not the utility functions) of every player over the set of outcomes are also independent of the particular position [that is, for all $G,H\in\Gamma^*$, $x,y\in\Delta$, and $i\in N$, $u^i(G)(x)>u^i(G)(y)$ if and only if $u^i(H)(x)>u^i(H)(y)$]. The only asymmetry among the positions in Γ^* stems from the identity of the player who is making the offer. In order to facilitate the derivation of the stable SBs for (γ^*,Γ^*), it seems reasonable to require that the SB reflect these properties, namely, that it be nondiscriminating.

Definition 11.3.1: *An SB σ for (γ^*,Γ^*) is* **nondiscriminating** *if for all τ and t with $t>\tau$, $x\in\sigma(G_t)$ if and only if $y\in\sigma(G_\tau)$, where for $i\in N$, $x^i=y^k$, $k\equiv 1+(i+t-\tau-1)mod(n)$.*

Assuming that "human rationality" involves the simplifications of both the representation [by (γ^*,Γ^*)] and the computation (requiring σ to be nondiscriminating), we have the following appealing result.

Theorem 11.3.2: *There exists a unique nondiscriminating OSSB, σ, for (γ^*,Γ^*). Moreover, σ is single valued and satisfies $\sigma(G_1)=\{(\alpha,\delta\alpha,\delta^2\alpha,\ldots,\delta^{n-1}\alpha)\}$, where $\alpha=(1-\delta)/(1-\delta^n)$.*

Herrero (1985) proved that if $\delta<1/(n-1)$ then there exists a unique subgame perfect equilibrium for the game tree T. In this case, $\sigma(G_1)$ coincides with the unique path in PEP(T). But, when $\delta>1/(n-1)$, PEP(T) coincides with all the possible paths in $\Pi(T)$. In particular, every offer in Δ, at any date, is supported by some (subgame) perfect equilibrium. In this case, the unique OSSB for (γ^*,Γ^*) refines the PEP correspondence σ^P. [Observe that the SB σ^P for the associated tree situation (γ,Γ) satisfies the (correspondingly modified) assumption of nondiscrimination. Indeed, let T^t and T^τ be two subtrees that correspond to the beginning of periods t and τ, respectively. Then, there exists a path $\xi\in\sigma^P(T^t)$ which terminates with the acceptance of the offer $x\in\Delta$ if and only if there exists a path $\eta\in\sigma^P(T^\tau)$ which terminates with the acceptance of the offer $y\in\Delta$, where for $i\in N$, $x^i=y^k$, $k\equiv 1+(i+t-\tau-1)\text{mod}(n)$.]

11.4 Lotteries

Situations in which the optimistic behavior is certainly justified are those where the inducing coalition can dictate what outcome from the solution for the induced position will prevail. (Such might be the case when, for example, the inducement correspondence is simple, since then the inducing coalition constitutes the set of players in the induced position.) But if the inducing coalition, S, can decide on the outcome in the induced position, H, why restrict S to pick a particular outcome from $\sigma(H)$ and not allow it to commit to a **lottery over outcomes in $\sigma(H)$**? Indeed, consider the following example.

Example 11.4.1: Let (γ,Γ) be the situation where

$$\boldsymbol{\Gamma=\{G\},\ N(G)\equiv\{1,2\},\ X(G)=\{(1,1),(10,0),(0,10)\},}$$

and for all $x\in X(G)$ and $i\in N$,

$$u^i(G)(x) = x^i,$$
$$\gamma(N|G,x) = \{G\}, \text{ and } \gamma(\{i\}|G,x) = \emptyset.$$

It is easy to see that σ is an OSSB if and only if $\boldsymbol{\sigma(G) = X(G)}$. But if $u^i(G)$, $i \in N$, is a vN&M utility function (that is, satisfies the expected utility hypothesis), then the players would object to the outcome $(1,1) \in \sigma(G)$, since they could agree to induce G and then choose, with equal probabilities, one of the two outcomes, (10,0) and (0,10), which belong to $\sigma(G)$ and yield both players the (expected) payoff 5 which is greater than 1.

Example 11.4.1 motivates Definition 11.4.2. Let (γ,Γ) be a position, and let σ be an SB for (γ,Γ). Assume that for every position $G \in \Gamma$, and every $i \in N(G)$, $u^i(G)$ is a vN&M utility function over $X(G)$. Let $B \subset X(G)$. Denote by $\boldsymbol{L(B)}$ the set of all probability measures (lotteries) over B, and for $p \in L(B)$, let $\boldsymbol{u^i(G)(B;p)}$ be (with a slight abuse of notation) the expectation of $u^i(G)$ on B with respect to p. That is,

$$u^i(G)(B;p) \equiv \int_B u^i(G)(x)dp(x).$$

For $G \in \Gamma$, define the "lottery ODOM" by

$$\textbf{LODOM}(\sigma,G) \equiv \{x \in X(G) \mid \exists\, S \subset N(G),\ H \in \gamma(S|G,x), \text{ and } p \in L(\sigma(H)) \text{ such that } u^i(G)(x) < u^i(H)(\sigma(H);p) \text{ for all } i \in S\}.$$

Definition 11.4.2: *Let (γ,Γ) be a situation. The SB σ for (γ,Γ) is a* ***lottery optimistic stable standard of behavior, LOSSB,*** *if and only if, for all $G \in \Gamma$,* $\boldsymbol{\sigma(G) = X(G) \setminus LODOM(\sigma,G)}$.

But if we allow the inducing coalition to offer a lottery among the outcomes in the solution for the position it induces, why not allow it to make, in addition, a lottery on the position it will induce? The following variant of Example 11.4.1 illustrates this point.

Example 11.4.3: Consider the situation (γ,Γ), where

$$\Gamma = \{G^1, G^2, G^3\},$$

for all $G \in \Gamma$,

$$N(G) = \{1,2\},$$
$$X(G^1) = \{(1,1)\}, X(G^2) = \{(10,0)\}, X(G^3) = \{(0,10)\},$$

and for all $i \in N$, $G \in \Gamma$, and $x \in X(G)$,

$$u^i(G)(x) = x^i,$$
$$\gamma(N|G,x) = \{G^1, G^2, G^3\}, \gamma(\{i\}|G,x) = \emptyset.$$

Since each position includes a single outcome, and no outcome Pareto dominates another, it is easy to see that $\sigma(G)=X(G)$, $G\in\Gamma$, is the unique OSSB as well as the unique LOSSB. But, as in the previous example, if the two players can decide to make a lottery, with equal probabilities, over which of the two positions G^2 or G^3 to induce, then they will object to the payoff $(1,1)\in\sigma(G^1)$.

Define, therefore, for $G\in\Gamma$, the "compounded lottery ODOM" by

$$\mathbf{CLODOM}(\sigma,G)\equiv\{x\in X(G)\mid\exists\, S\subset N(G),\ \{H^1,H^2,\ldots,H^K\}\subset\gamma(S|G,x),\ p^k\in L(\sigma(H^k)),\ k=1,2,\ldots,K,\ \text{and } q\in L(\{H^1,H^2,\ldots,H^K\})\ \text{such that } u^i(G)(x)<\sum_k q^k u^i(H^k)(\sigma(H^k);p^k)\ \text{for all } i\in S\}.$$

That is, players in S may take a lottery over which of the K positions, $H^1,H^2,\ldots,H^K$, to induce,[1] and then, depending upon which position k was chosen, to have a lottery p^k over the outcomes in the solution for H^k.

Assuming that the cardinal utility functions $u^i(G)$, $i\in N$, are vN&M over both the positions in Γ and the outcomes in $X(G)$, the above discussion leads to the following definition.

Definition 11.4.4: *Let (γ,Γ) be a situation. The SB σ for (γ,Γ) is a* ***compounded lottery optimistic stable standard of behavior, CLOSSB,*** *if and only if, for all $G\in\Gamma$, $\sigma(G)=X(G)\backslash CLODOM(\sigma,G)$.*

The two notions of LOSSB and CLOSSB might prove to be useful when the proposed approach is extended to social environments which involve uncertainty. A much more important and difficult task is to incorporate models with incomplete information into the theory of social situations.

11.5 Preferences over subsets of outcomes

The stability of an SB σ for a situation (γ,Γ) involves the comparison of a set of outcomes with a particular outcome that is proposed. Specifically, we require that for all $G\in\Gamma$, x belongs to $\sigma(G)$ if and only if there is no $S\subset N(G)$ and $H\in\gamma(S|G,x)$ such that "all members of S prefer $\sigma(H)$ in H, over x in G." It is because of the ambiguity of this expression (see the footnote in Section 2.3) that we needed the two extreme behavioral assumptions: optimistic and conservative.

Matters become much simpler and acute if we assume that for each $G\in\Gamma$, there exists a function $U^i(G):2^{X(G)}\to\mathbb{R}$, where $2^{X(G)}$ denotes the set of all subsets of $X(G)$. Then, instead of defining optimistic and conservative stability we could define an SB σ to be ***stable*** for (γ,Γ) if for all $G\in\Gamma$, $\sigma(G)=X(G)\backslash\mathbf{DOM}(\sigma,G)$, where

[1] We can require, more generally, that $q\in L(\gamma(S|G,x))$, that is, the support of q need not be finite.

$$\mathbf{DOM}(\sigma,G) \equiv \{x \in X(G) \mid \exists\, S \subset N(G) \text{ and } H \in \gamma(S|G,x) \text{ such that } U^i(G)(x) < U^i(H)(\sigma(H)) \text{ for all } i \in S\}.$$

The interesting problem is, of course, to derive the functions $U^i(G)$ from $u^i(G)$. (For an axiomatic approach see, e.g., Kannai and Peleg 1984, and Holtzman 1984, as well as the references in these papers.)

11.6 Individual stability

Another modification of the definition of stability results if we allow a coalition to object to a proposed outcome if it can induce a position which benefits some members and does not harm any other member.

Definition 11.6.1: *Let (γ,Γ) be a situation. The SB σ is an* ***individual optimistic stable SB (IOSSB)*** *if for all $G \in \Gamma$. $\sigma(G) = X(G) \backslash IODOM(\sigma,G)$, where*

$$IODOM(\sigma,G) \equiv \{x \in X(G) \mid \exists\, S \subset N(G),\ H \in \gamma(S|G,x), \text{ and } y \in \sigma(H) \text{ such that for all } i \in S,\ u^i(H)(y) \geq u^i(G)(x) \text{ and there exists } k \in S \text{ for which } u^k(H)(y) > u^k(G)(x)\}.$$

The notion of ***individual conservative stable SB (ICSSB)*** is defined analogously. Ron Holtzman (private communication) observed that Theorem 6.5.1 is valid also for individual stability, and that the unique IOSSB (which coincides with the unique ICSSB) for the stable bargaining set situation yields the "consistent bargaining set," a notion that was recently proposed by Dutta et al. (1987).

11.7 Nonemptiness of OSSB and of CSSB

By Claim 2.5.1, it is impossible for either an OSSB or a CSSB to be identically empty. But, the stability of σ does not imply that $\sigma(G)$ is nonempty for every G. (Indeed, several of the game-theoretic solution concepts that we derived from stable SBs can be empty.)

Let (γ,Γ) be a situation, σ be an OSSB or a CSSB for (γ,Γ), and $G \in \Gamma$. One sufficient condition for $\sigma(G)$ to be nonempty reduces to establishing the nonemptiness of the core of the cooperative game (N, v^G), where $N \equiv N(G)$ and the characteristic function v^G is given by

$$v^G(N) \equiv \{\xi \in \mathbb{R}^N \mid \exists\, x \in X(G) \text{ such that for all } i \in N,\ \xi^i = u^i(G)(x)\}$$

and, for all $S \neq N$,

$$v^G(S) \equiv \{\xi \in \mathbb{R}^S \mid \exists\, x \in X(G),\ H \in \gamma(S|G,x), \text{ and } y \in X(H) \text{ such that for all } i \in S,\ \xi^i = u^i(H)(y)\}.$$

That is, $v^G(S)$ consists of all the S-payoffs that belong to a position H that S can induce when some outcome, x, is proposed in G. The following is a simple observation which, together with Scarf's (1967) theorem, might prove to be useful.

Claim 11.7.1: *Let (γ,Γ) be a situation, σ be an OSSB or a CSSB for (γ,Γ), and $G\in\Gamma$. Then, $\sigma(G)\supset\{x\in X(G)|\{u^i(G)(x)\}_{i\in N}\in Core(N,v^G)\}$. In particular, if $Core(N,v^G)\neq\emptyset$, then $\sigma(G)\neq\emptyset$.*

11.8 *F*-stability

Uri Rothblum (private communication) introduced the following notion of F-stability, which extends von Neumann and Morgenstern's abstract stable set. Employing this notion, Rothblum obtained a partial analog of Theorem 4.5 for CSSB. (Theorem 4.10 demonstrates that the exact analog of Theorem 4.5 for CSSB is false.)

Definition 11.8.1: *A **friendship mapping** for the abstract system $(D,\angle)$ is a mapping $F:D\rightarrow 2^D$, where 2^D denotes the set of all subsets of D.*

Definition 11.8.2: *Let $(D,\angle)$ be an abstract system, let F be a friendship mapping for $(D,\angle)$, and let $K\subset D$. The **dominion of K with respect to F**, denoted $\Delta_F(K)$, is the set*

$$\boldsymbol{\Delta_F(K)=\{a\in D|\ \exists\ b\in K \text{ such that for all } c\in F(b)\cap K,\ a\angle c\}.}$$

That is, an element a in D belongs to $\Delta_F(K)$ if K contains an element b such that all b's "friends" that belong to K dominate a (according to the dominance relation $\angle$).

Definition 11.8.3: *Let $(D,\angle)$ be an abstract system, and let F be a friendship mapping for $(D,\angle)$. A set $K\subset D$ is an **F-stable set** if $\boldsymbol{K=D\backslash\Delta_F(K)}$.*

Observe that F-stability extends the notion of vN&M abstract stable set. Indeed, let $(D,\angle)$ be an abstract system, and let F^* be the identity friendship mapping for $(D,\angle)$, that is for all $a\in D$, $\boldsymbol{F^*(a)=\{a\}}$. Then, it is easy to see that **a set K, $K\subset D$, is F^*-stable if and only if it is a vN&M abstract stable set.** Using this more general notion, Rothblum (private communication) proved the following partial analog of Theorem 4.5 for CSSB.

Theorem 11.8.4: *Let (γ,Γ) be a situation such that if $H\in\gamma(S|G,x)$ then $H\notin\gamma(T|G,x)$ for $T\neq S$. The mapping σ is a CSSB for $(\gamma\Gamma)$ if and only if its graph C is an F-stable set for the abstract system $(D,\angle)$ that is associated with $(\gamma\Gamma)$, where the friendship mapping F is given by*

$$\boldsymbol{F((G,x))\equiv\{(G,y)|\,y\in X(G)\}.}$$

11.9 Incomplete and intransitive preferences

The abstract system $(D,\angle)$ we (following Shitovitz) associated with a situation (γ,Γ) implies that all that is required for stability is that every individual $i \in N(G) \cap N(H)$ be able to compare his welfare from an outcome x in position G to that of outcome y in position H. But the cardinal representation of these preferences (if at all possible) plays no role. This observation leads to the following generalization of the notions of situation and stability.

Let (δ,Δ) be a situation-form (see Definition 10.0.5). Denote by $N(\Delta)$ the set of all players in any of the position-forms of Δ, that is, $\mathbf{N(\Delta)} \equiv \cup\{\mathbf{N(D)} | \mathbf{D} \in \mathbf{\Delta}\}$, and for $i \in N(\Delta)$, let $E^i(\Delta)$ denote the set of all position-forms, together with their outcomes, to which i belongs, that is, $\mathbf{E^i(\Delta)} \equiv \{(\mathbf{D},\mathbf{x}) | \mathbf{D} \in \mathbf{\Delta}, \mathbf{x} \in \mathbf{X(D)}, \mathbf{i} \in \mathbf{N(D)}\}$. For each $i \in N(\Delta)$, let P^i be i's preference relation over elements in $E^i(\Delta)$, where $(\mathbf{F},\mathbf{y}) \in \mathbf{P^i(D,x)}$ is interpreted to mean that player i, when in position-form D and x is offered, prefers (F,y) to (D,x). Clearly, P^i need not be either complete or transitive. [In fact, it is possible that $(F,y) \in P^i(D,x)$ and at the same time $(D,x) \in P^i(F,y)$.] The triple $(\delta,\Delta,\{P^i\}_{i \in N(\Delta)})$ is called a ***generalized situation, and a standard of behavior (SB)*** for it is a mapping σ that assigns, to each $D \in \Delta$, a subset $\sigma(D)$, of $X(D)$.

Let $(\delta,\Delta,\{P^i\}_{i \in N(\Delta)})$ be a generalized situation and let σ be an SB for it. Define, for $D \in \Delta$, the generalized ODOM and generalized CDOM by

$$\mathbf{GODOM}(\sigma,D) \equiv \{x \in X(D) | \exists\, S \subset N(D),\ F \in \delta(S|D,x), \text{ and } y \in \sigma(F) \text{ such that } (F,y) \in P^i(D,x) \text{ for all } i \in S\}$$

and

$$\mathbf{GCDOM}(\sigma,D) \equiv \{x \in X(D) | \exists\, S \subset N(D) \text{ and } F \in \delta(S|D,x) \text{ such that } \sigma(F) \neq \emptyset, \text{ and } (F,y) \in P^i(D,x) \text{ for all } i \in S \text{ and } y \in \sigma(F)\}.$$

We shall say that the SB σ is a ***generalized optimistic (conservative) stable SB*** for the generalized situation $(\delta,\Delta,\{P^i\}_{i \in N(\Delta)})$ if for all $D \in \Delta$, $\boldsymbol{\sigma}(\mathbf{D}) = \mathbf{X(D)} \backslash \mathbf{GODOM}(\boldsymbol{\sigma},\mathbf{D})$ $[\boldsymbol{\sigma}(\mathbf{D}) = \mathbf{X(D)} \backslash \mathbf{GCDOM}(\boldsymbol{\sigma},\mathbf{D})]$.

Asheim (1988b) has recently used this more general setup to define and study the notion of renegotiation-proofness in dynamic (unbounded tree) games.

11.10 Epilogue

The above nine subsections constitute a small sample of possible directions in which the theory of social situations can (and perhaps should) be extended, generalized, and improved. My own beliefs concerning the potential of the theory of social situations are reflected by the following quote from a, deservedly, highly esteemed friend and scholar.

I thus feel tempted to conclude this book with a note of optimism. But optimism about an exciting subject is too easily wishful. So, to those who will extend the work in this area, I had better refrain from promising success. I will simply offer the modest advice that they are sure to learn a great deal from the proposed approach; and I will make the modest promise that it will be a lot of fun. (Jacques H. Dreze, presidential address at the Second World Congress of the Econometric Society, Cambridge, September 10, 1970, with minor modifications).

Proofs for Chapter 11

Proof of theorem 11.3.2: Let σ be a nondiscriminating OSSB for (γ^*,Γ^*). By Claim 2.5.1, $\sigma(G)\neq\emptyset$ for all $G\in\Gamma$. Moreover,

1. $x\in\sigma(G)$ implies $\Sigma_{i\in N}x^i=1$: Indeed, otherwise, there exists $y\in\Delta$ with $y>>x$. Since $x\notin\mathrm{ODOM}(\sigma,G)$ we have that $y\in\mathrm{ODOM}(\sigma,G)$. Hence, $y\in\sigma(G)$. Since for all τ, $G_\tau\in\gamma^*(\{i(\tau)\}|G_\tau,x)$, it follows that $x\in\mathrm{ODOM}(\sigma,G)$, contradicting $x\in\sigma(G)$.
2. For all $G\in\Gamma$, $\sigma(G)$ contains a single element: Indeed, since $\sigma(G)\neq\emptyset$, we need to show that $x,y\in\sigma(G)$ implies $x=y$. Assume, in negation, that there exist $G=G_\tau\in\Gamma^*$ and $i\in N$ such that (without loss of generality) $y^i>x^i$. If $i=i(\tau)$, then $G\in\gamma^*(\{i(\tau)\}|G,x)$ and $y\in\sigma(G)$ imply $x\in\mathrm{ODOM}(\sigma,G)$, contradicting $x\in\sigma(G)$. If, on the other hand, $i\neq i(\tau)$, then define $\tilde{y}\in\Delta$ by: $\tilde{y}^h=y^h$ if $h\notin\{i,i(\tau)\}$, $\tilde{y}^i=x^i$, and $\tilde{y}^{i(\tau)}=y^{i(\tau)}+(y^i-x^i)$. Since $x,y\notin\mathrm{ODOM}(\sigma,G)$ we have that $\tilde{y}\notin\mathrm{ODOM}(\sigma,G)$. Therefore, $\tilde{y}\in\sigma(G)$. But $\tilde{y}^{i(\tau)}>y^{i(\tau)}$ implies $y\in\mathrm{ODOM}(\sigma,G)$, contradicting $y\in\sigma(G)$.
3. Let $\xi\in\Delta$ be the (unique) outcome at the beginning of the game, that is, let $\sigma(G_1)=\{\xi\}$. Then, for $h=2,\ldots,n$, $\xi^{h \bmod n}=\delta\xi^{(h-1)\bmod n}$: Indeed, since σ is nondiscriminating and $G_2\in\gamma^*(\{2\}|G_1,\xi)$, we have that $\xi^2\geq\delta\xi^1$. Now, if there were a strict inequality, then by defining $\tilde{\xi}$ as $\tilde{\xi}^h=\xi^h$ if $h\in N\backslash\{1,2\}$, $\tilde{\xi}^2=\delta\xi^1$, and $\tilde{\xi}^1=\xi^1+(\xi^1-\delta\xi^1)$, we reach a contradiction as in (2). Hence, $\xi^2=\delta\xi^1$. In the same manner it is easily verified that $\xi^h=\delta\xi^{h-1}$ for all $h=2,\ldots.,n$.

Combining (1) and (3) yields that $\sigma(G_1)=\{(\alpha,\delta\alpha,\delta^2\alpha,\ldots,\delta^{n-1}\alpha)\}$, where $\alpha=(1,-\delta)/(1-\delta^n)$. By nondiscrimination, therefore, σ is unique.

Q.E.D.

Proof of Claim 11.7.1: Let $\xi\in\mathrm{Core}(N,v^G)$. Then, $\xi\in v(N)$, that is, there exists $x\in X(G)$ such that for all $i\in N$, $\xi^i=u^i(G)(x)$. We shall first show $x\notin\mathrm{ODOM}(\sigma,G)$. Otherwise, there exist $S\subset N(G)$, $H\in\gamma(S|G,x)$, and $y\in\sigma(H)$ such that $u^i(H)(y)>u^i(G)(x)$ for all $i\in S$. Since $\sigma(H)\subset X(H)$ it follows that $\zeta\in v(S)$, where for $i\in S$, $\zeta^i\equiv u^i(H)(y)$. But then, ζ blocks ξ, contradicting

$\xi \in \text{Core}(N, v^G)$. Thus, $x \in X(G) \setminus \text{ODOM}(\sigma, G)$, which by optimistic external stability implies that $x \in \sigma(G)$.

Modifying the above proof in the obvious manner yields that the claim is valid also if σ is a CSSB for (γ, Γ). Q.E.D.

Proof of Theorem 11.8.4: Let σ be an SB for Γ, and for $G \in \Gamma$ and $x \in X(G)$, let $F(G,x) = \{(G,y) | y \in X(G)\}$. Denote the graph of σ by C. Then, CDOM(σ, G) can be written as:

$$\text{CDOM}(\sigma,G) = \{x \in X(G) | \exists S \subset N(G),\ H \in \gamma(S|G,x), \text{ and } (H,y) \in C \text{ such that for all } i \in S,\ u^i(H)(z) > u^i(G)(x) \text{ for all } z \in F(H,y) \cap C\}.$$

That is, $x \in \text{CDOM}(\sigma,G)$ if and only if there exists $(H,y) \in C$ such that for every friend (H,z) of (H,y) that belongs to C, $(G,x) \angle (H,z)$. That is, $x \in \text{CDOM}(\sigma,G)$ if and only if $(G,x) \in \Delta_F(C)$. Therefore, $x \in X(G) \setminus \text{CDOM}(\sigma,G)$ if and only if $(G,x) \in D \setminus \Delta_F(C)$. Now, σ is a CSSB if and only if for all $G \in \Gamma$, $\sigma(G) = X(G) \setminus \text{CDOM}(\sigma,G)$, that is, if and only if $C = D \setminus \Delta_F(C)$. Q.E.D.

References

Abreu, D. (1988),"On the theory of infinitely repeated games with discounting," *Econometrica* 56, 383–96.

Alesina, A., and Rosenthal, H. (1989), "Moderating elections," mimeo.

Asheim, G. (1987), "Rawlsian intergenerational justice as a Markov-perfect equilibrium in a resource technology," Norwegian School of Economics and Business Administration, mimeo.

Asheim, G. (1988a), "Rawlsian intergenerational justice as a Markov-perfect equilibrium in a resource technology," *Review of Economic Studies* 55, 469–84.

Asheim, G. (1988b), "Renegotiation-proofness in finite and infinite stage games through the theory of social situations," Norwegian School of Economics and Business Administration, mimeo.

Asheim, G. (1989), "A unique solution to the *N*-person sequential bargaining," Norwegian School of Economics and Business Administration, mimeo.

Aumann, R. (1959), "Acceptable points in general cooperative *n*-person games," *Annals of Mathematics Studies* 40, 287–324.

Aumann, R. (1964), "Markets with a continuum of traders," *Econometrica* 32, 39–50.

Aumann, R., and Maschler, M. (1964), "The bargaining set for cooperative games," in *Advances in Game Theory,* Dresher, Shapley, and Tucker, eds. Princeton, NJ: Princeton University Press, 443–7.

Aumann, R., and Maschler, M. (1972), "Some thoughts on the minimax principle," *Management Science* 2, 54–63.

Beja, A., and Gilboa, I. (1987), "Value for two-stage games: another view of the Shapley axioms," Foerder Institute working paper 2587.

Berge, C. (1962), *The Theory of Graphs and its Applications*. London: Meuthen.

Bernheim, D.; Peleg, B.; and Whinston, M. (1987), "Coalition-proof Nash equilibria. I. Concepts," *Journal of Economic Theory* 42, 1–12.

Dasgupta, P.; Hammond, P.; and Maskin, E. (1979), "The implementation of social choice rules: some general results on incentive compatibility," *Review of Economic Studies* 46, 185–216.

Dutta, B.; Ray, D.; Sengupta, K.; and Vohra, R. (1987), "A consistent bargaining set," *Journal of Economic Theory* 49, 93–112.

Fudenberg, D., and Maskin, E. (1986), "The Folk theorem in repeated games with discounting and with incomplete information," *Econometrica* 54, 533–54.

Gekker, R. (1989), "Rights-exercising games through the theory of social situations," York University, mimeo.

Gibbard, A. (1974), "A Pareto consistent libertarian claim," *Journal of Economic Theory* 7, 388–410.

Greenberg, J. (1988a), ''A strategic aspect of the strong positive association condition,'' *Economics Letters* 26, 225–6.

Greenberg, J. (1988b), ''Payoffs in generalized bargaining games,'' *Economics Letters* 28, 33–5.

Greenberg, J. (1989a), ''Deriving strong and coalition-proof Nash equilibrium from an abstract system,'' *Journal of Economic Theory,* 49, 195–202.

Greenberg, J. (1989b), ''An application of the theory of social situations to repeated games,'' *Journal of Economic Theory,* 49, 278–93.

Greenberg, J., and Shitovitz, B. (1990), ''Conservative stability and subgame perfection,'' mimeo.

Greenberg, J., and Weg, E. (1987), ''Conservative stability in procedural voting by veto,'' Haifa University, Israel, mimeo.

Herrero, M. (1985), ''A strategic bargaining approach to market institutions,'' Ph.D. dissertation, London School of Economics.

Hoffman, E. J.; Loessi, J. C.; and Moore, R. C.; (1969), ''Constructions for the solution of the *m* queens problem,'' *Mathematics Magazine* 42, 66–72.

Holtzman, R. (1984), ''An extension of Fishburn's theorem on extending orders,'' *Journal of Economic Theory* 32, 172–5.

Howard, N. (1971), *Paradoxes in Rationality*. Cambridge, MA: MIT Press.

Howe, R., and Roemer, J. (1981), ''Rawlsian justice as the core of a game,'' *The American Economic Review* 71, 880–95.

Kahn, C., and Mookherjee, D. (1989), ''The good, the bad, and the ugly: Coalition proof equilibrium in games with infinite strategy spaces,'' University of Illinois, mimeo.

Kannai, Y., and Peleg, B. (1984) ''A note on the extension of an order on a set to the power set,'' *Journal of Economic Theory* 32, 172–5.

Kohlberg, E., and Mertens, J.-F. (1986), ''On the strategic stability of equilibria,'' *Econometrica* 52, 1007–29.

McKinsey, J. (1952), *Introduction to the Theory of Games*. New York: McGraw-Hill.

Mas-Colell, A. (1985), *The Theory of General Economic Equilibrium. A Differential Approach*. Cambridge: Cambridge University Press.

Mas-Colell, A. (1989), ''An equivalence theorem for a bargaining set,'' *Journal of Mathematical Economics,* 18, 129–38.

Moulin, H. (1983), *The Strategy of Social Choice*. Amsterdam: North Holland.

O'Neil, B. (1986), ''International escalation and the dollar auction,'' *Journal of Conflict Resolution* 30, 33–50.

Ray, D. (1983), ''Credible coalitions and the core,'' Stanford University, mimeo.

Richardson, M. (1946), ''On weakly ordered systems,'' *Bulletin of the American Mathematical Society* 52, 113–16.

Roemer, J. (1989), ''Rawlsian justice as a stable standard of behavior,'' University of California at Davis, mimeo.

Roth, A. (1980), ''Values for games without side payments: some difficulties with current concepts,'' *Econometrica* 48, 457–65.

Rubinstein, A. (1982), ''Perfect equilibrium in a bargaining model,'' *Econometrica* 50, 97–110.

Scarf, H. (1967), ''The core of an *n*-person game,'' *Econometrica* 35, 50–69.

Selten, R. (1975), "Reexamination of the perfectness concept for equilibrium points in extensive games," *International Journal of Game Theory* 4, 25–55.

Sen, A. (1970), "The impossibility of a Paretian liberal," *Journal of Political Economy* 72, 152–7.

Shafer, W. (1980), "On the existence and interpretation of value allocations," *Econometrica* 48, 467–76.

Shapley, L. (1953), "A value for *n*-person games," in *Contributions to the Theory of Games,* vol. II, H. Kuhn and A. W. Tucker, eds. Princeton, NJ: Princeton University Press, 307–17.

Shitovitz, B. (1989), "On the optimistic stable standards of behavior in repeated games," Haifa University, Israel, mimeo.

Shubik, M. (1971), "The dollar auction game: A paradox in noncooperative behavior and escalation," *Journal of Conflict Resolution* 15, 545–7.

Shubik, M. (1984), *Game Theory in the Social Sciences; Concepts and Solutions.* Cambridge, MA: MIT Press.

Sugden, R. (1985), "Liberty, preference, and choice," *Economics and Philosophy* 1, 213–29.

von Neumann, J., and Morgenstern, O. (1947), *Theory of Games and Economic Behavior.* Princeton, NJ: Princeton University Press.

Winer, Z. (1989), M.Sc. thesis, University of Haifa, Israel.

Index